THE ENCHANTED GLASS

THE ELIZABETHAN MIND IN LITERATURE

BY

HARDIN CRAIG

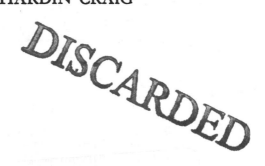

GREENWOOD PRESS, PUBLISHERS
WESTPORT, CONNECTICUT

Library of Congress Cataloging in Publication Data

Craig, Hardin, 1875-1968.
    The enchanted glass.

    Reprint of the 1952 ed. published by B. Blackwell,
Oxford.
    Bibliography: p.
    Includes index.
    1. English literature--Early modern, 1500-1700--
History and criticism. 2. Literature--Philosophy.
3. Great Britain--Intellectual life--16th century.
4. Renaissance--England. I. Title.
PR421.C67 1975   820'.9'003   75-11492
ISBN 0-8371-8200-X

Originally published in 1952 by Basil Blackwell, Oxford

Reprinted with the permission of Raemond Wilson Craig

Reprinted in 1975 by Greenwood Press, Inc.,
51 Riverside Avenue, Westport, Conn. 06880

Library of Congress catalog card number 75-11492

ISBN 0-8371-8200-X

Printed in the United States of America

10 9 8 7 6 5 4 3 2

To G. C.

PREFACE

THE following pages attempt to bring within the range of ordinary literary study, such as that pursued in colleges and universities, a body of scientific, philosophic, and social considerations sometimes unknown, often concealed from view, and oftener still disregarded. There is nothing difficult in the matter or the point of view, the former being usually commonplace and familiar things and the latter extremely simple and practical. The fundamental idea is that the literature of the Renaissance may be made more vital and significant by understanding it as fully as possible and by assuming with reference to it a point of view of immediacy both in knowledge and sympathy.

As to the outlines of the book, the author tries, first of all, to see man as part of a general formal order or cosmology, for the cosmology is a matter of importance in all mental life. We inquire how man received it and thought and felt about it. We observe that many of man's opinions in that bygone time are still valid, though error was permeative and omnipresent. Error, moreover, has an importance of its own in literary history, since it is not truth itself but what man believes to be truth that finds literary exemplification and emphasis. What, we ask, were man's chances to discover more of the truth about the external world than he then knew? How he thought he was related to the World Machine, his opinion of his own state, is seen to be a primary consideration in such an investigation. Man's distinguishing gift, as he knew then and knows now, is reason; the men of the

Renaissance made a determined effort to use reason operatively. Speech was recognized as the 'discourse of reason,' and the men of the Renaissance took unparalleled pains to employ speech in the service of reason, a circumstance which accounts, in part at least, for their literary preëminence. In accordance with the principles just referred to and with the aid of certain significant matters of history, the author attempts to determine the characteristic reactions of the Elizabethan mind as compared to our contemporary mind. Finally, he confronts the problem of how we are more truly to interpret Elizabethan literature, which is the expression of the Elizabethan mind. In the current study of literature are widespread analytical tendencies. What, we ask, are the nature and value of syntheses based on writers and groups of writers, and what are the feasible methods of forming literary syntheses?

Bibliographical notes do not usually aim at completeness, but record obviously needed references and list various works which the author has consulted. Not infrequently the books and authors enumerated at particular places serve to illuminate the general subject rather than the special thought of the text. The index does not include names which occur in the notes or those within quotations in the text.

The author wishes to express his gratitude to Professor George Coffin Taylor, of the University of North Carolina, and to Miss Madeleine Doran, of the University of Wisconsin, who have read the book and made valuable contributions to it; also, for a similar service, to his friend and former colleague, Professor E. N. S. Thompson, of the University of Iowa. Professor Richmond P. Bond, of the University of North Carolina, and the author's old friend Professor George R. Coffman, also of the University of North Carolina, showed the greatest kindness in reading the book, in making suggestions, and in participating with the author in discussions and debates which he found beneficial and enlightening.

The author wishes also to express his gratitude to the Trustees of the Henry E. Huntington Library and Art Gallery for the opportunities of study which they have afforded him.

Stanford University   HARDIN CRAIG
1 *October* 1935

CONTENTS

CHAPTER   PAGE

I. THE UNIVERSAL NATURE OF THINGS . 1

II. DERIVATIONS AND INFERENCES . . . 32

III. PREOCCUPATIONS AND PREJUDGMENTS . 61

IV. THE BINDING OF PROTEUS 87

V. THE NATURE AND CONDITION OF MEN . 113

VI. THE WELL OF DEMOCRITUS 139

VII. THE ELOQUENCE OF PERSUASIONS . . 160

VIII. THE WINDOW OF MOMUS 182

IX. INTERPRETATIONS OF TIMES 210

X. DISCLOSING AND EXPOUNDING OF MEN . 238

BIBLIOGRAPHICAL NOTES 265

INDEX 289

THE ENCHANTED GLASS

THE ENCHANTED GLASS

CHAPTER I

THE UNIVERSAL NATURE OF THINGS

And as for that censure of Salomon concerning the excess
of writing and reading books and the anxiety of spirit
which redoundeth from knowledge, and that admonition
of St. Paul, *That we be not seduced by vain philosophy;*
let these places be rightly understood, and they do excellently set forth the true bounds and limitations whereby
human knowledge is confined and circumscribed; and
yet without any such contracting or coarctation, but that
it may comprehend all the universal nature of things.—
Bacon, *The Advancement of Learning.*

EVEN before the days of Descartes a dualistic
philosophy of the material and the spiritual was
widely entertained;[1] today, however, as one
looks into it, one questions the validity of the distinctions fundamental to the system as then conceived.
In the Renaissance one searches in vain for a genuine
metaphysics, such as that of Berkeley. The metaphysics of Aristotle was corrupted or ill-understood. The
distinction between the material and the spiritual was
largely a distinction between the perceptible and the
imperceptible, or between ordinary matter and a more
finely attenuated substance thought of as spiritual.
To make this distinction was the utmost reach that
philosophy was then capable of making. One effect of
this form of thinking was to make the unseen and the
imperceptible a real thing, so that the supernatural
seemed ready at any time to pass over the margin and
assume a perceptible form.

Charron[2] argues emphatically that the soul, though
invisible and impalpable, is corporeal. In so doing he

attempts to distinguish between the corporeal and the material. Good spirits, devils, and human souls are wholly separated from matter, he says, but, according to the best authorities, have bodies and are of a bodily nature, and for these reasons: whatever is included in the finite world (as spirits are) is finite, i. e., limited in virtue and substance, enclosed within a superficies, and circumscribed within a place. Spirits are always in some definite place and cannot be in two places at once. They occupy space equal to their limited and finite substances and surfaces; else they could not change place and ascend and descend as Scripture says they do. If they can change place, it follows that they have the qualities of a body: they are movable, divisible, subject to time and the succession thereof (required in the passage from one place to another). They are affected by joy and sorrow, pleasure and pain, which are the accidents accompanying and dependent upon their substance or state of corporeality. Charron expresses the belief that spirits and souls are composed of a substance more finely attenuated than air or ether (the quintessence) and argues that they can be corporeal without being material, an argument as untenable in practice as it is confusing in theory.

The cosmology [3] of the age provided a world structure in conformity with the crude metaphysics just described, and the Platonism of the Renaissance was something more than parallelism between ideas and phenomena; it was also parallelism in the structure of two worlds. On the spiritual side were God in Trinity, the nine orders of the angels, minor spirits, and the soul of man; on the material side were the high heavens (where stood the throne of God), the solar system (including the fixed stars and centring in the earth), the earth (composed of the four elements), man on his corporeal side (divided into classes and orders within the church, the state, and the family), the animals, the plants, and the metals and minerals. These two vast series were, as said before, not spirit and matter respectively but, essentially, perceptible and imperceptible things. To each series and to each object in each series were assigned functions and places, and each series and all that it included found perfect correspondences [4] with the other or within the other. The system, though definite in its general outlines and doctrines, was complicated or vague in its details and inconsistent in its particular doctrines. It was a tissue of differing opinions, so that its clarity was specious. To work it out, to understand it, and to act in accordance with it were the ends and purposes of Renaissance thinkers. It afforded a motive for study, grand, authoritative, and was, in its promises and perplexities, loudly challenging.

It is the instrumentation and methodology of this task which constitute the various schools of thought and systems of philosophy of the Renaissance. Methods and purposes differed greatly. On one principle, however, practically all were agreed: the road to truth was ratiocination, not the free use of reason, but reason restricted to the discovery or rediscovery of a universe whose form and purpose were already known and whose laws were the legacies of a wiser past or the fiats of an unimpeachable God. Consultation of authority and the correct employment of logic, not the examination of phenomena, were the means by which truth would become known. Perhaps no age ever busied itself more incessantly about matters of thought, or had greater faith in the power of reason to discover the very body of truth. There was at that time a disposition to believe in the possibility, especially if a happy one, that mutually contradictory facts and principles might both be true and valid; faith

and reason began to be put into two separate compart-
ments of the mind, and fideism [5] was a characteristic
sequel to the invincibility of reason. Montaigne,[6]
grown weary of world-wide disputational inconclu-
siveness, states the theme of the *Apology for Raimond
Sebond* as follows:

Knowledge is truly a great and very useful acquisition;
they who despise it bear sufficient witness to their stupidity. Yet I do not value it at so excessive a rate as some
have done, as Herillus the philosopher, who sees in it the
sovereign good, and maintains that it has the power of
making us wise and contented, which I do not believe.
No more do I believe what others have affirmed, that
knowledge is the mother of all virtue, and that every vice
is the result of ignorance. If that be true it is capable of
being widely interpreted.

Further on in the same essay he is ready to say:

To us has been allotted inconsistency, irresolution, uncertainty, sorrow, superstition, solicitude about things to
come, even after we shall have ceased to live, ambition,
avarice, jealousy, envy, inordinate, furious and untamable
desires, war, falsehood, disloyalty, detraction and curiosity. We have indeed strangely overrated this precious
reason we so much glory in, this faculty of knowing and
judging, if we have bought it at the price of that infinite
number of passions to which we are continually a prey.

The opinion that reason is fighting a losing battle
is the basis of no small part of Montaigne's scepticism,
and the passages just quoted make clear by their
doubts the established trend in thought against which
he is revolting. How the learned world got into such
a state as Montaigne depicts is a story as long as the
history of civilization; we shall have to content ourselves at this time with such vague and imperfect statements as those just made. The significant thing is that

no complete agreement among thinkers, except in the most general features of the world machine and in some of the more elementary principles which governed it, is to be expected. The student of the field can often distinguish as the underlying thought of any particular literary work the dicta characteristic of usually more than one philosophic system. It is not to be supposed, however, that there is not consistency to be discovered in single works, the works of individual authors, and, if a scholar is adequately informed and imaginatively sympathetic, in, let us say, the Elizabethan age as a whole. The Renaissance in England was indeed a sufficiently unified movement to prevent the task of arriving at a fairly effective synthesis of its working philosophy from seeming hopeless. In other words, one may become an Elizabethan scholar, know one's way about in the age, and in one's feelings and opinions become a reasonably good subject of Queen Elizabeth.

Aristotelian doctrine is of course the most important single constituent of the complex, but Aristotelianism almost never appears alone or in pure form. It may be mingled with Neo-Platonism, modified by Christian dogma, or blended with Stoicism. Natural magic, an offshoot of Neo-Platonism, presented what was, by and large, the most intelligible and superficially the most practical intrument for reading the riddle of the universe; for Neo-Platonism had, so to speak, been present at the birth of the cosmology accepted by the Renaissance. But natural (or white) magic was never very generally accepted. It protested in vain its conformity with the Bible, the ancients, the physical and moral sciences, and all ascertained and ascertainable truth, but because of its black brother it lay under suspicion. It was an act of approved grace for the great Friar Bacon to renounce

magic; 'I'll burn my books' is the last outcry of Dr.
John Faustus; and even Prospero,[7] whose commerce
with the spirit world had brought only good, abjured
his potent art.

> I'll break my staff,
> Bury it certain fathoms in the earth,
> And deeper than did ever plummet sound
> I'll drown my book.

Christianity, whose cosmology was mainly Aristotelian, offered to the searcher a key more acceptable
than that offered by natural magic. The earth was
God's footstool, the stage on which His wayward
child must play his part; but not in isolation. Not only
had there been revelation in the days before the heavens grew astronomical, but a Comforter was ever
present, to inform, to guide, and to reprove. No other
approach to truth was necessary or desirable, not even
by way of the stars. The definiteness of the cosmological system in its general outlines and in many of
its particular parts, its tangibility and applicability,
made it present in the consciousness of all men. It was
conformable to Christianity, for the doctors of the
Church had helped to shape it; but in interpretation
of the cosmic machine Christianity always fixed a
boundary beyond which none but the hardiest thinkers
dared even to reconnoitre. Raphael's advice[8] to Adam
was general in the age:

> Solicit not thy thoughts with matters hid:
> Leave them to God above; him serve and fear.
> Of other creatures, as him pleases best,
> Wherever placed, let him dispose; joy thou
> In what he gives to thee, this Paradise
> And thy fair Eve; Heaven is for thee too high
> To know what passes there. Be lowly wise;
> Think only what concerns thee and thy being.

It must be remembered that the Renaissance conception of the universe was of just the sort that
Raphael recommends: it was built up out of what men
could ascertain with unaided human powers of observation—out of what mattered to man as regards his
earthly needs and his religious and moral hopes and
aspirations. One may therefore expect to find in the
cosmology of Shakespeare and his contemporaries an
immediacy and practical significance which perhaps
does not inhere in a philosophy of objectivity—one
based on mathematical physics, biological evolution,
and microscopy. The cosmological structure which
man had originally and primitively erected out of his
normal experience, the concept of the universal nature
of things, was not without truth and beneficence. One
should not think of it, in spite of its errors and limitations, as fiction or superstition. It was neither. It was
perhaps science in its infancy or a kind of traditional
knowledge resembling aphoristic wisdom. Particularly,
one should think of it as an instrument of thought, as a
means of understanding the life of man on earth, true
and efficient enough in its most general conclusions
and inferences. The system may even be said to have
fulfilled its chief purposes, a thing only to be expected, since it was the child of man's own needs
and served them. When its doctrines were carried beyond their primary group of assumptions, the final
causes which had given rise to the system itself, it
ceased to be a satisfactory philosophy of the universe.

What we have been describing is the situation that
existed before the beginnings of the shift, during the
seventeenth century,[9] from the cosmology of the followers of Aristotle to the cosmology which we associate with modern science. The ten general classes
(with various minor modifications) under which the
objects of human knowledge were arranged by the

Aristotelians—substance, quantity, quality, relation, place, time, situation, possession, action, and the state of being acted upon—continued during the Renaissance to offer the sole method of intellectual attack on the corpus of experience. The universe presented, so to speak, a flat surface. Quantity, now the primary concept of physical science, was as yet a mere category. Newton and his followers had not yet given new meanings to matter, space, and time in terms of forces, motions, changes in mass, temporal and spacial continua, and the like. Indeed, the advancement of science was not as yet a stated problem. Man looked out on a static world of nature present and intelligible to his mind and causally explicable in terms of his own good. He had not yet been demoted from his determinative position in the centre of the universe as the being for whom all things had been made and to whom had been granted the mastery and enjoyment of all things in return for a becoming glorification of an utterly generous Creator. That so obvious and inevitable a cosmology, quite aside from its theological aspects, should ever cease to retain validity for the minds of men is unthinkable.

Before we go further in the examination of this cosmological system, it is important that we should call attention to the significance of certain of its assumptions. One of the things assumed, as has been said, was a system of correspondences between a spiritual universe perfect in form, function, and operation and a material universe imperfect in these respects, the correspondences being, however, so shrouded in obscurity by the obstructions which the soul of man, enmeshed in clay, encounters in the exercise of its natural function of intuition that ideals and prototypes remained unknown. Analogy, controlled and directed by authority, was man's guide, and analogical reasoning was the sphere of action for the exercise of man's ingenuity. It was assumed that, since perfection was the intrinsic nature of the spiritual world, truth was knowledge of that world of spirit and not of this world of matter. As the earth approached the heavens in perfection it grew in beauty. Milton sees it before its ruin: [10]

> Yet not till the Creator, from his work
> Desisting, though unwearied, up returned,
> Up to the Heaven of Heavens, his high abode,
> Thence to behold this new-created World,
> The addition of his empire, how it shewed
> In prospect from his Throne, how good, how fair,
> Answering his great Idea.

Answering his great Idea! as Desdemona [11] answered it in the mind of Othello:

> but once put out thy light,
> Thou cunning'st pattern of excelling nature,
> I know not where is that Promethean heat
> That can thy light relume.

Since the ideal world was perfection, there could of course be no limits to the extent of its application to the imperfect material world. With reference to all action and policy there existed, it was thought, if man could but discover it, an adequate and appropriate doctrine. The very meticulousness with which Renaissance learning was applied to life is witness of the universal acceptance of this approach to truth; it accounts also for the high reputation of learning in that age and possibly in part for the greater stir in emotional content that life seems then to have had. So busy were the Elizabethans in learning and applying that they seem to us to have had, not too little science, but far too much. They thought they knew, or that there were those who knew the answer to every question, and they insisted upon applying to matters of daily life reams of stuff which appear to us false, or silly, or of no value.

By way of illustration consider the compendium of John Jones,[12] a Welsh physician, *The Arte and Science of preseruing Bodie and Soule in al Health* (1579). The book is learned, dull, eminently respectable. It is dedicated to the Queen and full of proper reverence for princes and nobles. It combines the contents of the two best known works of Sir Thomas Elyot, *The Castle of Health* and *The Gouernour*, with both of which the author is thoroughly familiar. Jones's plan for his book is to follow a child through from birth to maturity and lay down rules, both physical and ethical, for man's proper nurture. The book is not wordy, but it is detailed to the last degree, as are other similar learned works of the time, such as Elyot's own works, La Primaudaye's *The French Academie,* and Burton's *Anatomy of Melancholy.* Jones's work is based, he tells us, on more than three hundred authorities, cited carefully at appropriate places. The book, being the work of a stupid, sincere man, is invaluable as a historical document. There you will find (pp. 4-9) much attention paid to the choice of a nurse. On the authority of Hippocrates, Galen, Ætius, Montuus, and Mokerus we are told that the nurse is to be chosen according to the temperature of the babe. Galen, Plutarch, Quintilian, Crysippus, and Favorinus are quoted in favour of mothers' nursing their own offspring; but this practice is not convenient for English gentlewomen, let Sir Thomas More say what he will about the situation in Utopia. Avicenna, Montuus, Montanus, Hippocrates, Ætius, Gordonius, and Fallopius are consulted as to what kind of breasts

are meetest for the nurse. Another list of authorities
is cited as to the quality of her milk, which is an important matter, since the quality of the nurse's milk
was responsible for the sickliness of Titus, the cruelty
of Caligula, and the drunkenness of Tiberius. The
nurse's singing to the child and what she sings are
things not to be neglected. 'Lascivious Dymes, wanton
Lullies, and amorous Englins' should be avoided. The
psalms, commended by Clemens Alexandrinus, Basilius,
Eusebius, and Bernardus, and 'godly and cunningly
put into English' by Sternhold and Hopkins, will quiet
the child and put away ungodly affections in the
nurse. We are told (pp. 22-24) on the authority of
Elyot, Vives, and others that the nurse's nature, like
that of all women, should be mild, 'fearful,' gentle,
tractable, trusty, of sure remembrance, and shamefast.
Fulgentius, Valescus, Desiderius, Hippocrates, Galen,
and Avicenna are quoted on exercise; Actuarius,
Egidius, and Doctor Recorde on the urine, and so on.
The book illustrates the formalism of Renaissance
science and its faith in multitudinous authority and
shows it lost in a wilderness of indiscriminate details.

The laws and principles of the great *machina superior* were sound and comprehensible. Broadly
speaking, order (synonymously justice or natural law)
was conceived of as the fundamental cohesive principle of the cosmological system, and similitude or
correspondence as the means by which this principle
was operative in the universe.

Order or justice is in the very nature of God. It is
also in His nature to be all-powerful; He is the head
and ruler of all the harmonious universe. Harmony
means the proper functioning of every part in the
place designed for it. The spheres of heaven are arranged in descending order from the uttermost
empyrean to the earth in the centre of all. The ele-

ments have also their order: earth is the lowest, as it should be, for it is the heaviest; water is clearly above it, and air just as clearly above that; it follows that fire must be higher still. The principle of headship and of obedient subordination, evident in the workings of the universe, must of course be the pattern for human societies. It follows that monarchy is the best form of government and that all men must be contented with their stations in life, so that ambition becomes the most dangerous—and one of the most sinful —of all passions. It also follows that the father must be the supreme head of the family, with wife and children subordinate to him in obedience. A similar pattern must hold within man himself; souls or forms of souls are graded, the lower participating with the natures of plants and animals, the highest, which must be dominant if order is to be maintained, with the natures of the angels or pure intelligences. Obviously, the angels themselves must be arranged in hierarchies. Thus correspondences, all exemplifications of the cohesive principle of orderliness (resting upon the two poles of authority and obedience), are permeative and innumerable, to be sought for in the fields of religion, natural science, ethics, politics, psychology—throughout the whole field of rationalization. The idea of correspondences is seized on and carried on in its own right as a principle of cohesion. Man becomes a microcosm, formed on the pattern of the macrocosm. The very heavens themselves—the signs of the zodiac and the planets—must be found in him, and, of course, for effective purposes; for nothing that the Creator provided is idle and without purpose.

In the idea of correspondences there is an attempt to grasp an aspect of unity. One might go so far as to say that the principle of similitude meant effective cohesion for all the more immediate spheres of thought and action. But when the idea finds expression it often works itself out in the utmost triviality. Perhaps the idea, dimly seen intuitively, was too vague to be imaginatively sustained; when rationalized it assumed a definiteness on quite another level; it was thought to be exemplified in concrete ways from which the intuitive idea in its purity could not be abstracted. The result was that learning went about the world seeking and finding analogies without any common denominator, one set made on one level and one on another and both treated as if the common principle of analogy were enough to make them equal. Thinkers did not set for themselves terms to be adhered to throughout a given field of investigation. Moreover, correspondences were assumed which were incapable of factual verification, as, for example, the susceptibility of various parts of man's body to influence by planets and constellations. If correspondence was the key to the universe, then it must be exemplified in many ways not directly observable; as correspondences between the heavens and man's body ought to exist, it was therefore assumed that they did exist.

The easy statement of fundamental principles must not blind us to the extreme complexity in details of a system so comprehensive. One has only to examine the diagrams of macrocosm and microcosm [13] in Robert Fludd's *Utriusque Cosmi Majoris et Minoris Historia* (1619) in order to see the intricacy of schemes which a wide application of the idea of correspondences had brought into existence. Such diagrams are at once incredibly ingenious and hopelessly inconsistent. Correspondences were drawn from different levels of generality, the accidental was confused with the essential, and actual fabrication for the sake of symmetry was a frequent resort. It was perhaps the fallacy of misplaced concreteness [14] that was most delusive. The intellectual urge was to particularize more and more. If the picture was to be kept unified, one had to make continual small adjustments; one had continually to explain things away, to hunt for resemblances, or, if need be, to invent them. Science was in an advanced epicyclic stage and was, therefore, necessarily barren; no way was left for it to proceed except by the increase of its complexity.

So frequently was the world mechanism described, so necessary was it considered for the intelligibility of every intellectual conception or issue, so sublime and portentous was it felt to be in its outlines and applications that one can hardly escape it. All works which have to do with the grand divisions of learning, —theology, law, medicine, and the arts; or with any of their parts, as natural history, ethics, and politics; or with the encyclopædia of learning; or with the greater social and religious questions, such as the relation of the king to the law, the freedom of the will, and the immortality of the soul,—all these were made to spring from the doctrines of the macrocosm and the microcosm, or from what Hooker described as the manifestations of eternal law.

The world order was at once theological, legal, scientific, psychological, and moral. It was designed to provide for everything. It was, if you like, poetry at work in the world preparing a grand solution of the problem of human existence; it did not recognize itself as poetry, but thought of itself as constituting all the prosaic branches of human learning. Renaissance thinkers knew that the first poets had been the first philosophers, lawgivers, and teachers. What they did not know was that they themselves were even as the ancients. They thought of themselves as scientists, but they differed little except in literary form from the old poets. They built a philosophic world out of sense perceptions, generously and meticulously sprinkled with revelation, tradition, and superstition. Our scientists are not cosmological poets.

From the point of view of the history of philosophy, the major aspects of the Renaissance are two, the Neo-Platonic and the Aristotelian. We may say roughly that Neo-Platonism is a philosophy whose dualism was so strongly marked as to abandon the point of view of physical science. Specifically, it had constructed the vast fabric of the spirit world. Aristotelianism may be said to be a body of philosophic doctrines, dualistic to be sure, but still mainly occupied with the methods and materials of science and still bearing quite definite relations to the works of its founder. Further on in the chapter we shall illustrate the Aristotelianism of the English Renaissance from the works of Richard Hooker. Meantime, since in the study of literature we are not so much concerned with the cosmology as we are with its instrumentation and what were believed to be its sensible manifestations, it is especially desirable that we should consider the most persistent, ambitious, and intelligent attempt ever made to interpret dualistic cosmology for the benefit of man, namely, Neo-Platonism, which went by the name of Platonism. We shall not enter into any general explanation of the views of the Neo-Platonists or the relation of Neo-Platonism to Christian theology, although a complete and careful knowledge of these and other philosophic factors is necessary to an effective comprehension of the philosophy of Renaissance literature; nor shall we consider Stoicism, not so much a cosmology as a moral philosophy, and Epicureanism, but slightly known or regarded in Renaissance England. Instead of this we shall plunge at once into the midst of the Renaissance in northern Europe and trust that the consideration of a particular case will serve to make known the more general principles which underlie it.

Henry Cornelius Agrippa[15] was a follower of Reuchlin, who in turn was a follower of Pico della Mirandola and Ficino. This means that Agrippa was in the full tide of the revival of Neo-Platonism, whose exponent and apologist he became. It means also that Agrippa was a champion of humanism against scholasticism. What he calls Natural Magic is the operative aspect of Neo-Platonic doctrine.

In his prefatory epistle to *De occulta Philosophia* (1531), addressed to Ioannes Trithemius, abbot of St. James near Würzburg, an ancient bishopric and principality now part of Bavaria, Agrippa explains the reason why Natural Magic has come to be suspected and forbidden. Many false philosophers, he says, have assumed the name and status of magicians and have practised accursed superstitions and dangerous rites and ceremonies, such as are set forth in unlawful books, and have thus made the name of magic odious to good and honest men. Those, moreover, who have written on natural magic in the past have presented nothing but irrational toys and crude superstitions. Such persons (mainly Schoolmen) are, 'Roger Bacon, Robert [Grossetest] an Englishman, Peter Apponus [of Albano], Albertus [Magnus] the Teutonich, Arnoldus de Villa Nova, Anselme the Parmesan, Picatrix the Spaniard, and Cicclus Asculus of Florence.' The very list is a protest against Scholasticism. Moved by wonder at the possibilities of magic and by indignation at ignorance and error, Agrippa has determined to play the part of the philosopher, recover ancient magic from the errors of impiety, and present it purified and adorned. He repudiates the idea of counterfeiting dissemblers that magic must be learned from reprobate books of darkness. His work contains nothing at variance with the laws of nature, or offensive to God, or injurious to religion. The first book of *De occulta Philosophia* is Platonic or doctrinal, the second Pythagorean or universal, the third Cabalistic or ceremonial. Agrippa's doctrinal sources are mainly the group of treatises translated by Ficino. These he has supplemented from a fairly wide range of authors, particularly from Pliny's *Natural History*, Apuleius, the *De Mundo* and other Aristotelian works, Avicenna, and, particularly, Albertus Magnus, whose *De Cælo et Mundo*, *De Secretis*, and *De Virtutibus Herbarum* seem to have been constantly used.

The following from the fiftieth chapter of the second book will serve as a statement of Agrippa's thesis. It is not from the point of view of any age an absurd thesis, and from the point of view of his age it seemed to most thoughtful men entirely probable. He is talking about ceremonial magic, particularly about prayer: 'That humane imprecations do naturally impress their power upon externall things; and [that] man's mind through each degree of dependencies ascends into the intelligible world, and becomes like to the more sublime spirits and intelligences. The virtues of the terrene orb proceed from no other cause than Celestial. Hence the Magician that will worke by them, useth a cunning invocation of the superiors, with mysterious words, and a certain kind of ingenious speech, drawing the one to the other, yet by a natural force through a certain mutuall agreement betwixt them, whereby things follow of their own accord, or sometimes are drawn unwillingly. When we by the remembrance of its majesty being alwaies busied in Divine studies do every moment contemplate Divine things, by a sage and diligent inquisition, and by all degrees of creatures ascending even to the Archetype himself, [we] draw from Him the infallible vertue of all

things,... the understanding of Divine things purgeth
the mind from errors, and rendereth it Divine, giveth
infallible power to our works, and driveth far the
deceits and obstacles of all evil spirits, and together
subjects them to our commands; yea it compels even
good Angels and all the powers of the world unto our
service.' Occult ideas, he tells us in accordance with
Neo-Platonism, are the essential causes of every species
and of every virtue in the species. Therefore, magicians collect wonders from the threefold world of
the Elementary, the Celestial, and the Intellectual, a
practice which reveals the connexion between this
particular branch of pseudo-science and science itself.
The Chief Worker transmits the virtues of his Om-
nipotency by means of the angels, the heavens, the
stars, the planets, the four elements, animals, plants,
metals, and stones. Indeed, He speaks through the mind
of man in dreams and ecstasies and writes upon the
body of man in signs, so that man himself becomes
not only an interpreter of the Divine but a message
from God. It is reasonable, says Agrippa, for us to
ascend by degrees through each order of the universe
and draw new virtues from above. Magic is the faculty which instructs us concerning the differences and
agreements of things among themselves, uniting the
virtues of things through the application of them to
one another and to their inferior suitable subjects,
knitting them together through the power of suitable
bodies. Occult virtues are infused into the several
kinds of things by Ideas with the help of the world
soul and the rays of the stars. The virtues of things
natural depend upon the elements, which in their pure
forms are in the heavens and the stars, and in devils,
angels, and God. It is necessary to record these beliefs, or the matter-of-fact quality of natural magic
may not be understood.

After hearing Agrippa we can better appreciate the peculiar beauty of Adam's answer to Eve's question [16] in *Paradise Lost*, 'wherefore all night long shine these?'

> Lest total Darkness should by night regain
> Her old possession, and extinguish life
> In nature and all things; which these soft fires
> Not only enlighten, but with kindly heat
> Of various influence foment and warm,
> Temper or nourish, or in part shed down
> Their stellar virtue on all kinds that grow
> On Earth, made hereby apter to receive
> Perfection from the Sun's more potent ray.
> These, then, though unbeheld in deep of night,
> Shine not in vain.

Another principle of great importance in Agrippa's philosophy is this: the occult virtues of things have their causes hid, not only from the unobservant, but from the ignorant and the spiritually unfit. This obviously affords the blind of pretended superiority from behind which the impostor has always stalked his prey; but it is also a part of the obscurantist doctrine which appears in all the learning of the Middle Ages and the Renaissance, the doctrine, namely, of select souls and intelligences. Not even Bacon [17] is free from the belief that certain of the higher truths of science and philosophy neither can be nor should be opened to the consideration of common intelligences.

But there are other principles of importance for general Renaissance thought in Agrippa's remarkable exposition. Heraclitus declared that all things were made by enmity and friendship. One must understand, however, that powers resident in things are not of the things themselves but are infused by God through the soul of the world; there is a peculiar power of resem-

blances and intelligences overruling them and a con-
course of the rays and aspects of stars producing a
certain harmonious consent. Agrippa is disposed to
think that it is the world soul in the form of the
quintessence which as a medium unites virtues to
their subjects. But, in any case, everything turns itself
to its like, and the virtues of things must be found
out by way of similitude. If therefore we would ob-
tain any property, let us seek for such plants, animals,
or other natural objects as possess the desired property
in an eminent degree; nay more, since the virtue of
the whole resides in the parts, let us take that part in
which the virtue or property is most vigorous—the
blood of the bear for strength, and the foot of the hare
for speed—and bring the thing or part selected near
to the part to be affected. Natural things infuse their
powers into things which are near them. Does not the
loadstone impart its quality to steel and the looking-
glass of a harlot make the user wanton? But we must
pay attention to enmities as well as friendships. Mercury, Jupiter, Sun, and Moon are friends to Saturn,
but Mars and Venus are his enemies. Do not forget
that all planets except Venus hate Mars, and that all
except Mars love Jupiter. The whole world is full of
such consent and dissent. Of course Agrippa pillaged
Pliny and his followers for lore of this strange kind.
It is, Agrippa says, important to remember that natural virtues follow the species. The lion and the cock
are courageous and the fox is full of deceitfulness and
treachery. It was the virtue of the basilisk, to slay by
the sight of the eye.

From Proclus Agrippa quotes the important principle that all things inferior are subject to superior
things and are included in them. This introduces the
astrological problem, and, to be frank about the matter, it is not an easy problem. If you desire to receive

a virtue from a star, or part of the world, you must use those things which come under the star or body. To attract the virtue of the sun you must use those things which are solary; determinations of solary substances are not always easy to make. Some such agreements may be made known through the imitations of rays, or motions, or figures, colours, odours, and effects. Under Sol, for example, it is easy to recognize lucid flame (among elements), pure blood (among humours), gold (among metals because of its splendour), aetites and carbuncle (among minerals by their sparkle), chrysolite (because it comforts those parts which serve for breathing) as solary; likewise the bay-tree, mint, and cinnamon; the lion, the crocodile, the spotted wolf, the ram, the boar, and the bull; the phœnix, the eagle, the vulture, and the swan; the sea-calf, and the fish called strombi, which follow their king. In addition to these general means of determination there are also special means. All stars project their special natures in the form of certain particular seals or characters,[18] some of which are known and recorded in the science of physiognomy, and every herb, as well as every man, has its star from which it gets its peculiar virtue. At any rate, you must believe that all sublunary things are distributed among the planets, stars, and constellations—individuals, peoples, provinces, and kingdoms.

What are we to think of the hundreds of earnest, patient, intelligent men—of Raymond Lully, Cornelius Agrippa, Paracelsus, Dr. John Dee, and the great Cardan himself—whose misfortune it was to devote their lives to false hypotheses? What is to be said against the dignity of these men in the light of the authority Agrippa thought he could derive from St. Augustine?[19] 'For this is the harmony of the world that things supercelestial may be drawn down by the celes-

tial, and supernatural by the natural, because there is
one operative virtue which is diffused through all
kinds of things, by which virtue, indeed, manifest
things are produced out of occult causes.' Thus a
magician makes use of things manifest to draw forth
things which are occult, viz., through the rays of stars,
through figures, lights, sounds, and natural things
which are agreeable to the celestial; in which, besides
corporeal qualities, there is a kind of reason, sense, and
harmony, and incorporeal and divine measures and
orders.

The use of this principle as it applies to material
things is the special skill of Friar Lawrence[20] in *Romeo
and Juliet:*

> The earth that's nature's mother in her tomb;
> What is her burying grave that is her womb,
> And from her womb children of divers kind
> We sucking on her natural bosom find,
> Many for many virtues excellent,
> None but for some and yet all different.
> O, mickle is the powerful grace that lies
> In herbs, plants, stones, and their true qualities:
> For nought so vile that on the earth doth live
> But to the earth some special good doth give,
> Nor aught so good but strain'd from that fair use
> Revolts from true birth, stumbling in abuse:
> Virtue itself turns vice, being misapplied;
> And vice sometimes by action dignified.

It is obviously impossible to present in detail the
Aristotelian cosmology, nor is it necessary. Founded
as it is upon his physical and logical works Aristotle's
cosmology is scientific rather than idealistic, very vast
in extent and still in large measure credible to enlightened persons. It is, as before said, like Platonism dualistic, but not hospitable to so extensive a parallelism

between matter and spirit. God is to Aristotle an energy of self-contemplation, the unmoved Mover of all things; and, in accordance with his doctrine of form, the soul is the ultimate expression of a physical body; the science of the soul is a part of physical science. Even after St. Thomas Aquinas had rescued the soul from the physics in which Aristotle had enmeshed it, the soul never became with the Aristotelians a mere cousin of the disembodied spirits. In Christian Aristotelianism, with its ample provision for the immortality of the soul and for its life after death, the disagreement with Neo-Platonism is no longer seriously felt. Indeed, in the philosophy of human things it is not felt at all. Both Aristotelianism and Neo-Platonism join hands with Christianity in matters affecting human good. The opinions and beliefs of Agrippa may, in spite of his sincere efforts to achieve plausibility, seem mere vagaries to the modern reader. Not so the other doctrine. Let us turn to a noble example of the cosmological thinking of an enlightened Christian Aristotelian. The principles on which the philosophy rests will be apparent in its applications.

Richard Hooker begins his great theological work *Of the Laws of Ecclesiastical Polity* with a consideration of the nature of law, which he treats under two aspects—the law of Nature and the law of Scripture.[21] These he regards as harmonious, the one with the other, and as promulgated by the same authority. His definition of law is noteworthy and so carefully wrought that it applies to all matters of religion, science, and philosophy: 'That which doth assign unto each thing the kind, that which doth moderate the force and power, that which doth appoint the form and measure of working, the same we term a *Law*.' To determine the genus, species, property, and accident, to

govern the activity within the function, and to determine the position of each creature relative to other
creatures—that was the province of law. God is in His
property inexplicable. To understand Him is beyond
the capacity of man. Hooker therefore does not consider 'the natural, necessary, and internal operations
of God,' but only those in which God has a voluntary
purpose—eternal decrees which we term eternal laws.
God is in this aspect of His majesty a law both to Himself and to all other things besides. He is the First
Cause in whose workings Counsel or Wisdom is
used, Reason followed, and an orderly way observed.
Nothing is wrought without cause, and all is for an
end; nay, 'nothing else is done by God, which to leave
undone were not so good.' Though we cannot determine the particular drift of every one of God's eternal acts, yet 'that little thereof which we darkly
apprehend we admire, the rest with religious ignorance we humbly and meekly adore.'

The Eternal law is called by names appropriate to
the kinds of things which are subject unto it. These
are the grand divisions: the law of Nature which con-
trols all natural agents, Celestial law which orders the
Angels, the law of Reason which binds reasonable
creatures in the world, and Divine law which has been
revealed by God. Human law is made up of reasonable law plus divine law. Its basis is expediency.
Hooker here and elsewhere follows St. Augustine and
St. Thomas Aquinas, especially in his argument that
'the obedience of creatures unto the law of nature is
the stay of the whole world.' Of course those defects
(due to divine malediction after the Fall) in the matter of natural things may thwart the operations of
natural law, but nature's workings are always or for
the most part after one and the same manner, and appetite promotes obedience. All earthly things are en-

dowed with a desire which leads them to seek after perfection or goodness. Man resembles God in His manner of working and seeks naturally to attain the perfection of God. Not only so, but what we do as men we do wittingly and freely; for knowledge and will, both attributes of God, are the two principal fountains of human action. Man thus naturally seeks divine perfection in the various spheres of natural operation, but in his unity with God he is bound to strive for others' good and to prefer the good of the whole before the good of the particular.

These things man does through his nature expressed in appetite, which is primarily desire of sensible good. Affections, such as joy, grief, fear, and anger, are forms of appetite. Their stirrings as such are not in our power to control, and but for the provision of a controller we should be helpless before them; they are, however, under control of will, which in turn is subordinated to reason. The perturbations of the mind may thus be controlled indirectly through controlling the will. The light of reason is necessary to a true act of will, since only by that illumination may the way of nature be opened, and the good distinguished from the evil. Thus appetite is will's solicitor and will is appetite's master. Children, idiots, and madmen, having no use of reason, have no will except in their guardians. Likewise, things which are impossible are never sought by a reasonable will. If evil is desired, the cause of the desire is the goodness which seems to be (and is not) adjoined to it. Such a situation may arise from the claims of appetite. Sensible good is near-at-hand and potent, so that appetite is liable to be too strongly provoked. Sensible impression, especially when backed by custom, may prevail more than reasonable persuasion. Indeed, there may be set up a secondary world of evil in which will and even reason are deluded and seduced by sophistry. This evil world may take the place for a time of the natural world. There is thus provided a doctrine of evil sufficient to account for tragedy in the world and perdition in the human soul, but nevertheless temporary and destined to give way to natural good. 'If reason err, we fall into evil, and are so far forth deprived of the general perfection we seek.'

Hooker's doctrine of evil does not differ from that of Bacon as expressed in 'Of Goodness and Goodness of Nature': 'Goodness answers to the theological virtue Charity, and admits no excess, but error. The desire of power in excess caused the angels to fall; the desire of knowledge in excess caused man to fall: but in charity there is no excess; neither can angel or man come in danger by it.' This also Milton [22] confirms in the third book of *Paradise Lost* in the speech of the Almighty on freedom to choose:

> The first sort by their own suggestion fell,
> Self-tempted, self-depraved.

Satan's atheism in the fifth book and elsewhere shows the same conception of sin; as also Satan's momentary recoil from evil at the sight of Eve:

>   Her heavenly form
> Angelic, but more soft and feminine,
> Her graceful innocence, her every air
> Of gesture or least action, overawed
> His malice, and with rapine sweet bereaved
> His fierceness of the fierce intent it brought.
> That space the Evil One abstracted stood
> From his own evil, and for the time remained
> Stupidly good, of enmity disarmed,
> Of guile, of hate, of envy, of revenge.
> But the hot hell that always in him burns,
> Though in mid Heaven, soon ended his delight.

But it is Iago [23] who offers a grand perversion of the theory that good is the end and purpose of reason:

Virtue! a fig! 'tis in ourselves that we are thus or thus. Our bodies are our gardens, to the which our wills are gardeners; so that if we will plant nettles, or sow lettuce, set hyssop and weed up thyme, supply it with one gender of herbs, or distract it with many, either to have it sterile with idleness, or manured with industry, why, the power and corrigible authority of this lies in our wills.

Another important principle which Hooker develops has to do with the ways of knowing goodness. It is not necessary to know evil, since 'he that knoweth what is straight doth even thereby discern what is crooked.' There are two ways to know goodness: first, to know the causes whereby it is made such, and, secondly, to observe the signs and tokens always attached to goodness. In an age of 'common imbecility' such as his own it is not necessary to inquire deeply into causes. The most important of the tokens of goodness is the general and perpetual voice of men, which is 'as the sentence of God himself. For that which all men have at all times learned, Nature herself must needs have taught.' And yet Hooker admits that a commonly received error is never overthrown until we go from signs to causes. This passage from signs to causes is not impossible, since the main principles of reason are in themselves apparent. All the simpler axioms of reason, such as that God is to be worshipped and parents to be honoured, have been found out by discourse of reason. However, too much inquiry is perplexing. One may consider too curiously. Theophrastus said, 'They that seek a reason of all things do utterly overthrow Reason.' Apparently the most obvious of rational maxims is that the best and highest should head the rest—the soul the body, the spirit of

God within our minds the soul. The sentence of reason is clear, universal, and known to all; it may be mandatory, permissive, or admonitory. The point is that the dictates of reason are uninvestigable without revelation. They themselves tell us that such as keep the laws of reason 'follow the manner of Nature's works.' Lewd and wicked custom may have force to smother the light of natural understanding, which needs the perpetual aid and concurrence of God. As for the rest, reason leads men to make human laws for the government of politic societies and to establish also a Law of Nations. God has by Scripture made known such laws as serve for the direction of human conduct, which laws repeat, emphasize, and interpret the unrevealed natural law. There is no conflict, no inadequacy, and in nature no tyranny. All is perfect save in the unregenerate wills of the sons of Adam.

No such perfect statement of the nature, scope, and function of law can perhaps elsewhere be found; but Hooker's analysis is none the less explicative of the thought of the age. His explanation of human law as the outcome of the social contract [24] was not acceptable to the dominant political theorists of the reigns of James I and Charles I, a circumstance which possibly caused the later books of the *Laws of Ecclesiastical Polity* to be withheld from publication during their author's life and, in turn, brought about their publication after the forces of democracy had become dominant at the time of the Great Rebellion and the Commonwealth. But the opinion that human laws were the traditional result of human counsel and agreement, not an issue until late in the reign of Queen Elizabeth and not a burning one then, was common enough. The other view that laws might arise from the will of a divinely established monarch, though not fully asserted until after Hooker wrote his book, was even then more common and more authoritarian. Hooker derived his governing principles, in which there were no faults, from his conception of a universe perfect and divinely ordered in every part.

We have thus found in both major systems of philosophy (as popularly entertained) a cosmological dualism between matter and spirit, regarded as mutually correspondent. It only remains to say that man's body was believed to be made up of the material elements and his soul of spiritual substance. So constituted man might become a bridge across the chasm between mind and matter, spirit and substance; in him there might be formed a synthesis of originally irreconcilable elements, which synthesis was then as now his best hope. Such an agreement among composing elements and such a harmony between elemental and spiritual substance Antony attributes to the fallen Brutus: [25]

> His life was gentle, and the elements
> So mix'd in him that Nature might stand up
> And say to all the world, 'This was a man!'

If we understand Renaissance cosmology as the conception of the world then held as to the constitution of man's environment, both physical and spiritual, we may profitably inquire what were the consequences in opinions and conduct of such an environment. That inquiry we shall endeavour to make in the chapters which follow this. If a more definite realization of the significance of this now almost discarded cosmology in matters of thought and feeling is desired, it may be arrived at easily by a consideration of the effects and moral implications of cosmology in general and by a comparison of the situations in this respect between the modern world, both educated and uneducated, and the world of Shakespeare's time. Cosmology may be said to affect us according to the degree of its immanence and by its implications as to the lives we lead, or ought to lead; in other words, by what we see and feel and by what we believe is the significance of what we see and feel. A cosmology which is impersonally scientific, such as that which supplies us with our starry universe and our physical nature, will certainly seem coldly non-committal compared with the cosmology of the Renaissance. In the latter, the physical and the spiritual, the factual and the doctrinal, the casual and the purposeful were, to a far greater degree than in the modern world, of one piece. The Aristotelian cosmology, and much more its Neo-Platonic variant, were not only immanent but inclusive and inescapable. Man had an established part and place in them, which he understood because of his own simple dominance. The modern man may escape the influence of the modern cosmology because he does not understand it or perceive his own relation to it. The older universe spoke to him in a thousand ways; he could not get beyond the sound of its voice. Some one might say that the new physics has destroyed nineteenth-century determinism and left as large a scope for the freedom of the will as that suggested by the unpredictable atoms of Lucretius in *De Rerum Natura;* but, even so, this modern view cannot approach the Renaissance pattern on the side of its speaking intimation of a divine purpose, with man as the end of all.

In the gravity and reasonableness of Hooker and Cornelius Agrippa there is manifested a feeling of close intimacy between man and the universe. It is obvious even in the legitimate fields of learning occupied by these men. How greatly the aggressive nature of man's environment was enhanced in the realm of the fanatical and the superstitious can readily be imagined. These often more alarming voices could not but create in man an impression that he lived in an environment which demanded courage, caution, and eternal vigilance.

CHAPTER II

DERIVATIONS AND INFERENCES

For after the articles and principles of religion are placed, and exempted from examination of reason, it is then permitted unto us to make derivations and inferences from and according to the analogy of them.—Bacon, *The Advancement of Learning*.

WE HAVE attempted to see that regulated formal order of which the man of the Renaissance was a part; let us now inquire how man received and acted on it. The subject is of course both vague and complicated; but perhaps some idea of the situation can be arrived at by looking at the subject from two major aspects,—first, the aspect of science or the rational aspect, and, secondly, the aspect of religion. With the latter we shall consider certain political and moral effects and tendencies. The former has to do with credulity and scepticism and might be carried, as is customary, into the history of the birth of modern science; the latter has primarily to do with the accepted belief as to the nature and fate of the human soul, which had been placed outside the realm in which reason was allowed to operate. It is no small evidence of the intellectual hardihood of Bacon that he suggests even tentatively that 'it is permitted to make derivations and inferences from and according to the analogy' of the articles and principles of religion, which he has just exempted from reasonable examination. We shall consider the two cosmological pseudo-sciences of astrology and magic in an attempt to show that these disciplines met with at least partial acceptance, and shall then take up matters in other fields in some sense dependent on the doctrine of the soul. If the soul is conceived of as free, or if it is conceived of as in some sense enthralled, there are consequences in political, social, and individual conduct appropriate to both conditions.

Astronomical phenomena appear obviously and have immediate connexion with cosmological theory. We may therefore find it profitable to begin with astrology.[1] We may ask to what extent astrological influences were believed in by scholars and learned men in England in the sixteenth century. It is a typical question and fortunately very easy to answer. Astrology was the interpretative part of astronomy, was sanctioned by the writings of Ptolemy and by writings attributed to Aristotle, and seems to have held a place in the curriculum of the universities of the Middle Ages and the Renaissance. Astrology was tolerated if not sanctioned by the Church and was, as regards its validity as a science, believed in by all learned men. But there are necessary qualifications of this statement.

Let us begin with the case of one of the most intelligent of the literary men of the sixteenth century, Sir Philip Sidney. Fulke Greville,[2] who was himself something of a sceptic, has the following significant passage in his *Life of the Renowned Sir Philip Sidney:* 'Now though I am not of their faith, who affirme wise men can governe the Starres; yet I do beleeve no Stargazers can so well prognosticate the good, or ill of all Governments, as the providence of men trained up in publique affaires may doe. Whereby they differ from Prophets only in this; that Prophets by inspiration, and these by consequence, judge of things to come.' Among these wise men (those trained up in public affairs) he would reckon Sir Philip Sidney. Greville says that he takes no stock in star-gazers and that in political prophecy he would prefer Sir Philip Sidney's trained observations to astrological prognostications. A good many men no doubt felt as Greville did. He is voicing his own opinions and not those of Sidney, and yet in a general sense Greville probably expresses Sidney's views as well as his own. Sidney was indeed a man who, though he was an ardent student and believed in learned culture, trusted mainly in himself rather than in the stars and preached self-reliance. But, on the other hand, he knew a great deal about astrology, evidently wished his brother Robert to learn the rudiments of the subject, and used astrology very extensively and deftly in his works. The *Diary* of Dr. John Dee [3] records two visits by Sidney to Dr. Dee, one of which was immediately before Sidney set out on an expedition. His biographer, Mr. M. W. Wallace,[4] suggests that that particular visit may have been in order to learn the auspices of his journey. If so, it was a customary enough thing to do. *Arcadia* has many seriously intended allusions to horoscopes and astrological soothsayers; and still further confirmation of Sidney's faith in astrology is to be found in *Astrophel and Stella*, particularly in Sonnet xxvi:

> Though duskie wits doe scorne Astrologie,
> And fooles can thinke those lampes of purest light,
> Whose number waies greatnes eternitie,
> Promising wondrous wonders to invite,
>   To have for no cause birth-right in the skye.
> But for to spangle the blacke weedes of Night,
> Or for some braue within that Chamber hie,
> They shold still daunce to please a gazers sight.
> For me I nature every deale doe know,
> And know great causes, great effects procure,
> And know those bodies high, raigne on the low.
> And if these rules did fall, proofe makes me sure,

Who oft bewraies my after following case,
By onely those two starres in *Stellas* face.

The general credence given to astrology will be
made still clearer by a consideration of the opinions
of Robert Recorde, who was a humanist of very considerable breadth, a scholar, and the greatest mathematician of his time in England. What would such a
man think about the subject of astrology? He has not
left us in doubt. *The Castle of Knowledge* (1556) is
an excellent work by this man of high standing, whose
attitude toward branches of his general subject on
which he does not consider himself an authority may
be compared to that of many a modern scholar who
does not presume to wander from his own specialty,
because he respects the specialties of others. Recorde
is so modest that he regards astronomy, which he pro-
fesses, as ancillary to astrology, which he does not
profess. On the title-page of his book is engraved a
castle-like structure with the queenly figure of Astronomy on top of it; on the left is a female figure
holding aloft the *Sphæra Fati*, the Sphere of Destiny,
whose governor is Knowledge; on the right, another
goddess, blindfolded, holds a cord attached to the
crank of the *Sphæra Fortunæ*, whose governor is Ignorance. At the bottom is a piece of poetry:

> Though spiteful Fortune turned her wheele
> To staye the Sphere of Vranye,
> Yet dooth this Sphere resist that wheele,
> And fleeyth all fortunes villanye.
> Though earth do honour Fortunes balle,
> And bytells blynde hyr wheele aduaunce,
> The heavens to fortune are not thralle,
> These Spheres surmount al fortunes chance.

The book is composed of four treatises: (1) an introduction into the Sphere declaring the necessary

parts of it, both material and celestial; (2) a treatise on the making of the Sphere, as well 'in sound and massye forme, as also in Ring forme with hoopes'; (3) the uses of the Sphere and other things incident thereto presented for ease in learning without proofs or demonstrations; (4) a treatise on many things that were noted in the earlier parts together with the demonstrations and proofs before omitted. The Preface to the Reader, partly in verse printed as prose, declares that man was given eyes to view the heavens, so that he should not be so vain as not to realize the unimportance of earthly life. Man should study to understand the signs spread out in the heavens, since God wills that nothing should happen suddenly and without warning. Other men besides Noah could have read the signs of the approaching Flood. No great change in the world, no translation of empires—scarcely the fall of princes—no dearth and penury, have ever occurred of which God by signs in the heavens 'hath not and doth not premonish men.' This is too well known to require illustration. It belongs however to the judicial part of astronomy and does not, therefore, concern the author; yet he will, nevertheless, cite a few cases: There was an eclipse of the Sun before the building of Rome; signs also appeared at the time of the Fall of Rome at the hands of the Goths, and so on. He cites Manilius and Ptolemy to prove that eclipses of Sun and Moon, rainbows of unusual form, comets, etc., are God's messengers to say that earthly events are accompanied by heavenly signs. His object in writing this book on the Sphere is to render the calculations of those who consult the stars more accurate and easier of accomplishment. He wishes men, not merely to avoid calamity, but to become governors and rulers of the stars. Astronomy is of course important in other matters, particularly in navigation and, as shown by Hippocrates' 'Book of the Air' and Galen's 'Critical Days,' in medicine. Consider, Recorde says, the use of astronomy in sowing grain, in making the calendar, and in computing the seasons. Indeed, astronomy is useful in every art and science, even to grammar, rhetoric, logic, and history. The most important dialogue of *The Castle of Knowledge* between Master and Scholar advances the thesis that marvellous motions in the heavens correspond to strange perturbations on earth. But there is no astrology in the book; it devotes itself to a practical and sane, sometimes a brilliant, exposition of the operative part of astronomy, including several excellent demonstrations of the rotundity of the earth.

And yet contemporary with Robert Recorde, and long before and long after his time, there was a social exercise of the astrological art which such men as he must always have despised. The scorn of the learned for ignorant, and often dishonest, practitioners is beautifully expressed by Gabriel Harvey[5] in his *Marginalia:*

'The A.B.C. of owr vulgar Astrologers, especially such, as ar commonly termed Cunning men or Artsmen... Sum call them wissards. Erra Paters prognostication for euer. The Shepherds Kalendar. The Compost of Ptolomeus. Sum fewe add Arcandam: & a pamflet, intituled, The knowledg of things unknowne. I haue heard sum of them name Jon de indagine. Theise be theire great masters: & this in a manner theire whole librarie: with sum old parchment-roules, tables, & instruments. Erra Pater, their Hornebooke. The Shepherds Kalendar, their primer. The Compost of Ptolomeus, their Bible. Arcandam, their newe Testament. The rest, with Albertus secrets, & Aristotles problems Inglished, their great Doctours, & wonderfull Secreta secretorum.'

A volume could be written on this list of books. *Erra Pater*, the Esdras prognostications, exists in dozens of manuscripts, English and Latin, often accompanied by a widely circulated traditional series of lunations, prognostications for every day of the moon's age, and was published in English by R. Wyer about 1536. Never a book that a decent scholar would look at, it continued to appear in print at fairly frequent intervals until the middle of the eighteenth century. *The Shepherds Kalendar*, possibly Alexander Barclay's translation of the *Kalendrier des Bergers*, a poetical almanac describing the shepherd's life and work for all the months of the year, was published at Paris in 1503. R. Copland's translation, published first by W. de Worde in 1508, ran through fifteen editions by 1631. *The Compost of Ptholomeus* (published by R. Wyer, 1532?, 1535?, 1540?) is a wretched English translation of what seems to have been a poor French version of the *Centiloquium*, or hundred aphorisms, based on the *Tetrabiblos* of Ptolemy and supposed to give the 'Fruit' of the Ptolemaic teachings as applied to astrological ends. There was an edition of the book as late as 1635(?) and probably other editions intervening between it and Wyer's publications, it being the sort of cheap and vulgar book that would have been liable to complete loss. The *Arcandam*, described as 'the most excellent booke to fynd the desteny of euery man,' is another work of the same low character. It is one of the translations of William Warde through the French from a Latin original by Richard Roussat. The title-page betrays the book by describing it as *The most excellent, profitable, and pleasaunt book of the famous Doctor and expert Astrologian Arcandam or Aleandrin, to finde the fatal destiny, complexion, and natural inclination of every man and child, by his birth. With an addition of Phisiognomy,*

very pleasant to reade. It was published by J. Row-
botham about 1562 and ran through at least seven
editions by 1637. This same William Warde gave to
the world an English translation of *The Secretes of
the Reverende Maister Alexis of Piemont* (1558), a
book giving excellent remedies against divers diseases,
wounds and other accidents. This was a sort of peren-
nial book. Warde provided second, third, and fourth
parts, the fifth, sixth, and seventh being translated by
one R. Androse. With the books in Harvey's list, this
book, a copy of Vicary's wretched anatomy, and possibly a cheap herbal, a quack could defy the College
of Physicians and the Company of Barber-Surgeons.
For a complete equipment in superficial learning only
the *Pymander* would be needed, and that was to be
supplied by the next generation. An idea of the low
level of learned culture in the sixteenth century can
be gathered from the fact that William Warde was
Queen's Professor of Physic at Cambridge. The widespread abuse of astrology was found shocking to many
men of eminence in the medical profession. Among
them it is important to remember John Securis, one
of the most learned and careful almanac-makers of
the day, who in his *A Detection and Querimonie of
the daily enormities and abuses committed in Physick*
(1566) attacks quackery from the respectable ground
of sincere though erroneous learning. Of the final
members of Harvey's list, *Secreta Secretorum* and
Aristotle's *Problems*, nothing need be said. The former
is one of the most celebrated books of quackery in
the world, and the version of the *Problemata*, preserved as *The Problemes of Aristotle with other Philosophers and Phisitions* (published by the Widow
Orwin, 1595), is a degenerate specimen of a questionable work. One is moved to add to this pitiful
list of works of degraded learning Richard Grafton's

A Litle Treatise conteyning many proper tables and rules (Tottell, 1571), a vastly popular work and no doubt exceedingly useful to quacks and pretenders to learning; as was also the almanac of Nostradamus, which appeared in English first about 1558.

This ground is familiar, but the reader should remember a distinction probably worth making in connexion with it,—that between the honest, well-informed, and sincere practitioners of a false science and the dishonest, ignorant, and pretentious quacks from whose knavery the profession suffered disgrace. The matter was relative at any given time in the sixteenth century. It was not only relative but changing rapidly. Many works which were adequate expressions of the best learning of say 1550 had become the vulgar knowledge of 1580 and 1590; truer learning had meantime risen to higher planes. Quackery too underwent its changes. It grew more mystical and bombastic; but the ancient cheap stuff, much of which had troubled the Middle Ages, also lived on as it lives now more remotely. Let it not be thought that quackery was then or is now usually insincere; its insincerity was and is a variable factor. Dr. John Dee was a frank thinker and something of a scholar; he was much misled. Dr. Robert Fludd was one of the most learned, most sincere, most bombastic impostors that ever lived. He fooled himself far more than Dr. Dee was fooled by others.

The uses of these books by fanatics and impostors are primarily responsible no doubt for the *odium astrologicum* of which the literature of the time is full. Astrologers were cheats and charlatans. They lived in narrow lanes and dark alleys and dressed themselves like mountebanks. They were often crystal gazers and practitioners of the black art. They interfered in politics, lent their falsity to the causes of slander and prostitution, lived by cheating the foolish poor, and went wrong about the weather year by year and day by day. This attitude toward astrology is freely reflected in literature. It is not that anybody doubted that there might be significance in the behaviour of the stars, but that everybody knew that many astrologers were impostors; and yet the impression one gets from Renaissance literature is not prevailingly adverse to astrology.

There are scornful references in Jonson and other comic writers; specifically, there are John Melton's satire *The Astrologaster* (1620) and later Butler's famous portrait of Sidrophel in *Hudibras:* John Chamber's *Treatise against Iudicial Astrologie* (1601) and George Carleton's *The Madnesse of Astrologers* (1624), culminating in William Rowland's *Judiciall Astrology Judicially Condemned* (1652), are not only arguments against astrological beliefs but denunciations of astrologers. There were plenty of books written in favour of the subject, like Sir Christopher Heydon's learned and excellent *A Defence of Judiciall Astrologie* (1603), and so grave and serious are many of the allusions to the starry heavens by the dramatists that they not infrequently suggest religious reverence. Marlowe's heroes are conscious of their stars, as are Chapman's; indeed, the titanic Byron[6] fights against them. Shakespeare's treatment of astrology is respectful and considerate. One recalls the 'pair of star-cross'd lovers' and the 'yoke of inauspicious stars' in *Romeo and Juliet*. Shakespeare knows with Helena[7] that 'the fated sky Gives us free scope' and with Cassius[8] that

> The fault, dear Brutus, is not in our stars,
> But in ourselves, that we are underlings.

But he shows greater suspension of judgment, more awe, in the passage in which Hamlet[9] speaks of 'the stamp of one defect,' which is 'nature's livery, or fortune's star,' in the twenty-sixth sonnet, and in Prospero's [10]

> by my prescience
> I find my zenith doth depend upon
> A most auspicious star, whose influence
> If I now court not but omit, my fortunes
> Will ever after droop.

The famous skeptical passage spoken by Edmund [11] in *King Lear* may be intended to exemplify the speaker's rebellious and atheistical character:

This is the excellent foppery of the world, that, when we are sick in fortune,—often the surfeit of our own behaviour,—we make guilty of our disasters the sun, the moon, and the stars: as if we were villains by necessity; fools by heavenly compulsion; knaves, thieves, and treachers, by spherical predominance; drunkards, liars, and adulterers, by an enforced obedience of planetary influence; and all that we are evil in, by a divine thrusting on: an admirable evasion of whoremaster man, to lay his goatish disposition to the charge of a star!

The opinion of Shakespeare's Edmund the Bastard is not the common one; and, if further confirmation of this statement is needed, consider the eloquent words of Montaigne [12] in the 'Apology for Raimond Sebond' on man's indifference and his presumption in his doubts:

But, poor devil, what is there in him deserving of such a privilege? When we consider the incorruptible life of the heavenly bodies, their beauty, their grandeur, their continual motion by so exact a rule: ... when we con-

sider the domination and power those bodies have, not
only over our lives and the condition of our fortune,
...but even over our dispositions, our judgement, our
will, which they govern, impel and stir at the mercy of
their influence, as our reason discovers and tells us: ...
when we see that not only a man, not only a king, but
kingdoms, empires, and all this world here below, are
moved according to the lightest swing of the heavenly
motions: ...if our virtue, our vices, our talents and our
knowledge, if even this dissertation of mine on the power
of the stars, this comparison between them and ourselves,
comes, as our reason supposes, by their means and their
favour;...if this little portion of reason we possess has
been allotted to us by heaven, how can reason make us
the equal of heaven? How can it subject its essence and
conditions to our knowledge? All that we see in those
bodies fills us with amazement.

We have dwelt upon astrology at length because it
offers a crucial instance. It is cosmological, and it had
the best chance among the pseudo-sciences to win the
sanction of learned men and to escape the numerous
prohibitions of the Church, which was naturally jealous of all other agencies that sought to dispense a
knowledge of spiritual power or of the will of God.
But there are yet to be considered other even more
intimate and available means of cosmological interpretation, namely, magical arts and sciences. Of course
they are less in evidence in literature than is astrology,
but they are not absent or inconsiderable.

Agrippa has things, far reaching in their literary
effects, to say about the occult aspects of psychology;[13] for example, on the subject of fascination,
which is vitally connected with the all-important literary subjects of love and friendship. The instrument
of fascination is the spirit,—a lucid, subtle vapour

generated out of the purer blood by the heat of the heart. This spirit sends forth through the eyes rays like to itself. These rays strike into the eyes and possess the breast of him that is stricken; they wound his heart and possess in turn his spirit. References to this principle in the Elizabethan drama and lyric are numberless. Perhaps the most potent eye in literature, if we may believe Biron, is that of Rosaline [14] in *Love's Labour's Lost:*

> A wither'd hermit, five-score winters worn,
> Might shake off fifty, looking in her eye.

Fascination is the art of the witch; witches use for the purpose of fascinating their victims collyries, alligations, and ointments. But these magical influences seem to have been thought operative in many quite legitimate fields. It was known that the blood of doves will produce love fascination, the eyes of wolves fear. Physicians seem to have relied upon it. Montaigne [15] says quite definitely that they did:

Even the choice of most of their drugs is in some sort mysterious and divine: the left foot of a tortoise, the urine of a lizard, an elephant's dung, a mole's liver, blood drawn from under the right wing of a white pigeon; and for us who have the stone (so scornfully do they take advantage of our misery!), the pulverized droppings of a rat, and other such tomfooleries that are more suggestive of magic and spells than of a serious science. Not to mention their pills, to be taken in uneven numbers, the setting apart of certain days and festivals in the year, of certain hours for gathering the herbs of their ingredients, the grim scowl, the wise and learned looks and demeanour which they put on, and which even Pliny remarked upon with derision.

Souls by their powers of fascination, we are told by Agrippa, may repair dying bodies with other inferior souls; it is even possible, particularly in the condition of melancholy, to induce new spirits into men's bodies, according to the three apprehensions—sense-perception, imagination, and the passions of the mind.[16] These foreign spirits, aided by melancholy (natural melancholy and white choler), might enter an ignorant man, who might presently become a great painter or, if they entered his faculty of reason, he might become a philosopher or an orator; if the divine spirits entered his *intellectus* (or soul of intuition) he might perceive divine secrets and things eternal. It is thus that the Messianic prophecies of the Sybils are to be accounted for. So likewise those near to death or weakened by old age, since they are less hindered by bodily sensation, are capable of divination. Of the doctrine of the induction or transfusion of soul there are plenty of traces in literature, such as the story of the sons of Agape in the third book of the *Faerie Queene* and many references in lyric poetry which may not be wholly figurative; Sidney's sonnet beginning 'My true love hath my heart and I have his' is a case in point. As to the effects of weakened physical powers in increasing the insight of the soul, we have many examples. In *Hamlet* the Ghost of the murdered king[17] says of Gertrude,

> But, look, amazement on thy mother sits:
> O, step between her and her fighting soul:
> Conceit in weakest bodies strongest works:
> Speak to her, Hamlet.

There is no doubt that both the doctrine and its popular appeal appear in *Richard II.* The aged and dying Gaunt,[18] believing that

> the tongues of dying men
> Enforce attention like deep harmony,

says of Richard

> Methinks I am a prophet new inspired
> And thus expiring do foretell of him.

The magical power of the passions of the mind
arises from the fact that the spirits (such as those that
Lady Macbeth [19] longs to pour into her husband's
ear) alter the accidents or accessory qualities of the
body and thus the body itself by the moving of the
spirits within the person affected. Agrippa's doctrine
of the passions [20] or perturbations was that they derive their power, over soul as well as body, by the
means of imagination. This is a most interesting psychological doctrine as yet never worked out. Imagination becomes the agent of fascination, the actual
destroyer of distance (as in Shakespeare's sonnets),
and a misleader of the will within the individual. It
can work effects in other bodies besides its own. The
machinery which is set in operation is of this sort: in
joy the spirits are driven outward, in fear drawn back
to the centre, in bashfulness conveyed to the brain.
Joy dilates the heart; sadness restricts it. Lovers are
so tied together by the commingling of their spirits
that one suffers what the other suffers. By the imagination of the mother an infant in the womb may be
marked by a sign. Man's mind may be joined with the
mind of the celestials and wonderful virtues thereby
infused, because when the intellect is intent upon any
work the apprehension and power which is in all
things are obedient to it. Since the superior binds the
inferior, our minds can change, attract, and repel by
their excess of passion what they desire to influence
if it be inferior in station. Words have a magic power,
since speech is the distinguishing gift of man. Adam,
whose natural knowledge was perfect, named all

things according to their natures. Words are more potent in sentences and when written, for writing is the ultimate expression of mind. Hebrew is nearest the original magic of God's voice and is therefore the greatest of languages. It is thus possible by careful scrutiny and enlightened intelligence to lead the better life by making use of those things which God in His goodness has laid open to our observation.

Agrippa's second book is devoted to magical numbers, to figures and harmonies, particularly the mathematical harmonies supposed to reside in the celestial universe.

In his third book he dwells at length on evil spirits and their orders. His conception of malignant spirits as heathen gods and fallen angels is the traditional one which underlies Heywood's *Hierarchy of the Blessed Angels* and Milton's *Paradise Lost*. It may be that this section, which goes farthest in the direction of evil magic,[21] had much to do with the degeneration which Agrippa's reputation suffered in the later sixteenth century. He made a definite attempt to establish a new order of magic, and in a certain way he succeeded. Agrippa's magic is the characteristic magic of the Renaissance and differs, as he said it did, from that of earlier writers, in general, in its intelligence and in its attempt to establish its orthodoxy. These features did not prevent him and Paracelsus and even Cardan from acquiring popularly the reputation of wizardry. There sprang up many tales of the wonders he had wrought by his practise of the black art. His superiority and general plausibility were, however, fully recognized in the great revival of mysticism and cabalism in the seventeenth century. The remarks of his English translator J. F. (1651) in his epistle to the Judicious Reader reveal this: 'To have a bare notion of a Deity, to apprehend some motions of the

Celestials, together with the common operations
thereof, and to conceive of some Terrest[r]ial productions, is but what is superficiall and vulgar; But
this is true, this is sublime, this *Occult Philosophy;*
to understand the mysterious influences of the intellectual world upon the Celestial, and of both upon
the Terrest[r]ial; and to know how to dispose and
fit our selves so, as to be capable of receiving those
superiour operations, whereby we may be able to
operate wonderfull things, which indeed seem impossible, or at least unlawfull, when as indeed they may
be affected by a naturall power and without either
offence to God, or violation of Religion. To defend
Kingdoms, to discover the secret counsels of men, to
overcome enemies, to redeem captives, to increase
riches, to procure the favor of men, to expell diseases, to preserve health, to prolong life, to renew
youth, to foretell future events, to see and know
things done many miles off, and such like as these, by
vertue of superior influences, may seem things incredible; Yet read but the ensuing Treatise and thou
shalt see the possibility thereof confirmed by reason
and example. I speak now to the judicious, for as for
others, they neither know, nor believe, nor will know
anything but what is vulgar, nay they think, that
beyond this there is scarce anything knowable; when
as indeed there are profound mysteries in all beings,
even from God in the highest heavens to the divels
in the lowest hell; yea in very numbers, names, letters, characters, gestures, time, place, and such like,
all which this learned Author profoundly discussed.'

The doctrines of the demonology of the Renaissance
appear and reappear in Elizabethan literature. The
long struggle of rationalism against witchcraft was
not to be decided for more than a hundred years. It is
hard for a modern to conceive imaginatively of a

world surrounded and infested with spirits, good and bad. Such spirits must have been controlling agents in all human activities and in all walks of life. It has taken the full force of modernism to break down the belief in spirits. They were abundant in this universe, —the ranked and ordered angels, the unarmed youth of Heaven, the reprobate demons who like a flock of ravenous fowls followed their master to the ruined earth, spirits of fire, air, water, and earth, resident aliens from an almost forgotten paganism, and the ghosts of the departed dead.

> Nor think, though men were none,
> That Heaven would want spectators, God want praise.
> Millions of spiritual creatures walk the Earth
> Unseen, both when we wake, and when we sleep:
> All these with ceaseless praise his works behold,
> Both day and night.[22]

With whatever spiritual hosts the aggregated traditions of human imagination may have peopled all the vast world, the significant fact remains that theology had given to man a soul, and soul is spirit. The life of the soul is the religious life, and in that life resided the deepest interest of the age. So all-important was the subject of religion in every department of Renaissance life that those who seek to know the sources of Elizabethan thought must turn to it. The most fateful questions concerned the soul. Duty, human conduct, was a determinant factor in the soul's fate. Conduct cannot be divorced from responsibility. Was the soul responsible? Was it free? It could not be entirely responsible, entirely free, as long as it was a cog in the grand old cosmological machine. Let us now examine our second major aspect of cosmological thinking—religion [23]—and some of the things determined by it.

Much of the habit and belief of the old religion lived on undisturbed by the Reformation and carried with it throughout the Renaissance its atmosphere of formal order and permanence. It was the customary thing for large classes of people. Note, for example, the teachings of Robert Allott's [24] popular encyclopædia, *Wits Theater of the Little World* (printed for I. R. for N. L. 1599). Pliny, Allott says, has described the universal world; Strabo, Pomponius Mela, and Solinus, the particular world, dividing it into heaven and earth. Man belongs to neither of these, but is a little world or microcosm (so called by Aristotle), which corresponds in all details to the great world or macrocosm. God rules in both worlds equally. His organization of powers in the universal world, according to St. Denis, is as follows: (1) above Heaven, the Trinity; (2) In Heaven, the angels; (3) under Heaven, the prelates and ministers of God. From Isidore comes the following outline of the powers of Heaven itself, which, it will be noticed, correspond to the religious faculties of the human heart: *Epiphania*, divided into Seraphim (who excel in zealous love), Cherubim (who excel in knowledge), and Thrones (who excel in justice); *Epiphonomia*, divided into Principalities (who teach the lower states to revere their betters), Powers (who drive away evil spirits), Dominations (who teach men how to behave in spiritual conflicts); *Euphumia*, divided into Virtues (who work miracles), Archangels (who reveal miracles), and Angels (who are messengers and comforters). The avenue by which these powers may enter the human heart is prayer. This scheme is the merest commonplace, but it did not cease to function in men's minds until long after the Renaissance.

As to the nature of the soul, primary subject of religious thought, there is no reason to regard the views of Sir John Davies [25] in *Nosce Teipsum* and other writings as anything less than widely typical. To Davies, as to the Schoolmen, the universe was a duality of God and the world, and man was a duality of soul and body. The first part of *Nosce Teipsum* presents a detailed definition of the soul in positive and negative terms, its functions, and theories as to its origin. The conclusion is that the soul is 'a spirit, and heavenly influence.' An explanation of the relation of the soul to the body, which can hardly be regarded otherwise than as an advanced form of animism, closes the first part. The second part is devoted to answering the most engrossing question of that age (as of almost every other), namely, whether or not the soul is immortal. It is worth noting that the soul, operating through reason, retains in all circumstances her perfect power, which is necessary to her perfect freedom:

> So, though the clouds eclipse the sunne's faire light,
> Yet from his face they doe not take one beame;
> So haue our eyes their perfect power of sight,
> Euen when they looke into a troubled streame.

> Then these defects in Senses' organs bee,
> Not in the soule or in her working might;
> She cannot lose her perfect power to see,
> Thogh mists and clouds do choke her window light.

Much follows from this principle. For illustration consider the following lines which lay down the doctrine of the idiot. Idiots have as good souls as wise men; the inward senses of idiots are merely indisposed:

> Euen so the Soule to such a body knit,
> Whose inward senses vndisposed be,
> And to receiue the formes of things vnfit;
> Where nothing is brought in, can nothing see.

This makes the idiot, which hath yet a mind,
Able to know the truth, and chuse the good;
If she such figures in the braine did find,
As might be found, if it in temper stood.

The freedom of the soul, and hence of the will, was doctrinally so important, that even astrology had to admit that the stars incline but not compel. Nothing is more important than a knowledge of the doctrine held at any one time with reference to the immortality of the soul, because the conditions of its immortality often determine the degree of its freedom. If there is a warfare between reason and the will, it may take one of three forms: (1) the adversaries may be equal (a situation which may be disregarded); (2) reason may be superior, so that we may attain an Aristotelian peace in a life of contemplation; or (3) will may rule, with important results, for the supremacy of will is the fundamental principle of Machiavellianism, Calvinism, Puritanism, and Stoicism. It is obvious that the status of the soul as regards this conflict between will and reason is important in literature, and that Shakespeare, Bacon, and Hooker occupy the second position.

By and large, it is the old, formal, and peaceful religion which is usually to be found in both the learned and the literary works of the age. For example, consider this from Thomas Milles,[26] *The Treasvrie of Avncient and Moderne Times:* Book I, chapter i, furnishes us with a learned discussion of God, with arguments and elucidations drawn from Aristotle, Cicero, Damascene, Chrysostom, Origen, Anselm, Augustine, Dionysius Areopagitica, Justin Martyr, Philemon, and others, and of course from the Holy Scriptures, telling why we know there is a God and only one, what His names are and what they signify, and what is His essence. God in this account is a just, honourable and kindly being. The chapters following deal, in the same manner, with the creation, the orders of the angels, the earthly Paradise, Hell and what its fire is, Man and what is meant by his being created in the image of God, Satan in the serpent's shape with other devils, and death. The chapters are distinguished by their learning and their close logical reasoning, there being, for example, one of the finest possible distinctions drawn between 'Image' and 'Similitude.' It is the soul which is the image or form of God and possesses the three several dignities of God: Understanding, Will, and Memory; whereas similitude refers to the nature and attributes of God: Immortality, Virtue, and Wisdom. The similitude of God is the ruling principle of organized society.

What might be called the political value of the ancient religious system was held on to with some tenacity. Training in religion and piety was the first element in the education of the prince.[27] Bodin in *De la République* has much to say about religion and government. Book I, chapter xiii, tells how a Prince may suppress one religion by favouring another, there being many citizens who follow that which a prince favours. Book IV, chapter ii, declares that it derogates nothing from the majesty of God to seek in the stars indications of changes impending to empires, and later in the book (pp. 535-9) it is said that religion should be once settled and never after called in question, since disputations of religion are dangerous. If the Prince, being well assured of the rightness of his religion, wishes to draw others to it, he should not use force. Men cannot be compelled to believe, and, if forbidden to believe their own way, they may turn atheist, and atheism is worse than superstition. Bodin[28] presents an example of the indirect influence of humanism on religion.

A still more striking case is that of Regius, who confronts and describes a world whose primary aspect, as conceived by science, is endless variety and unceasing change. Regius [29] makes the unity of God's nature the basis of all form, order, decorum, and beauty; therefore, this unity is the basis of all learning, of which religion is the primary type. The inferior world is composed of contrary and conflicting elements; but the principle of unity must exceed the principle of contrariety, or chaos is come again. Heathen philosophers [30] have seen innate powers in the reasonable soul, as if it had been extracted from the Godhead before it came down to earth and forgot its original intelligence by the contagion of the flesh. But Christians reject such fatal necessity and believe that God, according to His pleasure, distributes to different persons different qualities, since the common good and preservation of society cannot endure without many estates, callings, offices, and works. This important philosophy of change and its various reconciliations in religion and elsewhere remains largely unstudied.

The older religious point of view is certainly the persistent one. Charles Butler writes excellently *The Feminine Monarchie, or A Treatise concerning Bees*,[31] which rests squarely upon the idea that religious instruction can be derived from bees. Their government is like the government of an ideal Christian state and God is present with them. Certain bees, he tells us, are known to have built a chapel, with windows, steeple, bells, and altar, for a bit of the Host, which they worshipped with a sweet sound. Bees are models of temperance, justice, and chastity. It is interesting also to find Person [32] in his *Varieties*, a book which bears the closest resemblance to Burton's *Anatomy* of any to be found, declaring that, though the plagues,

pestilences and deaths of beasts which follow earth-
quakes can be explained philosophically, God's liberty
to use these means of forewarning men should not be
abridged. The same principle appears in the ingenious
traditional argument offered by Huarte,[33] who says
take heed that you receive no hurt from leaving out
the Pope and his cardinals; for God, knowing the
uncertainty of men's reasons, enters into the midst of
the congregations of the Church, dispels errors, and
reveals a wisdom never attainable by human means
alone. One is not to think that the traditional religion
was usually less insistent on the punitive activities of
a jealous God. The sudden death of the wicked was
an act of divine judgment and a thing to be expected.
Religious faith was regarded as indispensable to correct conduct, a faith which relied for its efficacy on
lurid pictures of impending punishment. Without this
bulwark man, because of his degenerate nature, was
capable of every form of wickedness, and the denial
of religion, or even its minor tenets, was atheism, and
atheism was every form of vice. These features are
often attributed to Puritanism, but they are almost
equally characteristic of all forms of sixteenth-century
religion. The very fact of a general belief in the doctrine that every sin must and will be punished here
and now, and its other developing dogma to the effect
that the pangs of a guilty conscience [34] are inescapable, cannot but have important bearings in literature.

In England the greatest of religious events was the
coming of Calvinism [35] and the Puritanism which followed in its wake. These two established the religion
of conscience. It has been so much a matter of custom
in the study of English literature to depreciate Calvinism that it is possible the whole question of its
literary influences needs re-studying. It was not Scotland and New England only that felt the stress and

strain of the great reformer and his followers, but England itself had a bath in Calvinism both thorough and long. When we speak of Puritanism, to be sure, we ordinarily mean the sort of religious beliefs that prevailed longest in Scotland and New England. But Puritanism means much more than this, and we need to reconsider the fine humanistic body of teachings and teachers that entered England largely through a noble and learned group of Huguenots [36] during the last third of the sixteenth century. The influence of this humanistic type of Puritanism was felt by Sidney, Spenser, and certainly by the great mass of the greatest writers and thinkers of the age. The *Institutes* [37] of Calvin, as regards its reflection in literature, needs to be re-studied. It appears in various forms, which reflect various degrees and stages of religious thinking. We know Calvin's general theses, but we do not realize their significance: the knowledge of God is an inward knowledge, innate, which is an Aristotelian principle, to be supplemented by the purely Christian doctrine that God in pity for man's blindness and depravity, in a way which we do not understand but which came to be called election (a Stoical idea), has provided for man's redemption. Fairbairn has said rather shrewdly that Lutheranism saved everything not forbidden by Scripture, whereas Calvinism sacrificed everything not sanctified and justified by Scripture. It therefore tended to free the soul and to rescue it from its cosmological fetters. Calvinism is a primary critical force, and it is perhaps only the minor jealousies of the historians of culture that prevent them from recognizing it as possibly the greatest modernizing agent in the Renaissance world. Calvin's approach was humanistic. He was therefore strong in his educational policy and in his biblical scholarship. He was Stoical in his ethical sympathies and therefore turned attention to the side of polity. Calvinism is sometimes regarded as the source of modern democracy. Like Vives before him, Calvin turned for his ideals of private and domestic morals to that group of Greek and Latin Fathers—Tertullian, Ambrose, Augustine, Gregory, and Cyprian—who in their day had striven to save their charges from the contaminations of a degenerate society. The situations were parallel, and Calvin found there what he wanted—namely the Puritan code.

But Calvin and the Calvinists did more than this. They turned to logic. All critics who are effective must do that. They seized upon the philosophy of Aristotle as it had already been developed (and distorted) by the Schoolmen and made of it a most effective disciplinary instrument. In Aristotle's doctrine of form [38] as expressed in the doctrine of the four causes, current Christian Aristotelianism had made the final cause supreme and had identified it with the God of revealed religion. The formal cause was also important as indicating the revealed (and interpreted) mind of God. The material and the efficient causes were on a lower level. What Calvin did was to assume the importance of the final and the formal causes and endow the other two with a power and importance they had never before enjoyed. The thinkers of Puritanism seized upon the efficient cause as their point of argument or restraint, upon the formal cause as a complete justification of the acceptance of the Scriptures as the sole guide to truth, and upon the final cause, or will of God, as the source of perpetual remission of sins and full restoration to eternal life. Thus was the soul, freed from the rather gentle bonds of Scholasticism, shackled again by those of a revivified logic.

One wonders why the logical bases of Puritanism have not been more popularly recognized. There are few religious books written in England or America since the sixteenth century which do not to some degree rest upon this logic of religion. The subject is not dead and cannot die. We have heard it debated in our own day over and over, and we are still in doubt as to whether our own morals and those of society are better protected by removing the occasion and the opportunity for sin and vice, or by trying in some fashion to make ourselves and other men sin-resistant.

The clarity with which the principle was recognized by the Puritans will appear on almost every page of the *Anatomie of Abuses* by the notorious Philip Stubbes;[39] but, because it is rendered clearer in his case by his exaggeration and lack of perspective, one is not to believe that the principle is not almost universal among religious writers. What he has to say about fine clothes will exemplify his method as well as we could wish: 'The apparell in it owne nature is good and the good creature of God (I will not denie) and cannot hurt excepte it be through our owne wickednesse abused. And therefore, woe be [to] them that make the good Creatures of God instrumentes of damnation to themselves, by not using them but abusing them. And yet notwithstanding, it may be said to hurt, or not to hurt, as it is abused or not abused. And whereas they would haue the abuse of apparell (if any be) taken away, and the apparal to remain stil, it is impossible to supplant the one, without the extirpation of the other also. For truly it is sayd, Sublata causa, tollitur effectus. But not, Sublato effectu, tollitur causa. *Take away the cause and the effect fayleth*, but not contrarily, *take away the effect, and the cause fayleth*. The externe efficient cause of pride, is gorgeous attire: [the effect is pride it selfe ingenerate by attire:] but to begin to plucke away the effect, to wit, Pride, and not to take away the cause first, namely sumptuous attire, is as if a man intending to supplant a tree by the rootes, should begin to pull the fruit and branches onely, or to pull downe heaven, should dig in the earth working altogether preposterously, indirectly, and contrarily.'

But we need not stop with the narrowness of Philip Stubbes. If we remember that Milton based his argument for freedom of speech on a ground exactly opposite to that of Stubbes, we shall attach a far profounder importance to the question at issue between them. Milton believed that the efficient cause of sin and of virtue lies, not in external temptation, but within the human heart. Let us quote a familiar passage from *Areopagitica:* [40]

As therefore the state of man now is; what wisdom can there be to choose, what continence to forbear, without the knowledge of evil? He that can apprehend and consider vice with all her baits and seeming pleasures, and yet abstain, and yet distinguish, and yet prefer that which is truly better, he is the true wayfaring Christian. I cannot praise a fugitive and cloistered virtue unexercised and unbreathed, that never sallies out and seeks her adversary, but slinks out of the race, where that immortal garland is to be run for, not without dust and heat. Assuredly we bring not innocence into the world, we bring impurity much rather; that which purifies us is trial, and trial is by what is contrary. That virtue therefore which is but a youngling in the contemplation of evil, and knows not the utmost that vice promises to her followers, and rejects it, is but a blank virtue, not a pure; her whiteness is but an excremental whiteness; which is the reason why our sage and serious poet Spenser, (whom I dare be known to think a better teacher than Scotus or Aquinas,) describing true temperance under the person of Guion, brings him in with his palmer through the cave of Mammon, and the bower of earthly bliss, that he might see and know, and yet abstain.

From what has been said in this chapter an idea may be formed as to the main channels through which the ancient cosmology and its laws exerted their influence and as to the varied effects this influence was capable of working in the mind of the Renaissance.

CHAPTER III

PREOCCUPATIONS AND PREJUDGMENTS

In like manner, the use of confutation in the delivery of
sciences ought to be very sparing; and to serve to remove
strong preoccupations and prejudgments, and not to
minister and excite disputations and doubts.—Bacon, *The
Advancement of Learning.*

IT IS now apparent that certain formal ideas dominated the culture of the Renaissance. These ideas
were the classical, particularly the Roman, traditions; and these organizing agencies, in so far as they
determined the literary handling of materials, we
might call, but for confusion of terms, grammatical
forms. Certainly the dominance of the Latin tongue
itself—its indispensability—constitutes such a form.
Schools were Latin schools. Grammar was Latin
grammar. Learning to read was learning Latin, and
the study of Latin grammar was the recognized route
to the mastery of reading, writing, and speaking.
There were also logical, rhetorical, aphoristic, enu-
merative, cosmological, and theological forms,—the
whole picture being one of an assertive though not
consistent book-culture, rather than a popular or a
materialistic culture. But we must not be understood
as saying that the material, though subordinate in the
theory of school learning, was not during the Renaissance attended to as never before in the history of
learning since the days of Aristotle. The dominant
theory of the culture of the Renaissance regarded
things as the essentials of forms, which forms were the
various subjects of the encyclopædia of learning. In-

deed, it is doubtful if the entelechy of Aristotle, though not as yet fully comprehended, had ever been so well understood and so generally accepted at any previous time. The thinkers of the Renaissance recognized that the scholar, the rhetorician, the logician, the philosopher, and the theologian must have actual things to work upon. The chief movement of revolt was against the Schoolmen,[1] who were popularly thought of as working in a vacuum, on forms without content. There was in the intellectual system of the Renaissance an extensive use of the substance of knowledge, both casually and structurally. Renaissance scholars were also deeply interested in the moral significance of things. The moral is always the practical, and ethics recurs to the concrete case.

The opinion is definitely held in this discussion that erudition—science, pseudo-science, philosophy, history, school learning in general with all its vagaries and variations—has an important bearing on the interpretation of the literature of the Renaissance. This has never been denied and will be readily granted; but it may be that its manifestations have not been recognized and its full significance realized. It is at least true that there have been few definite attempts on a wide scale to determine why and how and to what extent learning as learning made itself felt in the literature of the Renaissance. We shall not discuss such an elementary proposition as this, that the literature of every age must be composed, both materially and structurally, of the current ideas and accepted beliefs of that age. We must abandon to the solace of its advocates the mystical view of creative literature. Those who believe that the poet and the literary genius are independent of time, place, and social circumstance and that a God to whom present, past, and future are as one, does actually and directly speak to and through poets and reveal to them ultimate truth and beauty—those holding such doctrines will see no occasion for these remarks. They must perforce be addressed to those who, holding a different opinion as to the nature of genius, believe it to be the possession of ordinary powers to an extraordinary degree and admit that not even Shakespeare and Dante could know and reveal the future as fact or opinion or present those aspects of the past about which they had had no information. What is said here may be of some significance to those who believe that neither Bacon nor Shakespeare could possibly have thought in terms of Darwinian evolution, that both of them thought of Julius Cæsar on the basis of Cæsar's own writings, of Plutarch, and of the historians of the Roman Empire, that both Bacon and Shakespeare were influenced in their thinking about Cæsar by contemporary Tudor and Stuart opinion on the supreme importance of monarchy, and that neither Shakespeare nor Bacon could or would have held the views about Cæsar which are advanced by Mr. H. G. Wells.

The point of view of historical criticism[2] which has just been illustrated is widely held and must, for practical purposes, be henceforth assumed. We know that the writers of the Renaissance expressed the opinions of their age as these opinions had been coloured and modified by them themselves as individuals. We know that they embodied and presented the emotions, the desires, and the learning of their time in characteristic forms and in accordance with principles which they themselves accepted. Correct literary interpretation depends on this general principle, and data for its employment are still inadequate. These data we may help to supply; we may also come to a

clearer understanding of the inter-relations of literature and learning; for the question, as regards the
Renaissance, needs to be restudied.

We must consider, in the first place, the limitations
of science with reference to extent, to methods, to
presuppositions and beliefs, and with reference also
to the fidelity with which the learned men of the
Renaissance mastered such science as they had; and,
in the second place, we must prepare, for the sake of
clarity, a critique of Renaissance learning. The 'beliefs' referred to at this point are not in reference to
the value of science as known, but rather in reference
to our answer to the question of whether or not the
sciences as they existed were imperfectly mastered
and capable of further exploitation.

We should try to ascertain the value of Renaissance learning, not only according to our modern
seemingly absolute standards of validity, but also according to the standards of those times, which we
believe showed often a factitious value now lost. This
is in agreement with the dictum, not the truth but
what men believed was the truth is important. In this
borderland of relativity, one contents oneself with
pointing out the obvious fact that in literature those
matters which are given importance by the emphasis
of feeling, thought, and literary skill, must be the
matters important in the lives and opinions of the
authors and, only by accident or by the recurrent patterns of human life and art, the things which are important to us.

We wish to get an idea of the validity of Renaissance science,[3] and we ask: Are men, generally speaking, limited in their imaginative reconstructions, in
their understanding of the world, to what can be seen
and handled? Is it not true that, when the current of
the patently and normally accountable is broken, men

are, in spite of all the development and extension of science and invention, still readily perplexed or carried beyond their depths? Let it be admitted that men in the modern world are not so ready to resort for explanation to the supernatural and to abandon their belief in the possibility of a rational explanation of unknown phenomena as were persons in an unscientific or less scientific age, such as that of the Renaissance. The people of our age neither lapse into fear so readily, nor so habitually seek fanciful or formal explanations of those things not explicable on obvious grounds, but we do not always understand or realize that we have found in authority a substitute for magic. It may be, however, that in a superstitious age men domesticated the supernatural and felt relatively calm in the presence of the uncanny. To the mass of educated people in the modern world the radio is an example of a modern mystery. People are usually entirely ignorant of the mechanism with which they are confronted, of the forces controlled by the mechanism, and the manner of the control; but its existence is accepted without any sense of mystery because of the belief that there are those who do understand. Some modern machines and devices must no doubt be felt, realized, and understood; but such things must usually be visible though not necessarily simple.

Was the age of the Renaissance a credulous age? Was it, when all allowances have been made, a more credulous age than our own? Topsell, or rather Gesner,[4] says that one must not believe anything which is against reason. How can we reconcile this with his, to our minds, credulous acceptance of satyrs and sphinxes, and of various strange actions on the part of beasts? He seems to us to have no consistent point of view about credibility, to be illogical, and to be credulous. Many similar statements of respect for

truth and the evidence of alertness and caution show
that Gesner thought of himself as viewing his science
rationally and intelligently. He disclaims credulity.
The monsters and marvels he accepts are often incredible from our point of view; they cannot have
been incredible from his or that of his age. It is a
mistake to think that a cautious attitude of mind
toward the enlargement of factual knowledge implies
withholding belief until we have satisfied ourselves
by our own experience of the existence of an asserted
fact.

The basis of the credible is that a thing shall be conceived of as possible in the world as we know it. We
possess an extensive and well articulated body of scientific knowledge that limits for us with some definiteness the possible. The Renaissance had a vague,
loose, less trustworthy body of knowledge, which
gave far greater extension to the limits of the possible,
the range of which was also increased by theological
sanction of the marvellous. The actual presence of
supernatural beings in the world served also to widen
the field of reference. The world of the marvellous
and the monstrous lay open to the men of the Renaissance in a way in which it does not to us. The scope
given to analogy had the same effect. For example,
fables and myths were approached then pretty much
as they are now. The learned man was forbidden to
accept them literally, but, since he accepted them as
having allegorical reference to the facts of experience,
they assumed great importance in his mind. Authority
had greater actual sanction in that age than in ours,
but probably did not play relatively a much more
important rôle. The point is, not that the authorities
followed in the Renaissance were more numerous or
less reliable, but that they ruled in a different realm
of truth.

The scientists of the Renaissance had their field of reference and thus a point of view not unlike that of scientists in more recent times, but they had different guiding principles and many special difficulties. Sir Thomas Browne,[5] after carefully weighing authorities for and against the existence of the griffin, renders a formal decision to the effect that the griffin, described as having the wings and beak of an eagle and the limbs and body of a lion, is an anatomical impossibility, a line of reasoning which would rule out the Australian duck-bill and show us more credulous than Sir Thomas. We should decide against the existence of the satyr with great facility, but Gesner had the satyr forced on him by weight of authority. What could be done in presence of Pausanias, Macrobius, Albertus, and others, reinforced, let us say, by St. Jerome, who in his life of Paul the Hermit gives an account of a visit to St. Anthony by a hippocentaur? The account concludes in Topsell's version [6] in these terms:

I am a mortall creature, one of the inhabitants of this Desart, whome the Gentiles (deceiued with error) doe worship and call *Fauni*, Satyres, and *Incubi:* I am come in ambassage from our flocke, intreating that thou wouldst pray for vs vnto the common GOD, who came to saue the world: the which words were no sooner ended, but he ran away as fast as any foule could fly. And least this should seeme false, vnder *Constantine* at Alexandria, there was such a man to be seene aliue, and was a publike spectacle to all the World, the carcasse whereof after his death was kept from corruption by heat, through salt, and was caried to ANTIOCHIA that the Emperor himselfe might see it.

If the nature of the field is known and if we allow for the fact that Renaissance scientists had not yet learned the principles and methods of verification, we may acquit them of credulity in so far as that means a predisposition to accept more of the marvellous than was thrust upon them and of greater illogicality than characterizes the learned men of every age. Mental attitudes remain so much the same that the actions and practices of the modern man, with reference both to the things which come within the range of familiar comprehension and those which do not, cannot possibly be different in kind from those of men who lived a few hundred years ago. One would not say that motives and mental habits are the same. The matter will become sufficiently clear for present purposes by raising a question. Can we find encroachments of modern discoveries in the various fields of science upon the operative content, the determinant opinions and feelings, of the mind of the modern man [7] in other realms besides the mechanical? The most promising region to explore is possibly the realm of desire. Affective states readily intrude themselves, as desires and appetites, into the focus of volition. The modern man may differ from the Elizabethan in being more acquisitive, since he is accustomed to the use of more things. Probably, more individuals in the current world are caught by complex desires, and it is a most interesting question whether suspended responses are more characteristic of human mentality in our days of enlightenment, when the range of choice is much greater, than they ever were before (a question to which we shall return later), and again whether there are any differences in kind.

We might illustrate an aspect of the problem from the greatest of Elizabethan arts. The plays of Shakespeare, Jonson, Chapman, Webster, Ford, and their contemporaries are actually extremely difficult both in language and in thought, and yet they were popular, played in public theatres before audiences who were man for man, from top to bottom, less well educated than any modern audience.[8] These plays were certainly understood and enjoyed. Who can doubt that, in intelligence as distinguished from education, those audiences were at least not inferior to the audiences of our times?

Elizabethan psychology [9] and, to a certain extent, Elizabethan science in general were, on the principle under consideration up to a certain point, as good as our own, for this reason: the science of the Renaissance was, though overlaid with traditional error and explained by impossible hypotheses, the result of applying to the observable phenomena of human environment human powers unaided, not reinforced and extended by instruments. The Elizabethan man could see as much, hear as much, feel as much, and judge as truly as we can. Indeed, since the Elizabethan scientist had to rely solely on his own powers, the limitation bred in him a habit of observation and an intimacy with detail which the modern man has often turned over to somebody else. The Elizabethans became great empiricists, and it must be admitted that their science had a fair chance to conform to fact if not to develop sound theory. Their observations within certain fields were from their very origins often easily subject to verification or rejection. The tools of fabrication, being unaided human powers, were on hand for purposes of correction. The Elizabethans made progress in ships and shipping and in the art of war, particularly at sea. They were actually pre-eminent in certain applied sciences [10] within the range of intimate use, such as pharmacology, animal husbandry, horticulture, and many of the arts of peace. The details of Renaissance science were often truer than its laws, its practice often better than its theories. This is borne out by an examination of the particular branches of science in which Aristotelian and Neo-Aristotelian science met with success,[11] if we may judge success by currency and validity, by tests of time and use.

As has just been said, faculty psychology, the most intimate of the early sciences, has remained intelligible in its details. It still forms a very satisfactory working basis, though its theories, both as to soul and body, have been completely swept away. Its doctrines explanatory of mental state, physical appetite, and the passions of the heart stand like the tools of a carpenter's shop—axes, saws, chisels, hammers, and augers—superseded, many of them, by expert power devices, and all more or less remote from the modern science and art of architecture, but still usable, still capable of performing the essential operations of building. The absurdity of the word *humour* causes no more difficulty than the *rising* and *setting* of the sun. These words, though the relics of imperfect scientific theory, are completely valid as symbols for the expression of ideas. One may, at some risk of arguing in a circle, declare that Renaissance science (ancient science revived) was largely valid in detail, though varying in its validity from science to science and from region to region within particular sciences. This validity is manifest in the permanent utility of much of the older science in the midst of a more scientifically enlightened age. Though the older theories of causation and instrumentation are almost utterly exploded, the fact remains that, in the practical work of meeting the most insistent of the needs of man as an immortal soul and a social animal, the ancient science was and is, by and large, a satisfactory instrument. It has written and, with a certain supplementation, stilll writes our poetry and drama. That it is still operative is not an indication of mere human inertia and blind tradition (only, altogether, or principally), but of the adequate conformity of large parts of the most ancient science with the observed and observable phenomena of life on earth. To say that one died of a *broken heart* was originally a literal record of physiological and psychological theory. The truth about it, although the ancient explanation is lost, is that the expression has never become a mere figure of speech.

From this point of view it will be seen that modern science and invention do not always descend as familiar factors into the region of ordinary life. In other words, there is what has been called a 'cultural lag.' Science often relies on devices for extending the hand, the eye, and the ear; the ordinary human being is not equipped with tools and instruments and has little consciousness derived from their use. Such consciousness is no doubt progressively active; but, generally speaking, the situation in which we stand in the modern world, in reference to our new science and invention, is perfectly revealed by the Aristotelian dictum: 'Tools to those who can use them.'

One cannot say that even discarded ancient theories, beliefs, and hypotheses were entirely without validity. It is far truer to say that most of such intellectual figments were good up to a certain point. They were often the best explanations of fact then available and are examples of imperfect scientific laws, like the Ptolemaic hypothesis awaiting correction at the hands of Copernicus and Kepler. The materials for such theories are often still available, as, for example, the theories of Richard Hooker on the social structure of the world set forth in his *Of the Laws of Ecclesiastical Polity*.[12] Hooker conceived of the social world in terms of orderly progression and saw as a fact the existence of ranks, classes, and degrees. We

may or may not agree with him that the spectacle
of higher and lower gradation is a reflection of God's
mind and an outstanding feature of God's plan, but
we cannot ignore the facts on which he operated or
fail to appreciate the clarity and truth with which he
grasped the details and functions of the social organization of his time.

The idea of stability in gradation is in Plato and the
Platonists and is fundamental to Shakespeare's political and most of his social thinking. The idea is
found in many places in his works, the fullest and
most magnificent being the speech of Ulysses [13] to the
Greek generals in *Troilus and Cressida:*

> The heavens themselves, the planets and this centre
> Observe degree, priority and place,
> Insistiture, course, proportion, season, form,
> Office and custom, in all line of order;
> And therefore is the glorious planet Sol
> In noble eminence enthroned and sphered
> Amidst the other; whose medicinable eye
> Corrects the ill aspects of planets evil,
> And posts, like the commandment of a king,
> Sans check to good and bad: but when the planets
> In evil mixture to disorder wander,
> What plagues and what portents! ...
>   O, when degree is shaked,
> Which is the ladder to all high designs,
> The enterprise is sick! How could communities,
> Degrees in schools and brotherhoods in cities,
> Peaceful commerce from dividable shores,
> The primogeniture and due of birth,
> Prerogative of age, crowns, sceptres, laurels,
> But by degree stand in authentic place? ...

We may still see the social classes that Hooker and
Shakespeare saw. We may explain them economically
as resulting from control over the necessities and

possibilities of life, or socially as resulting from dominance in matters of opinion. We may think biologically of the social degrees and orders of the world as degrees of advantage in environment; or traditionally these orders of society may seem to be religious or political interpretations of man's sense of his own inferiority or superiority. Similarly, to account for the differences between man and the lower animals, the differences between genera and species in the animal kingdom itself, the differences between plants and animals, all of which, together with the differences between living creatures and inanimate objects, were seen by Hooker as stages in God's perfectly graduated plan, we resort to the theory of evolution in the operation of natural causes. Hooker accepted, explained, and in minor ways improved a wide hypothesis to account for the universe about us, namely, as the plan of the Creator. That hypothesis rested squarely on unchanging fact then as now. It does explain much and is, therefore, to a certain practical extent (perhaps for that age an adequate extent) a valid hypothesis.

It may be fairly contended that, when given an equal chance, the scientists of the Renaissance were the equals of the scientists of the present. The only situations in which Renaissance scientists could have an equal chance are those in which they, having free access to materials and no hampering social fetters or authoritarian inhibitions, had no need of artificial extension of eye, ear, and hand.

The physical sciences lagged far behind other disciplines in development, partly because science was authoritarian and, therefore, merely aggregative, and partly because large stretches of its territory still utterly defied analysis. The first of these limitations affected most obviously the field of natural history; the second, that of the physical sciences. In an approach unaided by instruments and unassisted by the devices of isolation and record, chemistry is a recondite science, since chemical action in the material world works itself out to a state of apparent quiescence. The products of chemical change are often notoriously unlike the original agents, so that to unaided observation chemistry is a baffling science. Anthony van Leeuwenhoek was not born until 1632, so that the microscopic world was almost totally unknown. The scientist of the Renaissance could neither see anything below the range of human vision nor think that there was anything to be seen there which was worth seeing. The telescope [14] no doubt widened men's scientific curiosity in the seventeenth century, but we are limited in our consideration mainly to the days before Galileo.

Medicine, natural history, physics, and other branches of Renaissance science had the same sort of imperfect validity as that which adhered to faculty psychology. Since these subjects lie on the physical side of psychology, their imperfections were usually greater; but on the social side of the subject of psychology the results from the test of enduring utility are indeed remarkable, for they lead us into the ancient scientist's best and freest field of operation, the field of ethics. As moral philosophers, ancient thinkers have not been superseded. The social data on which Plato and Aristotle worked remain relatively unchanged, and thus far in the history of human progress show some stubbornness in yielding to our scientific method. In their study of ethics and the social sciences Renaissance students were, roughly speaking, on a par with us; whereas, in the laboratory sciences, we have incredible advantages. The relations between man and man, man and the state, and man and God were as patent to the ancients as they are to us. The factors which give importance to the ethics and the social science of the ancients are operative in less restricted fashion in the field of law. In religion ancient superiority lies in religious institutions and in religion as a purely personal activity, rather than in the science of religion. In ancient politics, as it appeared in the Renaissance, there is considerable excellence, though political thought was warped and hampered by the ensconced position of monarchy in the practical world. It was left for the eighteenth century to rediscover the *Politics* of Aristotle.

The line of demarcation between what was possible to the Renaissance scientist and what was not will be rendered clearer by two considerations. The development of physical science has been dependent on the experimental method, which was in abeyance even in Bacon's hands. Even Bacon did not succeed in distinguishing it wholly from empiricism. Experimentation [15] had long had its connections with magic, and magicians were perhaps the first to experiment. But the vast instrument of controlled experimentation was not available to the scientists of the Renaissance. Secondly, when Bacon faced the great and original task of sifting the learning of the world, he recognized that certain sciences were well and sufficiently developed, and these he set aside as not in need of exploitation. In order to form a true estimate of the value of Renaissance science, we should do a similar thing. Most of Bacon's salvage comes from those fields of human learning not closely dependent on the experimental method or the use of the microscope, or, it must be added, dependent on mathematics, whose fundamental importance Bacon [16] never realized.

We can also advance our critique by locating certain points of conflict between the learning which was new to the Renaissance and the learning of mediæval tradition. There is, for example, the issue between Aristotle and the Aristotelians, which arose from the use of a truer interpretation of Aristotle [17] as a means of defeating traditional Aristotelian science and theology. Scholars who came to understand Aristotle saw that he was an independent seeker after truth. Generally speaking, one finds that in every science Aristotle touches a new light dawns when the true Aristotle appears. The fifteenth century curricula of English and French universities were well supplied with Aristotle. The new *studium generale* [18] of the University of Leipzig, adopted in 1409 from the course of study at Prague, presents for the whole course a formidable array of the works of Aristotle. Since the official curriculum was set primarily as the basis of lectures, it must be that few minds came into actual contact with Aristotle, learners being held at a distance from the actual corpus by some intermediary corpus. What was actually studied must have been epitomes and commentaries rather than the classics themselves. When, in the sixteenth century, the genuine Aristotle began to be felt, it is certain that the true friends of Aristotle were often his professed enemies, i.e., enemies of Aristotelianism, the formal system which had grown up under his name. It seems also that the many spurious scientific works which stood unchallenged in the Aristotelian canon prevented until Bacon's time, or even later, discrimination between true and false Aristotelian science. Finally, the harvest of ancient learning was delayed by the difficulty of its comprehension.

There is, for example, little reason to believe that the learned men of the sixteenth century, aside from Bodin, Regius, and a few others, actually understood the *Politics* of Aristotle, a much more difficult book than the *Ethics*. Again, the attitude of the mathematicians of Cardan's time towards Euclid was that of the modern schoolboy. The question before them was not one of advancing the science of geometry, but of understanding Euclid; and so in other fields. We must picture our sixteenth-century scientists as men travelling in a great forest, much of which was uncharted, and the men themselves as having partial, false, or imperfect charts, which they were not always able to read. Their difficulties were very great.

The issues extend in characteristic forms into each of the school disciplines. In studying these issues one must bear in mind the fact that contests between opposing major forces are often fought out on minor objective differences of opinion. The Renaissance, as compared to the Middle Ages, was possessed of new and different ideals and wished to exploit other and new fields of culture.

Inanimate nature does not, as already stated, manifest much operative detail, so that as an explanation of what is to be seen, the hypothesis of the four elements with the doctrine of commixtion formed an obvious but entirely inadequate hypothesis. Its very simplicity was its defeat. Unfortunately there is not enough differentiation in physical phenomena themselves to have rendered its inadequacy more quickly evident. There was no known measure of 'commixtion' and no true basis for elemental unity. We know—the scientists of that time did not—that, in current terminology, fire is a chemical activity, air a mixture of elements, water a compound of two common elements, and earth a mixture of elements and compounds. No effective basis of comparison obtruded itself upon the scientist. There was no variation not subsumed under commixtion; no clash not accounted for as warfare between these four aboriginal forces. In vain did the thinker endeavour to superimpose

upon physical nature analogies from divine government and the human state. We may pity and even
respect the alchemist,[19] whose sole stock in trade,
though he did not know it, consisted of a few isolated
and unrelated chemical and metallurgical processes.
There is a reason, intelligible in the conditions of un-
guided observation, for the duration of the almost
completely erroneous and disastrous hypothesis of the
four elements, but it is the worst of ancient scientific
laws. It was a veritable house builded upon the sands.
For historians of science the salvage from its downfall is considerable, especially because the elements
were not conceived of as four distinct substances but
as conditions in which universal matter existed; but for
the historian of literature the salvage is even greater.
Men lived in that unstable house for two thousand
years and thought of themselves as men living the
lives and thinking the thoughts of men who dwelt in
just such a tabernacle. Man was formed of the four
elements,[20] was tempered by their commixture, and
subject to their rare harmonies and their never-ending
discords. 'Does not our life consist in the four elements' asks Sir Toby Belch in *Twelfth Night*. 'I am
fire and air,' says Cleopatra; 'my other elements I give
to baser life.' It was by 'overgrowth of some complexion,' says Hamlet, that men 'in the general censure
take corruption.' Even when nature had done her best
to mix the elements within Brutus, he was yet deceived
by his friends and beaten to the pit by enemies. Iago
is sure of his destruction of Desdemona, because 'she's
framed as fruitful As the free elements.'

If one were to criticize the hypothesis of the four
elements, one would point to the principle which ultimately prevailed against it. Ramus borrowed from
Posterior Analytics (I) of Aristotle a dictum which he
called the Rule of Reason,[21] and Bacon approved it. It

required, he thought, that all things be disputed in logic according to their natures, general things to be treated generally and special things specially. The age was prone to the use of analogies with no common denominator and to the treatment of abstractions drawn from different levels as of equal scope and application. The hypothesis of the four elements was just such a fallacy, since the elements had no common origin. There was already a wide application of the Rule of Reason in other fields; but, as Bacon clearly perceived, it could not get its innings in the field of physical science until more had been learned as to the properties of things. Aside from a few great principles, such as the conservation of matter, and a few special discoveries, such as those of Archimedes, modern physics had not been born. Few scientists were even moving in the right direction.

Of false science accepted and acted on as true there are innumerable examples. False science and pseudo-science entered into almost every field and made themselves factors in many sorts of literature. The middle of the seventeenth century saw a recrudescence of magic in England, and Charron's *De la Sagesse*, a book of psychology, ethics, and politics of the older tradition, was still an authority in the days of Alexander Pope. The doctrine of the four humours broke down slowly before William Harvey's discovery of the circulation of the blood; but it is surprising how slowly the science of medicine [22] relinquished phlebotomy, the doctrine of similarity and contrariety, and a *materia medica* based largely on some form of magic or on the belief that for every ill found in nature there is in nature also a remedy.

If it is true, as it is, that the daily lives of modern men are less fearful because less hag-ridden by superstition, is it not worth asking whether the old means of arousing the emotions, as for example the appeal to fear and conscience, have not undergone severe loss of effectiveness? Men are clever enough at manufacturing new horrors, and the sum total of human fear may possibly remain the same; but it is probably a different sort of fear. The losses in the field of the emotional appeal which Elizabethan literature has suffered from the development of better science are certainly considerable, that is, if the things lost are viewed as stimuli. The losses are probably mainly in the realm of conjecture and are certainly not to be regretted, although they may need to be restored intellectually and imaginatively in order to understand and appreciate Renaissance literature. From this point of view they may be worth restoring. The tribe of ghosts and witches are the most obvious emigrants from the literary world. Griffins, hobgoblins, fairies, naiads, and dragons were during the Renaissance already practically gone. Magicians of the Merlin type, devils, attendant spirits, witches, and ghosts were to a less degree parts of the celestial machinery than at an earlier time, but were undoubtedly still potent. These have certainly lost their emotional appeal to us, as have certain animals, such as the crocodile, the ostrich, the elephant, and the pelican. We have probably lost a certain element of wonder in our attitude towards all animals. The cat, the owl, and the snake still retain for us some power of appeal. The plague [23] is a less insistent and a less mysterious dread. Though we do much in our society to repeat the violence [24] of sixteenth-century England, Ireland, France, and Scotland, there is in modern life much more security than during the Renaissance, with a consequent diminution of emotional instability. Violence is less likely to intrude into high places. There can be no doubt that *Hamlet*, *King Lear*, and *Macbeth*, with many other plays of violence of the time, were reinforced in their appeal to audiences because those audiences had lived through and were living through a time when murder stalked its prey in royal courts. Consider, for example, the crimes in the Scottish court in the youth of James VI and in the French court in the days of Catherine de' Medici and the Massacre of St. Bartholomew. Elizabethan dramatic poets can usually be trusted to bring back this atmosphere of horror, but not to restore lost beliefs and inhibitions of an important though somewhat milder character; such as the veneration for kingship as such, for fatherhood and priesthood, for the authority of husbands and the docility of wives, the inquiring wonder at a potent sky, the association with a material world whose every event and aspect might be significant, and the daily round whose every step was under the command of a completely absolute God. No one who regards frankly the fortuities and inexorable destinies of life in any age can fail to understand the anxiety of the Renaissance man. Jerome Cardan,[25] one of the cleverest men of the time, walked through the world as a hunter might stalk through an unknown and enemy-infested forest. His foot catches in the bedclothes as he gets up in the morning, and all that day he is afraid to go out because he does not know the significance of that event. He is puzzled and disturbed by it for days, and it is only the next of his many calamities that shows him the true significance of the undoubted portent.

Changes in the world of thought are no doubt only relative, and the losses we have suffered since Elizabethan times have abundant compensation in the better known universe which has been conferred upon us. But it might be offered at least conjecturally that we are intellectually poorer than the Elizabethans were in precisely those fields in which the thinkers of a

bygone age had an equal chance with us. The Elizabethans seem to have known and thought more about
conduct than we do. They exalted duty and courage
and attended to the nature of these things. They bore
their hardships with fortitude and understood the reasons why men should practise that virtue. They loved
wisdom and saw its applications in the *ars vivendi*.
They were able to think, and did habitually think,
with clarity and fruitfulness, in regions of the mental
and emotional life into which the modern man more
rarely enters, such as filial piety and the nature of
true love. The wisdom of Shakespeare is a wisdom of
family and state, of peace and war, of love and friendship, of death, and of a good life. In these fields he
is still pre-eminent, and so stable are certain of the
ways of men from age to age that he has a fair chance
to preserve this pre-eminence.

There seems to be about Shakespeare [26] an enduring
validity, which may be explained by a number of
circumstances in addition to those just mentioned,
though most of all, no doubt, by the nature of the
man himself. He developed his genius, however, in
a happy time, before the optimism of Aristotle and
Plato had given place to the pessimism of Seneca and
Epictetus; for he belongs in his philosophy of life with
Sidney and Spenser rather than with Marston and
Chapman. Shakespeare, for the most part, stayed off
the shaky ground of unsubstantial science and pseudo-
science and did not go too near the pit of vulgar
popularity. He had also the gift of great art. But, most
of all, this opinion as to his enduring validity rests
upon the belief that the thing that matters most of all
in literature is the conception held by a given writer
about human life, about man's individual fate, and
about the conditioning factors of human life. This is
not the only thing that matters, but this is the thing

that will determine the credibility, value, and importance of the writer.

If, in general, the writer falls in with the best, or even with the most widely held opinions of his time, he will, if his art is adequate, be what is called popular. If his thought has currency after he is dead, he will live on in literature. To what extent refined skill alone will operate as a means of making his art live after him, it is not for us to say, except this, that perdurable art seems to depend, in some measure at least, on perdurable thought. A solution of the problem may be found in the inseparability of thought and form. It is doubtful whether the art of Shakespeare as a dramatist is finer than that of Middleton and Jonson; his superiority over these men as a great literary man seems in part at least to lie in his truth to life as subsequent ages have determined it. In other words, Shakespeare's greatness is primarily a greatness of thought—of vision, imagination, criticism, interpretation, sympathy, and wisdom, and his life in literature is a popular reprieve. The world has saved him from sentence of death by oblivion because it has believed in the significance of what he had to say about humanity.

A unity in opinion as to the human situation may be apprehended in its outlines for the period of the English Renaissance, however difficult it may be to distinguish the Renaissance from the Middle Ages and however much the Renaissance may have anticipated the points of view which were most current in the seventeenth century. The smallness of the English literary world in the later sixteenth century and its centralization help us to do this. Indeed, it is possible to determine in general and in particular the conditioning factors of this unity in the intellectual life of the time. The difficulty comes in knowing where to stop, for the field is very large. It will assist us in our task if we adopt, with immediate recognition of its narrowness, the simple point of view above expressed, namely, that the important thing is to search the mind of the Renaissance in order to discover, not what we of the current world believe is true, but what the poets and literary men of the Renaissance believed was true. We shall need to observe the moving forces in Renaissance literature. It is not in general difficult to perceive and understand them, whether in the moral, the æsthetic, or the intellectual field; but it is difficult to sympathize with them, respect them, and adopt them vicariously either in those cases in which our science and ethics have declared them erroneous or vicious, or in those cases in which our own suggestibility has caused us to read back our modernity or our superior insight into the literature of that age. Beliefs respecting man's fate as a natural or social animal, and as an individual human soul—all that pertains to conduct, to duty, to freedom of action, to chances of escape and success, to physical well-being or the reverse, to man's conception of himself and his inborn obligations, and to mental consequences—these conditioning factors in man's understanding of himself are now, and must always have been, both the substance and the occasion of all that man has had to say about life. The poets and sages of the Elizabethan age did not say exactly the same things about life that poets and sages now say. Aside from a scarcely to be questioned superiority in style, the hard thing to comprehend is that the Elizabethans did not say necessarily better or worse things about life than poets and sages now say, but that they said what seemed good to them as we say what seems good to us. They said in part the same things and in part different things. We suggest that there be made a discrimination of these matters by the use as an instrument of the body of advanced learning which the Renaissance possessed. The universal faith in learning and thirst for it gives learning we think some value as a determinant.

A recent writer [27] has rejected Webster's *The Duchess of Malfy* as a contemptible piece of work, because the careless dramaturgy of Webster's age permitted him to leave standing in his version of the story he was telling inconsistencies and implausibilities of which, we are assured, no experienced modern playwright would ever be guilty. The shortcomings and delinquencies complained of are no doubt to be found in the play, but apparently Webster's audience did not heed them. It follows that a modern reader or auditor whose more refined dramaturgic sensibilities are shocked by Webster's carelessness must, in order that he may see imaginatively and enjoy emotionally *The Duchess of Malfy*—must, shall we say? forgive Webster for his transgressions. He must go even further if he wishes to borrow the artistic delights of a dead century, and gather pleasure and not merely the raw materials of historical criticism and alms for the wallet of his self-conceit. He must, as far as it is possible, see as that century saw and feel as it felt. In the case cited, we must accept the Websterian dramaturgy not only as a matter of course but as an adequate though careless art form. Historical criticism has no occasion to praise or blame, no occasion to allocate the performances of a past age with those of our age and say, 'This is better or that worse,' unless it acknowledges that what seems to us good or bad seems so because we believe in it or disbelieve in it, or because it conforms or does not conform to our standards of excellence. There are other criteria which, for all that is said here, may be of more importance both social and individual; but the task of the historical critic demands rather strict adherence to the point of view of historical criticism. Of course the literary critics of the age we are studying could never have taken, any more than many of our modern critics can take, the historical point of view. With the Renaissance value was absolute. It was no small or restricted body of learning which was available for the use of literary men in the Renaissance, but it was learning seen on a flat surface and without perspective. It had one purpose, one colour, one underlying subject. It was about man. The learning of the Elizabethans was to a very large degree ready-made for them and delivered to them for their good. It was, nevertheless, full of what they wanted to be true rather than what their experience was to teach them was true; but, because the whole learned corpus pertained to man, it may be said that even the errors of Renaissance science led into the heart of the literary world.

CHAPTER IV

THE BINDING OF PROTEUS

For like as a man's disposition is never well known till he be crossed, nor Proteus ever changed shapes till he was straitened and held fast; so the passages and variations of nature cannot appear so fully in the liberty of nature, as in the trials and vexations of art.—Bacon, *The Advancement of Learning.*

WE HAVE seen that, in spite of pervasive and omnipresent error, many of the learned opinions of the Renaissance are valid, so that the age has claims to intellectual importance. We have mentioned many of the difficulties of the Renaissance thinker and investigator. Let us now, for the sake of knowing him better, consider his opportunities for making progress in the advancement of learning. We shall begin with the fact, sometimes disregarded, that there were many practical elements in the Renaissance system of education. These served to bring the Renaissance man into immediate and inescapable contact with the realities of existence and gave expression to the practical nature of the age.

The Renaissance indeed looked both ways. It knew the value of the contemplative life and understood the issue between thought and action:

> They tax our policy, and call it cowardice,
> Count wisdom as no member of the war,
> Forestall prescience, and esteem no act
> But that of hand: the still and mental parts,
> That do contrive how many hands shall strike,
> When fitness calls them on, and know by measure

> Of their observant toil the enemies' weight,—
> Why, this hath not a finger's dignity:
> They call this bed-work, mappery, closet-war;
> So that the ram that batters down the wall,
> For the great swing and rudeness of his noise,
> They place before his hand that made the engine,
> Or those that with the fineness of their souls
> By reason guide his execution.

So says Ulysses [1] in *Troilus and Cressida*, but on another occasion he is also ready to say,

>   Take the instant way;
> For honour travels in a strait so narrow,
> Where one but goes abreast: keep then the path;
> For emulation hath a thousand sons
> That one by one pursue: if you give way,
> Or hedge aside from the direct forthright,
> Like to an enter'd tide they all rush by
> And leave you hindmost.

The Renaissance always heeds the call to action. Sometimes it discards its learned doctrines in favour of its native tastes. Sidney in a familiar passage confesses his own 'barbarousness' and says, 'I never heard the old song of Percy and Douglas that I found not my heart moved more than with a trumpet; and yet it is sung but by some blind crowder, with no rougher voice than rude style; which being so evil apparelled in the dust and cobwebs of that uncivil age, what would it work, trimmed in the gorgeous eloquence of Pindar?'

Christian teaching as to the supremacy of the passive virtues was never very generally accepted by men of the Renaissance. From the earliest times their minds were on the practical aspects of study. This is true of the early writers on education in Italy [2] and, indeed,

of all writers on education all over Europe. Vives
made liberal provision for the study of both quadrivial
branches and nature. Melanchthon[3] spent much time
in the development of the study of mathematics,
physics, medicine, and Roman law. He delivered a
famous address on the history of mathematics in antiquity (1536), edited *De Sphæra* of John Holywood,
and knew Euclid, Aristotle, Pliny, and Pomponius
Mela,—all practical authors. There were striking advances in the study of the quadrivium at the Collège
de Guyennes, with considerable extensions down-
ward into the grammar school grades. Elyot urged the
study of geography in its relation to history, and the
study of cosmography. The authors he recommended
are Strabo, Solinus, Pomponius Mela, and Dionysius.

There can be no doubt that in its first intention
Renaissance education favoured practical subjects,[4]
although these branches, under the influence of men
like Sturmius and Ascham, were often shoved aside in
favour of rhetoric, logic, and the classics—the grammar
school curriculum as later presented by John Brinsley.
This does not mean that the quadrivial studies were
equally subordinated in all places or that they were
ever suffered to be completely neglected. Cambridge,
for example, was more practical in its intentions than
was Oxford, and yet there was much practical study
at Oxford itself. In so far as the quadrivial studies were
neglected at the universities and public schools, their
needs were served by private instructors and by metro-
politan institutions. The demand for technical instruction was a very real one, and in France and Germany
as well as in England there arose in the later sixteenth
century a demand for academies which would teach
the subjects neglected in grammar schools and colleges. Strangely enough, the demand came, not altogether from mercantile classes, as has been so often

said, but from the upper-classes themselves. Such a demand is voiced by Sir Humphrey Gilbert[5] in *Queene Elizabethes Achademy*. This demand was for training in arms, the mathematics of warfare, manly exercises, natural philosophy, modern languages, as well as Latin, itself a subject of great practical utility. Gilbert is not so such a revolutionist as a restorer of the full curriculum of the Seven Liberal Arts. He demanded Latin, Greek, Hebrew, logic and rhetoric (significantly presented in the Ramist tradition as one subject), cultivation of the vernacular, history, natural philosophy, mathematics, warlike tactics, geography, astronomy, navigation, surgery and medicine, French, Spanish, Italian, German, and music.

These subjects were not new. Renaissance education had always demanded them. Manly exercises and practical disciplines were part of Vittorino da Feltre's[6] program. They were strong points with Guarino, who recommended swimming, snow-balling, dancing, walking, ball-playing, and mimic war. Elyot in *The Gouernour* recommends games and sports, especially wrestling (an English sport). For other sports he cites classical parallels: running from Epaminondas and Achilles, swimming found useful by Horatius and Cæsar, hunting practised by the Young Cyrus, as by Theseus, Alexander, and Pompey. Dancing Elyot presents from Italian models of Alberti and Agricola. Milton in the *Tractate on Education* goes as far in the recommendation of practical subjects and manly sports as any Renaissance writer on education, and in so doing he is merely aligning himself with Vittorino, Alberti, and Elyot; for it must be understood that this inclusiveness is in part responsible for the versatility of the Renaissance. The curriculum of education is both a source and a sign of the spirit of general participation in all-round achievement. More recent times are less versatile in part because they specialize in their interests and inhibit their more generous impulses. Glendower [7] proudly replies to Hotspur's taunt:

> I can speak English, lord, as well as you;
> For I was train'd up in the English court;
> Where, being but young, I framed to the harp
> Many an English ditty lovely well
> And gave the tongue a helpful ornament,
> A virtue that was never seen in you.

The ideal lies back of Ophelia's lament:

> O, what a noble mind is here o'erthrown!
> The courtier's, soldier's, scholar's, eye, tongue, sword;
> The expectancy and rose of the fair state,
> The glass of fashion and the mould of form,
> The observed of all observers, quite, quite down!

It appears also most interestingly in the conversation between the Archbishop of Canterbury and the Bishop of Ely. They are surprised at the reformation of the new king and speculate on how his culture has been acquired:

> Hear him but reason in divinity,
> And all-admiring with an inward wish
> You would desire the king were made a prelate:
> Hear him debate on commonwealth affairs,
> You would say it hath been all in all his study:
> List his discourse of war, and you shall hear
> A fearful battle render'd you in music:
> Turn him to any cause of policy,
> The Gordian knot of it he will unloose,
> Familiar as his garter: that, when he speaks,
> The air, a charter'd libertine, is still,
> And the mute wonder lurketh in men's ears,
> To steal his sweet and honey'd sentences;

So that the art and practic part of life
Must be the mistress to this theoric:
Which is a wonder how his grace should glean it,
Since his addiction was to courses vain,
His companies unletter'd, rude and shallow,
His hours fill'd up with riots, banquets, sports,
And never noted in him any study,
Any retirement, any sequestration
From open haunts and popularity.

To this Ely, seeking parallels in nature, replied analogically,

The strawberry grows underneath the nettle
And wholesome berries thrive and ripen best
Neighbour'd by fruit of baser quality:
And so the prince obscured his contemplation
Under the veil of wildness; which, no doubt,
Grew like the summer grass, fastest by night,
Unseen, yet crescive in his faculty.

It must be said, on the other hand, that, because of this ideal of versatility, the ordinary educated man of the Renaissance was likely to be a smatterer, basing a pretense of scholarship on snippets drawn from books of extracts, and that the educational theorist, particularly if he had the upper-classes in mind (as he usually did), encouraged superficiality. It follows that geniuses thrived well in the schools of the Renaissance; ordinary persons, not so well. It is interesting in this connexion to follow a chain of transmission in the education of Sir Philip Sidney. Hubert Languet, under whose guidance Sidney is pursuing his studies, instructs Sidney in the theory of the education of a gentleman, Sidney transmits similar instructions to his brother Robert (who is meantime urged by his father Sir Henry Sidney to follow his brother's lead in every-

thing), and Sir Philip finally embodies and exemplifies
these instructions in his heroes Pyrocles and Musidorus
in *Arcadia*. During the period of his foreign study, particularly while he was at Padua, Sidney applied himself earnestly to the study of astronomy and geometry.
This was with Languet's approval and advice, but
Languet felt that Sidney should not carry these studies
too far, since they required too great an exertion of
the mind and would thus tend to undermine the
health. Italian, French, and German (which Sidney
found difficult) are present in Languet's program for
Sidney, and there is particular stress laid upon history,
contemporary as well as ancient, on ethics, and on
politics. There is full recognition of the value of foreign travel and the advantages to be derived from
meeting persons of importance. (*Letters* X and XI.)
When Robert Sidney's[8] turn came to go abroad for
the completion of his education, Sidney poured out his
best advice for Robert's guidance. There is not only
the famous letter XXXVIII, written probably in 1579,
in which Sidney discusses the function, or objects, of
travel,[9] but a very significant, more personal letter
(No. XLII) in which Sidney gives advice on actual
studies to be pursued. Robert is to read the historians
and search out historical causes, doing his best at the
same time to become a discourser, a thing the wiser
historians (such as Livy, Tacitus, Plutarch, and Dion
Nicœus) will help him to become. Robert is to make
a table of these interesting side-lights to be gained
from the historians. 'Now (deere Brother),' Sidney
continues, 'take delight likewise in the Mathematicalls,
Mr Savell is excellent in them. I think you understand
the Sphere. If you do I care little for any more Astronomie in yow, Arithmetick and Geometry, I would
wish yow well seene in, so both in Matter of Nomber
and Measure yow mighte have a Feeling and Active

Judgment: I would you did beare the Mechanicall
Instruments wherein the Dutch excel. . . So you can
speak and write Latin not barbarously, I would never
require great study in Ciceronianism, the chiefe abuse
at Oxford, *Qui dum verba sectantur*. . . Now, Sweete
Brother, take delight to keep and increase your Mu-
sick, yow will not believe what a want I find of it in
my melancholy times. At Horsemanshipp when you
exercise it reade Grison Claudio, and a booke that is
called *La Gloria del cavallo*, withall, that yow may
joyne the through contemplation of it with the exercise, and so shall yow profite more in a moneth than
others in a yeare, and marke the bitting, sadling, and
curing of horses. I would by the way your worship
would learne a better hand, yow write worse than I,
and I write evell enough; once againe have care of
your dyet, and consequently of your complexion, remember, *gratior est veniens in pulchro corpore virtus*
. . . When yow play at weapons I would have yow
gett thick capps & brasers, and play out your play
lustilie, for indeed tickes, & daliances are nothing in
earnest for the time of the one & the other greatlie
differs, and use as well the blow, as the thrust, it is
good in it selfe, & besides exerciseth your breath and
strength, and will make you a strong man at the
Tournei and Barriers. First in any case practize the
single sword, & so shall yow come home to my comfort and creditt. Lord how I have babled, once againe
farewell deerest brother.' The letter is signed 'At
lesterhouse this 18. of October. 1580.'

One had a right to expect from the preoccupation
with the practical, as exemplified in the ideals of
Renaissance education, that sooner or later progress
would be made in the discovery of scientific truth;
and, indeed, this expectation was fulfilled. But there
was another element in the cultural heritage of the

time which superficially at least showed great promise. Scepticism accomplished less in the end in the advancement of learning than did the practical tendencies of the age; its voice, however, is not to be disregarded. We shall find that Bacon combined in himself a strong utilitarian with an equally strong sceptical quality.

It would be a mistake not to point out that to the average learned man of the Renaissance there was little idea of the active possibility of discovery. That the mysteries of nature had ever been penetrated, meant to the Middle Ages and the Renaissance that there had been some sort of revelation in ancient days. The educated man of the time asked, not 'Is it true that adamant, the hardest known substance, can be broken only in goat's blood?' but, 'How did man ever make this discovery?' Magic itself, that great formula for the reading of the obscure present and the unrevealed future, must, it was thought, have come to man as a sort of revelation, possibly introduced from the East as a part of the store of Oriental wisdom, a wisdom far off and in its very nature beyond the reach of human powers. Bacon's enlightened doctrine of the wisdom of the ancients rests upon his belief in the existence of ancient, probably revealed wisdom. He saw in myth and fable something supremely valuable as a key to the temple of truth, better than normal science and reason afforded. Bacon therefore proposed that the wisdom of the ancients [10] be made a branch of human learning and exploited for man's benefit. He made noble and, it may be, fruitful studies in the field himself. Erasmus [11] and others, influenced by Ficino, who in turn followed Plotinus, had had the same idea that there was embodied in the myths of the ancient world a superior sort of wisdom. And, according to the beliefs then current, why not? If Adam before his fall was perfect in knowledge, then the height of science was at the most remote point in time. It might well be that there had survived of the old superfluity at least parts and outlines of the illimitable wisdom of God. The doctrine, changed in basis and rationalized far beyond the point of Bacon's rationalization, still survives. It now takes the form of a belief that primitive men leading their primitive lives [12] may have learned things about human life as such and embodied these things in the principles of their religion and the morals of their folk-lore. The belief that there must have been inspired originators of scientific truth [13] is in Pliny and other ancients and in Agrippa and many moderns. This belief had possibly given way to a conception, not a bad one, of the major hypotheses of science and pseudo-science as a body of valuable truth handed down from antiquity, part of man's birthright, which deepened and strengthened respect for authority and joined hands with the perfect submission of man to God inculcated by Christianity.

Then again, as to the nature of scepticism, it was not magic, astrology, or alchemy whose truth was called in question, but the sincerity and competency of magicians, astrologers, and alchemists. 'Alchemy,' [14] Bacon says, 'pretendeth to make separation of all the unlike parts of bodies which in mixture of nature are incorporate. But the derivations and prosecutions to these ends, both in the theories and in the practices, are full of error and vanity; which the great professors themselves have sought to veil over and conceal by enigmatical writing, and referring themselves to auricular traditions, and such other devices to save the credit of impostures. And yet surely to alchemy this right is due, that it may be compared to the husbandman whereof Æsop makes the fable, that when he died told his sons that he had left unto them gold

buried under ground in his vineyard; and they digged
over all the ground, and gold they found none, but by
reason of their stirring and digging the mould about
the roots of their vines, they had a great vintage the
year following: so assuredly the search and stir to
make gold hath brought to light a great number of
good and fruitful inventions and experiments, as well
for the disclosing of nature as for the use of man's life.'
Again elsewhere Bacon reveals a complete and respectful understanding of the principles of alchemy when
he says, 'If then it be true that Democritus said, *That
the truth of nature lieth hid in certain deep mines and
caves;* and if it be true likewise that the Alchemists
do so much inculcate, that Vulcan is a second nature,
and imitateth that dexterously and compendiously
which nature worketh by ambages and length of
time; it were good to divide natural philosophy into
the mine and the furnace.'

The scepticism [15] of a man like Sir Walter Ralegh is
of precisely the same sort as that of Bacon though by
no means so far advanced and so close to the fundamentals of disbelief. The attitude is old. Philostratus [16]
in the *Vita Apollonii* betrays a contempt for magicians and wizards and defends his hero from the
charge of belonging to such a class, dirty people who
violate the laws of nature, live in caves and hovels,
and cheat peasants and shopkeepers. He does not
deny astrology or even magic; with him it is a matter
of social class and moral behavior. The life of
Apollonius, known in the Middle Ages as the *Golden
Flowers of Apollonius* and frequently republished in
the Renaissance, is, in fact, in spite of its incredibilities,
a book of great good sense, which contains some of
the best science of the ancient world.

The distrust of the practitioner was certainly a
great deterrent to the acceptance of the superstitious

arts. To what extent it was a growing and effective element in the breakdown of the old order is hard to say. Certainly, much importance must be attached to the gentleman's attack on superstition, or rather on the faker and his dupe, which is obvious in Bacon and is the stock-in-trade of Jonson and the comic dramatists; but it is, as before said, an old thing. Rhetoricians [17] and men of letters, such as Cicero, Seneca, Plutarch, Lucian, and Favorinus, rebelled against the claims of pundits and professors, much as their modern representatives do against the claims of specialists. In the sixteenth century there is a definite school of sceptics, led by Henry Cornelius Agrippa and represented in England by Stephen Gosson, whose history is worth tracing, but is possibly less important for reform than the scoffings of Rabelais [18] and certainly less significant than the rationalistic attitude of Montaigne.[19] The usual attitude perhaps is that of Seneca, who has in him a great deal of genuine scepticism, but whose thinking is none the less controlled by a system. He matches scepticism with superstition, and what he gives with one hand he takes away, like Cardan, with the other. For example, Seneca, in spite of his scepticism, endorses and exploits ghosts and portents, which he regards as parts of a grand series. He has rationalized them in order that they may become credible. Our question relates to the beliefs of intelligent men when they sat in Elizabethan theatres and watched the dramas of the Neo-Senecans. Did they feel about the supernatural as Seneca felt, or as we feel?

It is probable that they felt as Seneca felt and gave an endorsement at least to the possibility of apparitions which we would not give. There was at least always the logic of supposed fact. There must be, they thought, occult virtues in natural objects, since, otherwise, why was it that a wild bull will be tamed when tied to a figtree. There was no disposition to deny fact, and from it deduction follows. Casual distrust, such as Pliny's question as to why a ship bearing the right foot of a tortoise will have its progress expedited, was easily answered. Any shrewd thinker would know that the virtue of a whole inheres in its parts. Even animistic beliefs are intelligible. Man had learned about his own nature from his observance of animals.[20] The fox had taught him to conceive of cunning, and the ox of laborious patience. Bacon argues plainly that, since 'man did give names unto other creatures in Paradise, as they were brought before him, according unto their proprieties,' he must have possessed 'the pure knowledge of nature and universality.' In other words, Adam named a certain creature 'lion' because of his royalty and another 'ass' because of his stupidity. Who was ready to deny human traits to animals and call in question well authenticated stories of their reason and their emotion? Did not the horses of Hector weep, and had not many animals shown religious veneration to God and his saints? Pure animism is but a step away, and the widely held theory of the structure of the universe demanded inanimate objects as its lowest order. They too, as well as animals, were possessed of spirit in lesser degree according to their station.

The serious disruption of this established world was begun, not by sceptics, but by practical investigators, who worked without much regard to theory. They were men whose normal interests caused them to observe nature so truly that they discovered what was actually there rather than what Pliny had said was there. A good deal of this valuable but unobtrusive discovery was made in England during the sixteenth century.

The intellectual life of the sixteenth century was in practice no doubt much like that of other times; effectual culture tended to connect itself with groups of co-workers and series of masters and pupils. Progress rarely comes at a single stride or as the work of a single discoverer. The advancement of science is and has been a matter of cooperation, and it is certainly true that no adequate account has been made of the inter-relations during the later sixteenth century of men of science with each other and with men of letters. Sixteenth-century poets and prose writers, distinguished by their hospitality to philosophy and science, were in the universities with the greater lights of science and philosophy and probably were often associated with them in later life. We know only a few particular things, such as Sidney's pre-occupation with Ramist logic; the mass of the investigation remains to be made. This idea of the inter-relations of men of learning could be illustrated from the group of mathematicians, such as Sir John Napier, Henry Briggs, Edward Wright, and Edmund Gunter, or from the group of anatomists headed by William Harvey; but possibly still another and more miscellaneous group will be more significant.

Long before Bacon became engaged in the actual work of science the spirit of inquiry into nature had manifested itself in many places. Dr. John Caius (1510-1573),[21] refounder and co-founder of Gonville and Caius College, Cambridge, had a most interesting career and one closely connected with the scholarship of the sixteenth century. He had his first training at Gonville Hall, an institution closely connected with the growth of humanism in Cambridge. It was there that Erasmus, Sir John Cheke, and Sir Thomas Smith had laboured successively in promoting the study of Greek. To this tradition belonged Roger Ascham and

Thomas Wilson. Caius's first work, like that of Linacre, was as a classical humanist in the study of medicine. It must be remembered that learning was not yet departmentalized and did not become so throughout the sixteenth century. There were no lines between science and literature except such as the individual chose to draw, the inter-relations of all subjects were freely recognized, and the conception of learning was at once unified and encyclopædic. In 1539, at the age of twenty-eight, Caius went to Padua to continue his medical studies, medicine under Johannes Baptista Montanus and anatomy under Andreas Vesalius, in whose house Caius resided for eight months. He made at the time of his departure from Padua a tour through Italy in order to make observations on libraries and on the state of learning—Venice, Florence, Urbino, Ferrara, Siena, Bologna, Pisa, Rome; also a similar journey through France and Germany. He became acquainted with all the most important men in the world, including Cosimo de' Medici, Melanchthon, Camerarius, Conrad Gesner, and Sebastian Munster.

Specifically, Caius was engaged in collating all the best manuscripts he could find in order to prepare accurate texts of Galen and Hippocrates, thus operating as a humanist in the first stage of modern culture—attempting to secure accurate versions of the teachings of antiquity. But he was something more than that; he was also an investigator. In 1552, after his return to England and after some years spent in the practice of medicine, he published the first version of his work on the sweating sickness[22] (1552), compiled some years before at Shrewsbury. His account of the symptoms of that disease is one of the truest pieces of medical observation since the days of Hippocrates. One wonders, when one hears Bacon speak of the need of recording cases in medicine, whether Bacon was ignorant of the work of Caius. Caius wrote for Conrad Gesner's use in his *Historia Animalium*, a tract, *De Canibus Britannicis Libellus* (1570), which was translated by Abraham Fleming as *Of Englishe Dogges*[23] (1576). This tract has the interesting and novel quality of resting on experience for its knowledge. For example, in his account of the Shepherd's Dog he says, 'This dog either at the hearing of his master's voice, or at the wagging and whistling in his fist, or at his shrill and hoarse hissing, bringeth the wandering wethers and straying sheep into the selfsame place where his master's will and wish is to have them... And sometimes the straying sheep, when no dog runneth before them, nor goeth about or beside them, gather themselves together into a flock, when they hear the shepherd whistle in his fist, for fear of the dog (as I imagine): remembering this (if unreasonable creatures may be reported to have memory) that the dog commonly runneth out at his master's warrant, which is his whistle. This we have oftentimes diligently marked, in taking our journey from town to town. When we have heard a shepherd whistle, we have reined in our horse and stood still a space, to see the proof and trial of this matter.' Dr. Caius does not hesitate even at this early time to attack, on the basis of his own experience, the authority of Hector Boethius. Hector Boethius has given an account of a dog called the Fisher, 'which seeketh for fish by smelling among rock and stone.' Caius has asked both fishermen and huntsmen and heard nothing of such a dog. He concludes either that there is no such dog or that Boece had taken the beaver or otter for a fish and thus had in mind the otter hound. He rejects the ancient Latin classification of dogs in favour of one based on actually known English breeds.

Dr. Thomas Penney (d. 1589),[24] botanist and entomologist, although his experience did not enable him to make a full classification of spiders, described in detail and put into classes those that he knew. He is reported to have remarked significantly that he doubted if Actorides 'had seen all things.' Penney's friend, Dr. Thomas Moffett, made use of Penney's studies in the preparation of his important scientific work, *The Theater of Insects* (Latin 1634, English 1658), and one can see from that work how Penney was anticipating the scientific methods of the late seventeenth century.

Now, Thomas Penney was a Cambridge man in the time of Caius (M.A. 1559). He assisted Conrad Gesner in Switzerland, and was also a friend of Camerarius. Thomas Moffett (1553-1604) studied medicine under Thomas Lorkin and John Caius. His fellow students were Peter Turner, Timothy Bright, and Thomas Penney, all of whom were eminent as physicians, and nearly all of whom were eminent in other sciences besides medicine. In 1579 Thomas Moffett visited Italy and Spain and studied the culture of the silkworm. The result of this was his poem, *The Silkwormes and their Flies; Lively described in Verse* (1599). It is not a very good poem but is doubtless excellent vermiculture. It is interesting that he, like Fracastoro, should have written his science in verse. In his *Theater of Insects* Moffett seems to have built upon the work, not only of his fellow student Penney, but of Gesner and of Edward Wotton (1492-1555), an Oxford man, a Greek scholar, and a naturalist, whose *De Differentiis Animalium* (1552) is possibly to be brought into the complex of English natural history at an earlier time. Thomas Lorkin (1528?-1591), an associate of Caius, was regius professor of physic at Cambridge and author of a work on medical education, entitled *Recta Regula et Victus Ratio pro Studiosis et Literatis* (1562). The Turners,[25] father (William d. 1568), son (Peter, 1542-1614), and even grandson (Peter, 1586-1652) are one of the interesting families in the history of English learning and show numerous connexions with scholars and learned men. William Turner, the grandfather, Dean of Wells, was a Marian exile and a bitter anti-papistical controversialist. He travelled and studied in Italy, and at Zürich was intimate with Gesner, whom he seems to have assisted. Turner's *Herbal* (1551, 1552, 1558) marks the beginning of scientific botany in England. He was also learned in stones, metals, and fishes. He belonged to the Cambridge of Cheke, Nicholas Ridley (his Greek teacher), and Hugh Latimer. Peter, his son, was a physician of eminence who wrote a book (1603) against the use of amulets (known as 'plague cakes'). Peter Turner, the grandson, was a mathematician, who succeeded Henry Briggs as professor of geometry at Gresham College. Dr. Timothy Bright (1551?-1615) [26] was the inventor of modern shorthand and a leader of that group of scientists who attempted to solve the problem of insanity along the lines of the physiological psychology of Aristotle and his followers. Bright's *Treatise of Melancholie* (1586) enjoyed an international reputation.

It is apparent that the group of men just discussed was, so far as the development of science is concerned, moving in the right direction and was, to some extent, anticipating the objects and methods of the modern scientist; but most scientists concerned themselves with books and not with natural objects, and did not know how faulty their science was. They objected to being pushed beyond the satisfactory limits of their known world. They despised what they did not know

and thought unimportant the activities of those engaged in unknown or new fields. We have had a good
deal to say about the limits and difficulties of Renaissance science. In order to see, finally, how great was
the complex we have only to mention again as an additional burden the general belief in correspondences,
affinities or appetites, and antipathies. The nature of
this obstacle appears in the work of Bacon. An illustration drawn from his advanced method will indicate the
road which it was necessary for science to travel. As
conceived even by the shrewdly analytical Bacon,
who affirmed that the secret of truth lay in definition,
the concept 'motion' included (1) change of place,
(2) appetite, (3) chemical affinity, (4) interaction
between bodies, (5) passion, and (6) thought.

Bacon seems to have a qualitative conception of motion, for he speaks of kinds of motion as appetites and
inclinations of matter; he possibly attaches no quantitative aspect to it. He regards the knowledge of motions as of primary importance. Apparently motion as
conceived by Bacon was an active agency having
kinds; whereas to us motion is a change of position,
having directions but not kinds. To him motion was a
force or active agency, not as to the modern scientist
the result of a hypothetical force. In his *Confession
of Faith* he says that the Laws of Nature are commands which God has laid upon the universe. God's
continuous will that these laws shall function keeps
them functioning. Bacon probably thought of motion
as an emanation from this constant and conserving will
of God. His conception of motion is thus probably an
inheritance from older philosophies, since he uses the
traditional terms *appetitus* and *inclinatio;* it finds expression, for example, in the essay 'Of Truth': 'Certainly, it is heaven upon earth, to have a man's mind

move in charity, rest in providence, and turn upon the poles of truth.' Such moral and spiritual excellence is also motion.

In the *Filum Labarynthi, sive Inquisitio legitima de Motu* [27] is a scheme of tables of motion—not actually constructed but consisting of a series of aphorisms or final observations. The first stage of the process of investigation (*machina intellectus inferior*) is that pertaining to ordered collections. The following headings are really incipient hypotheses, although Bacon does not think of them as such:

A. Concerning forms and diversities of motion
   1. Motion of exterior application or adherence
   2. Motion of interior application or mingling
   3. Motion of application to the fibres
   4. Assimilation
   5. Signature or impression
   6. Excitation
   7. Apparent Generation

B. Concerning things which are moved—subjects or containers of motion
C. Bearers of motion
D. Operations and consequences of motion
E. Courses and times of motion
F. Circle or region of power of motion
G. Hierarchy of motion
H. Association of motion
I. Affinities of motion
J. Powers of union in motion
K. Forces of custom and novelty in motion [suggestive of inertia]
L. Concerning all other motions

In his Table of Anatomy or Table of the Second Division adapted to the study of motion Bacon provides for

A. The exterior axiom or table of the second division
B. Table of the apparently impossible
C. Table concerning aid or use
D. Anticipation or interpretation of the amassed material
E. The bridge or chart of new charts

When he comes to *Machina intellectus superior*, which should be the result of tables of second appearances, Bacon does not outline them, but simply unites *Chartæ novellæ*.

This outline for the study of motion, found in part in a different form in *Novum Organum*, II, xlviii, Bacon intended as a substitute for the outlines of the subject in physics as made by other physicists, which he explains and discards in *Cogitationes de natura rerum* (III-VIII). The principles of investigation hitherto followed he calls 'inactive,' because they 'tell us of what elements things are made up and consist, but not by what force or in what manner they come together.' These things do not bear materially on the enlargement of the power and operation of man. The vague and impractical themes actually discoursed of are these: whether impulse is communicated to matter by privation, whether there is conformation of matter to idea, whether there is coalition of like particles, whether there is a fortuitous play of atoms *in vacuo*, whether there is an enmity and friendship among substances, whether there are reciprocal actions between heaven and earth, whether there is a commerce of elements through contributing qualities (*symbolizantes*), whether there is an influence of heavenly bodies, whether there are occult and curative virtues and properties, what are the nature and function of fate, fortune, and necessity—all generalities, 'spectres and appearances that float and play on the surface of things, as on water.' Bacon expresses belief in the conservation of matter and seeks a means in the investigation of nature to confine and bind matter (like Proteus in the myth) so that we shall not be deceived by apparent disappearances.

The common division of motion is into generation and corruption (in which bodies in the progression of their motion assume new forms or lay aside the old), increase and diminution (in which bodies, their configuration remaining the same, acquire new quantity or measure of dimension), alteration (in which, mass and outline remaining the same, bodies undergo change in quality, operation, and properties), removal to place (in which the body, unaltered in figure, matter and quantity, undergoes change in place and that only). This division Bacon regards as merely descriptive, giving information as to the successive courses motions have to run, but conveying no real distinctions—adjusted to the forms of scholastic logic, but unproductive of physical knowledge.

Bacon's chances to isolate phenomena and hold nature fast in the investigation of motion with such an heterogeneous corpus for examination were indeed not great. His success would have depended on the axioms arrived at in his second table. Meantime, from his consideration of the subject of motion it is possible for us to perceive the outlines of an unknown world stirred and controlled by the will of God pervading all things by reason of its intentness—creating, annihilating, stopping, accelerating, reflecting, and enigmatically blotting out from sight.

Bacon's outline of procedure will make clearer what we have to say about the state of scientific method. We should like to indicate, as well as we can in so dark an area, general features of the mental habits arising from centuries of scholastic learning and ecclesiastical dominance. We shall, however, merely present certain practical matters suggestive of intellectual habit.

In the epistle to the Reader in John Molle's translation (finished 1612?) of *The Walking Librarie* of Camerarius is the statement that the author in his spare hours was wont to read histories and to cull from them delightful, memorable, and profitable observations which he made his own by reflecting on them. Camerarius was wont to compare what he had heard from others or had observed himself with those of ancient times, and again ancient with modern. History, regarded as a kind of philosophy by the ancients and delivered by examples, was the study which Camerarius most followed. The many precepts in the book, collected from the best writers, show us what in life to imitate and pursue and what to avoid. Generous spirits, we are told, may be incited to Piety, Wisdom, Justice, Magnanimity, Temperance, and other fair virtues and be deterred from vices by a consideration of what fearful punishments and calamities are most commonly the concomitants of these vices.

This is the usual didactic method of the time and consists in the enumeration of principles, the citation of authorities, and the presentation of examples. Beyond this there was in literary composition little organization of the body of discourse, and even Bacon, who saw advantages in the aphoristic method, was concerned rather in the .completeness of the single aphorism, a kind of 'demonstration in circle,' [28] which by its avowed devotion to a single aspect might invite men to inquire further, than in a concatenated plan. Bacon objected to the specious and misleading completeness of the customary sort of learned discourse, which, proceeding on the basis of a few axioms, observations, or *dicta*, is illustrated and reinforced by authority and example and digested by formal art into apparent unity. There was also current the method of question and answer, which, when it was fairly used, had certain advantages in its freedom.

Bacon's criticisms [29] are revelatory, and all the more so because of his attack upon the principle of universality. He dwells on the handling of final causes as a deterrent to 'the severe and diligent inquiry of all real and physical causes.' Plato 'ever anchoreth upon that shore,' as also Aristotle and Galen. 'For to say that *the hairs of the eyelids are for a quickset and fence about the sight;* or that *the firmness of the skins and hides of living creatures is to defend them from the extremities of heat or cold;* or that *the bones are for the columns or beams, whereupon the frames of the bodies of living creatures are built;* or that *the leaves of trees are for protecting of the fruit;* or that *the clouds are for watering of the earth;* or that *the solidness of the earth is for the station and mansion of living creatures* and the like, is well enquired and collected in Metaphysic; but in Physic they are impertinent.' Elsewhere he criticizes the presuppositions of all natural science, such as the principle of like to like, imparted power, sympathy and antipathy, the virtue of the whole resident in the part, and the doctrine that the inferior is subject to the superior; but before his day, and popularly long after it, we find miscellaneous collection for moral purposes, blind veneration for authority with its consequent aggregative procedure, the method of similitudes, and the endless making of hypotheses.

For example, with reference to the interpretation of Scripture, Henry Cornelius Agrippa [30] is orthodox enough. Interpretation, he tells us, by the demonstration, definition, division, and composition of the Schoolmen is useless. The way to know God's meaning lies between this and the prophetical vision; that is, an equalization of truth with our purged understanding. Truth is manifold and lies hidden in the Holy Scriptures. The following are the true kinds of interpretation: literal, moral, tropological (where they are turned to the secrets of the church), anagogical (referring all things to the mystery of God's glory), typical (referring all things to the changes of times, alteration of kingdoms, etc.), and physical or natural (searching out powers and virtues of the natural world). He adds to this the statement that no one can find out or declare God's meaning; one can only know His word and declare it. Bacon's discussion of the subject, though complicated, is again significant. Sound interpretation of the Scriptures,[31] he says, is 'methodical,' by which he means the reduction of divinity to an art and the making of the Scriptures into a 'cistern' from which streams of doctrine are derived; and 'solute, or at large,' by which he means the immediate extraction of doctrine from Scripture. He has much to say about the weaknesses of the 'methodical' interpretation, and throws out anagogical interpretation, and, partly, philosophical interpretation, on the ground that they are drawn from two things known only to the inditer of Scripture, namely, the mysteries of the kingdom of glory and the perfection of the law of nature, which things are not attainable by man. He endorses literal, moral, and allegorical interpretation as just, because God knew the secrets of the heart of man and the future succession of all the ages. Thus Bacon, though his method of progress may have been at fault in certain particulars, clears away some at least of the errors of his age; but for most men, even in part for Bacon himself, these errors were still truth.

One may conclude after this survey that the beginnings of modern science were already present in sixteenth-century England, and that both critical and exploratory elements were greatly increased by Francis Bacon. Our habit of mind makes us watch for this thing and adds importance to it, as if human happiness were certainly and immediately connected with the advancement of science. The spectacle of a clearer and more triumphant mind in the race is indeed gratifying—the conquest of ignorance and error, imposture and credulity—but, if we are reading this story aright, we shall see that, if we forget Sidney's and Shakespeare's fine enthusiasm for beauty and goodness in human life, we shall leave something of value behind.

CHAPTER V

THE NATURE AND CONDITION OF MEN

Which merit was lively set forth by the ancients in that feigned relation of Orpheus theatre; where all beasts and birds assembled, and forgetting their several appetites, some of prey, some of game, some of quarrel, stood all sociably together listening unto the airs and accords of the harp; the sound whereof no sooner ceased, or was drowned by some louder noise, but every beast returned to his own nature: wherein is aptly described the nature and condition of men; who are full of savage and unreclaimed desires, of profit, of lust, of revenge, which as long as they give ear to precepts, to laws, to religion, sweetly touched with eloquence and persuasion of books, of sermons, of harangues, so long is society and peace maintained.—Bacon, *The Advancement of Learning.*

WHAT man thinks are his nature, his earthly condition, and his fate is a matter of importance in the depictions he makes of himself. The man of the Renaissance was a fallen creature, unable to save himself from the consequences of his original and his inevitably recurrent sin, because his nature was such that when he would do good evil was present with him and sure to prevail. His environment was also ruined. His companionship was with creatures of his own kind and was detrimental to him and to them. Science and religion agreed on these points. The real hardships of the age supplied an all-too-obvious confirmation. What then did the man of the Renaissance think of his own nature and state?

Psychology,[1] the subject but not the name, had been well known from the times of Aristotle and Galen. The treatises of Cornelius Africanus and of

Nemesius are almost as complete and detailed as those of Melanchthon and Vives. But in the study of psychology there occurred a sudden and essentially unsound exploitation in the last fifteen or twenty years of the sixteenth century. At that time psychology seemed all at once to realize the extent of its own claims. As an old subject, widely known and deeply realized, it had entered into the warp and woof of literature, science, and philosophy. It suddenly came out of its seclusion and declared that it knew how to cure disease, solve the problems of education, and elucidate the vagaries of human action. After a century of the wildest career it found itself discredited and bankrupt and ready for the ministrations of John Locke. Its more extreme developments arose from the Galenic or Stoical theories of the passions or perturbations of the mind. These theories began to be most actively entertained in England about the turn of the century.

In taking up the important subject of faculty psychology we should remind ourselves that our task demands for its basis, not a history of the development of science, a subject which Bacon would describe as 'adequately laboured,' but an intelligible description of the doctrines of science at particular times. We need to realize the implications of such a description in all the ways in which the feelings and opinions of men were affected and controlled. What we now confidently regard as scientific truth can serve us only as it makes apparent the complex of truth and error which passed for truth during the English Renaissance and had for that particular time the power of truth. Not the truth, as before said, but what they believed was the truth was the controlling motive of the men of the Renaissance, as appears in the records they made of life. We need therefore a history of error as well as of truth if we are to understand those records.

It has been said that psychology underwent popularization in the last years of the sixteenth century; it was applied at that time to the practical ends of education and medicine and came into more frequent and more technical use by literary men as a means of studying character and action. The language of the subject had long been a *milieu* of expression.[2] A science false in its principles cannot stand exploitation in practice. When applied in detail its falsity becomes revealed. Ancient psychology as a body of doctrine for the explanation of human mentality had and has a sort of general validity. As long as it was devoted to the relatively simple ends of its founders and sought to explain mental phenomena on the basis of the external criteria of human life it served and still serves well. Psychology showed indeed a surprising adaptability; in the earlier stages of its exploitation during the Renaissance it met adequately the needs of sonnet, lyric, and drama. This was its ancient use and is as easily illustrated from Euripides and Chaucer as from Shakespeare himself. As one sees in the later cantos of the *Faerie Queene*, Book II,[3] man had, even when beset by passion, a fair chance under this system to maintain his equilibrium, to save himself. Milton[4] gives Adam this chance:

> 'I yield it just,' said Adam, 'and submit.
> But is there yet no other way, besides
> These painful passages, how we may come
> To death, and mix with our connatural dust?'
> 'There is,' said Michael, 'if thou well observe
> The rule of *Not too much*, by temperance taught
> In what thou eat'st and drink'st, seeking from thence
> Due nourishment, not gluttonous delight,

Till many years over thy head return.
So may'st thou live, till, like ripe fruit, thou drop
Into thy mother's lap, or be with ease
Gathered, not harshly plucked, for death mature.'

Men under stress of passion, according to the older
system, grew violent or even insane, but were still
men.

A false piece of theory, arising from a mechanistic
physiology, made now its appearance, or rather its re-
appearance, since, as before said, it is part of the psychology of Galen and the Stoics. As the extreme
aspects of the subject developed and approached the
stage represented for us in Burton's *Anatomy of Melancholy*, the faults of the system begin to be obvious.
Perhaps we should rather say that, as literary men insisted more and more on applying psychology to human life, psychology suffered from an *argumentum ad
extremum*. Jacobean tragedy as compared with Elizabethan tragedy shows us an unconvincing spectacle of
man when obsessed by passion. The theory of the
domination of the reason by the passions rested on the
hypothesis of a crude physical device according to
which one passion of the heart replaced another as
one liquid might replace another in the emptying and
filling of a cup. This theory was useful for diversion
and cure, but as a psychological theory it made no
provision for the suspensions of natural inhibition and
judgment, or the inertia of habitual action, these being
the functions of a reason which was *ex hypothesi* dethroned. A man's character became, so to speak, an
accident rather than a property. Man and man under
passion were different machines. Everyone must have
noticed the difference between the natural and
motivated jealousy of Othello and the sudden and un-

accountable jealousy of Leontes. One finds in Jacobean tragedy monsters instead of men—De Flores,
Vindici, Flamineo. The Machiavels of the earlier
period were, relatively speaking, crudely conceived
fiends. The villains of the later tragedy were manu-
factured according to formula. Other examples of the
overwrought condition of the science are to be seen
in Huarte's classification of men by their humours and
Burton's frank treatment of love as a disease of the
body.

One is not concerned in this account with psychology as such, but with it mainly as it helps to reveal a
conception of man and man's life.[5] No doubt life in
the Renaissance, with its plagues and brawls, was un-
certain enough to bring about a theory of its instability, but the theory is none the less ancient and well
grounded in science and theology. Cardan[6] gives us
as the seven major calamities: *Terrae motus, inundatio,
ventus, animalia, pestis, bellum,* and *fames.* Many disasters interfere with longevity, but calamity may be
fitly discussed, he says, under the captions supernatural, natural, and accidental. Even the greatest of men
are subject to misfortune, and Boethius gave perfect
warrant to the belief that philosophers are subject to
affliction.

It was generally believed that there had never been
so vicious an age as that of the Renaissance, and that
the youth of the time were thought of as a menace.
Thomas Fortescue declares in his dedication to *The
Foreste* (1571) that he had travelled abroad not long
before and found the world in disorder and tumult.
Justice was not administered, all mechanical arts and
all sciences were surceased. In schools the chairs were
void of learned doctors; no man delivered laws from
Justinian; Hippocrates, the solace of the sick, and

Galen were unknown. The Scriptures were not taught, the tongues were all forgotten, and philosophy was a stranger. The land was in a state of war.

Not only was man thought of as unfortunate in his situation; he was also unstable in himself. He desired change for the sake of change. Since man's qualities must be excused, it was said that he was in his very nature liable to concupiscence. Man was, however, responsible for his own misery. He must live a life at war with reason and suffer all the defeats and sorrows of such a life; even his wit destroyed his blessedness. At best there was, they held, a mixture of virtue and vice within us, but vice had the better of it; men were naturally prone to every sin, and could be saved only by faith and the mercy of God's grace. Man disobeyed God and fell from his high station; the animals, created for man's comfort, saw that because of sin man was no longer worthy of the dignity of being placed above them and straightway began to disobey him. Animals must not be blamed and persecuted for this, since man has brought the calamity on himself. This reckless, vacillating, unstable, discontented creature man lived unhappily, usually died in agony, and spent eternity in torment. His chances for earthly happiness were very few at best and mainly to be found in the mean estate.

If one confers upon such a creature a psychology of mechanistic change—in point of fact the psychology was deduced from the condition—and makes of that psychology a controlling factor in behaviour, so that man may suddenly fall a prey to a group of feral and venal passions, one lifts man out of the normal world and makes his situation altogether special. A more exaggerated psychology is one of the things that distinguishes the Baroque from the Renaissance, for the mechanistic conception of man's inward nature became more and more current as the Renaissance gave way.

On the psychology of Vives and Melanchthon, on other older and less detailed treatments (such as that in *De Proprietatibus Rerum* and in *Margarita Philosophica* of Gregorius Reisch), on the Schoolmen, the Church Fathers, and the ancients was based the traditional psychology carried by the great Elizabethans into their literary works. Perhaps the very extended treatment of the subject in *The French Academie*[7] helped to disseminate a knowledge of psychology and an interest in it. Levinus Lemnius, *The Touchstone of Complexions*, translated by Thomas Newton (1565 and later editions), Pierre Boaistuau, *Theatrum Mundi*, translated by John Alday (1566? and later editions), and Sir Thomas Elyot, *The Castle of Helth* (1534 and many editions) must have helped to popularize the subject. Indeed there was no lack of material. Toward the end of the century there was a perfect flood of psychological works in the vernacular: Timothy Bright, *Of Melancholy* (1586); Juan de Dios Huarte Navarro, *Examen de Ingenios*, translated by R. Carew (1594); Sir Richard Barckley, *The Felicitie of Man* (1598); Pierre Charron, *De la Sagesse* (1601, early translation by Samson Lennard); Sir John Davies, *Nosce Teipsum* (1599); John Davies of Hereford, *Mirum in Modum* (1602); Robert Allott, *Wits Theater of the Little World* (1599); Thomas Wright, *The Passions of the Minde in Generall* (1601), and others.

Bright's *Of Melancholy* marks the development of the medical aspect of psychology, a development which culminated in the great work of Robert Burton, *The Anatomy of Melancholy*. The special study of melancholy as a disease had of course long engaged people's minds, but Bright's work shows a reawakening of interest. Bright's Epistle Dedicatory[8] to Peter

Osborne outlines clearly his medical point of view and shows the application of pseudo-medical principles to the subject in hand. The most noble part of physic, he says, is that part which restores the brain when it is disordered from not being well tempered. So great is the power of physic to cure these distemperatures that many have thought ill of the soul. If one understands the philosophy of the subject, one understands such questions. Physic devotes itself to what Bright calls natural melancholy; it does not pretend to cure those cases in which God in his demand for penitence has laid a heavy hand upon the sinner. 'More needs she the divine than the physician,' says the Doctor of Lady Macbeth. The passions, Bright says, gain power over the soul and force it from its proper serenity, through the evil-disposed instruments of the body. These the physician may restore and thus indirectly restore the mind, an idea now currently accepted. One cannot tell to what extent such medical writers as Bright were known to Elizabethan and Jacobean writers, but certainly much technical psychopathic information appears in the literature of the time.

Among the important aspects of the renewal of interest in psychology which occurred in the latter part of the sixteenth and the earlier part of the seventeenth century, there is one which might be considered now. It has to do with a phase of applied psychology, namely educational psychology, and its history remains to be written.

It concerns mainly the work of Juan de Dios Huarte Navarro,[9] who in psychology was a follower of Vives. His *Examen de Ingenios*, which enjoyed great popularity in England, is a sincere, learned, and strictly logical book, and one with a practical idea as its basis. If, he says, it is true, a thing which nobody denies, that each individual has one special faculty preëminent above all the rest and if it is true that a man's success in any particular calling depends upon his possession of the temperament demanded by that occupation or profession, it follows that if one knew one's own temperament, one would know what calling to follow. Now, to learned men there is no particular difficulty about determining the temperament of any given individual. Temperament is merely the resultant of a mixture of the qualities of hot and cold, moist and dry, and each individual is, so to speak, written all over with physiognomic signs, easily read. For those already embarked on a fruitless voyage little can be done, but for the youth much. What qualities are required in a successful soldier, lawyer, doctor are well known. Wise men can easily tell the qualities of individual youths. Put these together, and the result is success. Put a wrong two together, and the result is failure. Hence Huarte's book. Let nobody think that Huarte is anything less than learned, practical, wise, and ingenious, or look down with scorn upon this early scheme for vocational guidance. The book went through many editions, must have been read by many parents and schoolmasters, and have enjoyed great influence during the seventeenth century. It would be interesting to know more of the history of Huarte's theory.

The idea that parents should know the natural constitutions of their children is expressed by Peter Paul Vergerius (d. 1428);[10] also by Mapheus Vegius.[11] Erasmus, *De pueris statim ac liberaliter instruendis* (1529) and *Philodoxus*, stresses natural fitness according to temperament of various youths for various professions, and it was probably from Erasmus that Vives took the idea. It also appears in Silvio Antoniano, *Tres libri della educatione christiana dei figliuoli*

(Verona, 1583) and in Antonio Possevino, *Cultura ingeniorum*. Klein thinks that a concurrent exploitation of physiognomy also entered the field and caused psychology in the sixteenth century to take a practical turn, but this is supposition perhaps unnecessary since there is little physiognomy as such in Vives, and the physiognomy in Huarte takes a medical and observational turn rather than the conventional form of the traditional subject. Still there is no doubt that Huarte did both know and use physiognomy, and there is no reason to question the statement that out of a combination of the pedagogical psychology of Vives and the general interest in physiognomy arose the work of John Huarte. The subject of physiognomic study in the sixteenth century needs further investigation.

But it is with the literary uses of psychology that we are naturally most concerned. Literary men, aware that man becomes interesting under the sway of passions, used their knowledge of psychology to clarify and reinforce their conceptions. The earliest group of great Elizabethans usually reveal a more or less extensive knowledge of psychology which is to some extent casual—the early dramatists, Lyly, Peele, Greene; as also Sidney and Spenser. Then come a group of writers who show a knowledge of the details of the science and employ it in an obvious and often penetrating way in their work—Marlowe, Shakespeare, Marston, Chapman, and Jonson. They are at home with the terminology of the subject; it is integral and poetized. Lastly, there is a Jacobean group, persons who know psychology and take it as a matter of course. They no longer explain psychological principles or lard their discourses with psychological terms; but they are really more advanced psychologists than their predecessors, for they have taken the Stoical theory of passions to heart. They are absorbed in the spectacle of man in the grasp of unruly spirits and driven to insanity, crime, misery, blindness, or possibly to such folly as to become a mere ridiculous cartoon of humanity. Such men are Beaumont and Fletcher, Tourneur, Webster, Middleton, and Ford. Shakespeare and other writers show more than one of these three arbitrarily chosen phases of the psychological wave of the period. Other men, usually those of a less highly trained type, manifest only the older undeveloped stage of psychological study. Dekker, for example, was a less learned psychologist than were his contemporaries; whereas Ford [12] seems to have made a most extensive and deliberate use of Burton's *Anatomy of Melancholy*.

A relatively unemphasized and normal use of psychology is characteristic of the plays of didactic formalism like *Gorboduc, Damon and Pithias, Selimus,* and of Greene, Marlowe (the greatest psychologist of the group), Peele, and the early Shakespeare. Yet this is no uniform rule. Marlowe's *Dr. Faustus* and his *Edward II* certainly show superior maturity in their use of formal psychology, for Marlowe was apparently much interested in the subject. His pre-eminence is apparent in *Tamburlaine,*[13] and enough of psychological terminology appears in *Dr. Faustus* and *Edward II* to convince one that Marlowe knew the subject particularly well; his plays, moreover, show this technical knowledge transmuted into the realization of character and not merely fitted into a formal pattern. Strangely enough the same advance in culture is obvious in *Arden of Feversham.*[14] There is little of the formal language of psychology in the play, less than in many later plays; but there is, on the other hand, what seems to be great realization of psychological states and conditions and even enough technical language to indicate conscious reference to the subject. For example, Mosbie says:

> Disturbed thoughts dryves me from company
> And dryes my marrow with their watchfulnes,
> Continuall trouble of my moody braine,
> Feebles my body [like] excesse of drinke.

But even this passage is surpassed in affective consciousness by Richard's speech in the first scene of the second act (ll. 79-86) of *3 Henry VI:*

> I cannot weep; for all my body's moisture
> Scarce serves to quench my furnace-burning heart:
> Nor can my tongue unload my heart's great burthen;
> For selfsame wind that I should speak withal
> Is kindling coals that fires all my breast,
> And burns me up with flames that tears would quench.
> To weep is to make less the depth of grief:
> Tears then for babes; blows and revenge for me!

Dekker uses psychological principles to some degree in the structure of his plots, and there is also a fair showing of incidental allusions. In *The Honest Whore*, Part I,[15] the sudden repentance of Bellafront after Hippolito's long and eloquent indictment of her wickedness is a parallel, psychologically speaking, to the suddenness of Claudius's repentance [16] in *Hamlet*. Both are explained by the theory that one emotion or passion drives out another, and that the substitution is immediately operative. The doctrine is enough to account for many of the sudden changes in character, changes without transitional stages, which appear frequently in Elizabethan drama. Bellafront's pretended madness and the madhouse scene reveal Dekker's knowledge of what behaviour was to be expected from an insane person and what measures were taken by the medical fraternity for the cure of insanity. The play contains a good deal of the widely current psychological knowledge of the time. One learns that the spleen swells in anger. The sea of a lover's rage comes rushing with so strong a tide that it beats and tears down all respects of life, honour, friends, and foes. Viola's brother has swaggering humours. The doctor who has administered to Infelice the potion which makes her seem dead explains its action. The vital spirits are bound up fast by a sleepy charm and throw an icy rust on her external parts. When she begins to recover she must not be spoken to, and, as in *King Lear*, music is played to set in order her spirits. Princes have high spleens which swell for empery; such men are not easily managed. Candido is a monstrous patient man; his blood is immovable. He hasn't a thimbleful of blood in his belly, or a spleen as big as a tavern token. You could sooner raise spleen in an angel than rough humour in him; for he was a man made up without gall; nothing could move him or convert his meek blood into fury. All love is lunatic and a disease. Bellafront is so vexed at her page that she will have the 'mother' presently; Hippolito tells Bellafront that when she interrupted him he was on meditation's spotless wings; like a storm she beat his ripened cogitations down; like a thief she stole devotion from that holy land (His soul had been freed from his body). Bellafront had no sooner laid eyes on Hippolito than her eye conveyed him straight to her heart. The Duke begs Hippolito to send away his milder spirits and let wrath strengthen the force of his sword; and so on. This is a familiar way of talking with Dekker, as it is with Heywood and other dramatists.

But there is a group of dramatists who put psychological theory to uses of far greater importance. The first of these is Marston. It may be that he was the leader of the fashion. Not only do Marston's works teem with ordinary psychological comment and explanation in general, but his dramas and the satires show how deeply he was impressed with the importance of the humours in the determination of character. He seems also to have been a student of dream-lore and to some extent at least of madness. The second is Jonson, who created a new type of comedy in which the eccentricities of men are presented in terms of the doctrine of the humours, and who furthermore constantly presents character and motive for action in what can fairly be called psychological terms. The third is Chapman. Chapman was pedantic. It pleased him to make clear his psychological distinctions and interpretations in the terms of the science itself. So true is this that one could almost reconstruct the subject of Elizabethan psychology from his plays alone. Finally, there is Shakespeare, who seems to have begun his work without anything more than the usual general knowledge of psychology employed in describing action and character, but, later, in plays after about 1600, shows a mastery of the science. He uses it skilfully as a tool. Perhaps he was following dramatic fashion in so psychologizing his plays. Perhaps he studied the subject seriously for the first time then. But one cannot doubt that he knew the subject well and considered it an important angle from which to regard human life. He rarely introduces anything which is improbable even from the point of view of the superior knowledge of our day, but employs formal psychological principles only when they further his dramatic ends and illuminate the characters and situations with which he is dealing. He seems never to be merely illustrating psychological principles; there is an organic quality about his use of the features and distinctions of the subject. Disregarding the more disputable questions as to Shakespeare's conscious employment of psychological theory in the depiction of such characters as Hamlet, Macbeth, and King Lear, we may indicate the manner of his procedure by a few characteristic examples.

Shakespeare [17] understood the relation of passion to action and the necessity of gaining and holding an efficient head of passion. Lady Macbeth's famous advice to her husband seems a case in point:

> *Macbeth.*   If we should fail?
> *Lady Macbeth.*   We fail!
> But screw your courage up to the sticking-place,
> And we'll not fail.

King Henry V before Harfleur definitely recommends the use of corporeal means to pump up a sufficient height of courage for the assault:

> In peace there's nothing so becomes a man
> As modest stillness and humility:
> But when the blast of war blows in our ears,
> Then imitate the action of the tiger;
> Stiffen the sinews, summon up the blood,
> Disguise fair nature with hard-favour'd rage;
> Then lend the eye a terrible aspect;
> Let it pry through the portage of the head
> Like the brass cannon; let the brow o'erwhelm it
> As fearfully as doth a galled rock
> O'erhang and jutty his confounded base,
> Swill'd with the wild and wasteful ocean.
> Now set the teeth and stretch the nostril wide,
> Hold hard the breath and bend up every spirit
> To his full height.

The phrase 'bend up every spirit' betrays Shakespeare's consciousness of psychological theory in this passage, for strength of courage was at once strength of body and strength of spirit. Julius Cæsar, for ex-

ample, expresses pride in the strength of his spirit
when he says to his flatterers,

> Be not fond,
> To think that Cæsar bears such rebel blood
> That will be thaw'd from the true quality
> With that which melteth fools.

Shakespeare seems also to have grasped a relation
only recently re-advanced in psychology, that control
of the outward expression of passion is the control of
the passion itself. 'Sleek o'er your rugged looks,' says
Lady Macbeth to her husband and later makes the
even more significant statement:

> O, these flaws and starts,
> Impostors to true fear, would well become
> A woman's story at a winter's fire,
> Authorized by her grandam. Shame itself!
> Why do you make such faces?

And again there seems anticipation of permanent
psychological truth in Shakespeare's grasp of the principle of the fixed idea unhinging the reason. Iago's
expression of it can hardly be surpassed:

> The Moor already changes with my poison:
> Dangerous conceits are, in their natures, poisons,
> Which at the first are scarce found to distaste,
> But with a little act upon the blood,
> Burn like the mines of sulphur.

The psychology of *A Woman Killed with Kindness* [18] by Thomas Heywood is conventional, and the
play is consciously written within the lines of Elizabethan formal thought in matters of ethical and psychological import. The play, which is based on a
belief in the menacing quality of the passions, will
repay brief consideration.

In remorse for what he has done, after the killing

of Sir Francis's followers, Sir Charles lays the blame
on anger (I, iii, 49-56):

> Forgive me, God! 'twas in the heat of blood,
> And anger quite remooved me from my selfe:
> It was not I, but rage, did this vile murther;
> Yet I, and not my rage, must answer it.
> Sir Francis Acton, he is fled the field;
> With him, all those that did partake his quarrell,
> And I am left alone, with sorrow dumbe,
> And in my heighth of conquest, overcome.

Sir Francis, having procured the imprisonment and
ruin of Sir Charles, approaches Susan to taunt her
with her poverty. But he falls in love with her at
sight (III, i, 88-95):

Ha, ha! Now will I flout her poverty,
Deride her fortunes, scoffe her base estate;
My very soule the name of Mountford hate.
But stay; my heart, or, [oh?] what a looke did flye
To strike my soule through with thy piercing eye.
I am inchanted, all my spirits are fled,
And with one glance my envious spleene strooke dead.

He recalls that she is poor (and therefore unfit for
matrimony) and the sister of his enemy. He is amazed
at his passion (III, i, 105-114):

> How now, Franke? turn'd foole
> Or madman whether? But no; master of
> My perfect senses and directest wits.
> Then why should I be in this violent humor
> Of passion, and of love? And with a person
> So different every way; and so opposed
> In all contractions, and still-warring actions?
> Fie, fie, How I dispute against my soule!
> Come, come, Ile gaine her; or in her faire quest
> Purchase my soule free and immortall rest.

When Frankford steals into the house to discover
whether Wendoll is with Mrs. Frankford, his nervous

excitement is represented with the immediacy of faculty psychology (IV, iv, 23-34):

> A general silence hath surpriz'd the house,
> And this is the last doore. Astonishment,
> Feare, and amazement beate upon my heart
> Even as a madman beats upon a drum.
> O, keepe my eyes, you Heavens, before I enter,
> From any sight that may transfix my soule;
> Or if there be so blacke a spectacle,
> Oh, strike mine eyes starke blind! Or if not so,
> Lend me such patience to digest my greefe,
> That I may keepe this white and virgin hand
> From any violent outrage or red murther!—
> And with that prayer I enter.

Although there is little formal terminology here, it is obvious that an Elizabethan conception of psychology lies behind the behaviour of Anne and Wendoll. In him there is a conflict of soul (II, iii) between loyalty to Frankford and his passion for Frankford's wife. He cannot pray without meditating on her: therefore he strives to arm himself against thoughts of her and still more against her infatuation. When he comes into her presence (II, iii, 15-16) he will

> Hale these bals until my eye strings cracke,
> From being pull'd and drawne to looke that way.

It is the fascination of eye that he wishes to avoid because it will be fatal to him. At that moment (II, iii, 17-18) she passes by, and Wendoll is undone.

> O God, O God! With what a violence
> I'me hurried to mine owne destruction.

He is still sensible of his villainy and ingratitude (II, iii, 45-52):

> Hast thou the power straight with thy goary hands,
> To rip thy image from his bleeding heart?

To scratch thy name from out the holy booke
Of his remembrance; and to wound his name
That holds thy name so deere? or rend his heart
To whom thy heart was knit and joyn'd together?
And yet I must; then Wendoll be content;
Thus villaines when they would, cannot repent.

Surely this is pitiful villainy and false psychology,
one recorded struggle and the sudden termination of
mental conflict! But, after all, psychology provided
for these to us unnatural suddennesses in the doctrine
of the domination of a single passion, brought about
by physical spirits in the heart. Passion has overcome
Wendoll's reason, possessed his will; that is all there
is to it. Will is now in passion's service. A similar
thing happens in the case of Mosbie in *Arden of
Feversham* and in scores of other cases. Of course
striking drama calls for sudden surprises and brilliant
contrasts; Elizabethan drama learned to produce them
in accordance with learned theory.

The same crippling nature of emotion underlies
the conception of Mrs. Frankford. She is a good
woman until she is beset with temptation. One would
call her weak if Renaissance philosophy did not oblige
her to carry all her sex with her. Women were frail
and susceptible by nature. Hence a world of chap-
eronage and the doctrine of the removal of occasion.
To the Renaissance natural goodness was not regarded
as a sufficient safeguard for women against the temp-
tations of the flesh; for they were strong in passion,
weak in reason. To be tempted was to fall. Vives [19]
is strict, not only in his injunctions that women be
brought up to be modest, chaste, mild and obedient,
but also, no matter how good they are, that they must
not go out in the street any more than necessary, and,
when they do, they must keep their eyes straight in
front of them that they may not be caught by the

lures the devil has prepared for their eyes. Their composition is warm, soft, and impressionable. They must never be in the company of men without some member of their families or some sage matrons by to guard them from temptation and occasion. Even Montaigne,[20] the liberal, repeats Plato's statement that women are like dissolute boys. Wendoll's attack is one calculated to soften a soft nature (II, ii); he reveals his love, throws himself on Anne's mercy, appeals to her pity. She must choose between duty, which means cruelty to a submissive and helpless suitor, and pity. She feels a responsibility for the condition her lover is in and for his danger. She is weak in judgment, strong in pity; she is a woman. There is plainly a pre-conceived notion of what a woman would do in the circumstances. One does not quarrel with this; one thinks it a pitiful sort of determinism. And there is also another difference. We should hardly think of a good woman who respected and honoured her husband as going so far in her compassion as actually to yield to such a man, unless she loved him mightily. Even we would allow the excuse of a great passion. But Anne does not appear to love Wendoll (II, iii, 142-4); her texture is soft and warm. She does not love him later; she had had no inclination to him earlier. Anne's yielding to Wendoll is the psychological convention of the frail woman put to the test. Very important, for Jacobean drama, was this staging of psychological doctrines.

> You move me, sir, to passion and to pitty:
> The love I beare my husband is as precious
> As my soules health.

Wendoll replies that he too loves her husband; he promises to be secret (an ancient Court of Love convention), and she says in bewilderment (II, iii, 142-4, 152-63):

> What shall I say?
> My soul is wandring, and hath lost her way.
> Oh Master Wendoll! Oh!
> *Wen.* Sigh not, sweet saint;
> For every sighe you breathe drawes from my heart
> A drop of blood.
> *Mrs. F.* I ne'er offended yet:
> My fault (I feare) will in my brow be writ.
> Women that fall, not quite bereft of grace,
> Have their offences noted in their face;
> I blush and am asham'd. Oh Master Wendoll,
> Pray God I be not borne to curse your tongue,
> That hath inchanted me! This maze I am in,
> I feare will prove the labyrinth of sin.

Her confusion is the shattering of such reasonable will as Elizabethan psychology allowed her. From the first she is exhibited as a yielding, modest, obedient woman. We, rather than the Elizabethans, would condemn her for lacking a will of her own; to them she was the most favoured ideal (III, ii).[21] She represents the ease with which the best of women might fall. In the card scene (IV, ii) and those that follow, she manages to keep the knowledge of her infidelity from her husband; but she does not protest affection and act the hypocrite as Alice Arden does. Anne really wishes Frankford to remain at home, and, when he is gone, she takes no joy in being with Wendoll. She is a mere and unwilling victim. Surely sin was never more joyless! Her repentance is genuine and pitiful (IV, v). It has in it another element; it is formal. Her grief is for her offence to her husband *qua* husband, rather than for the personal sorrow she has caused him. She sorrows for the breach of her vow. The

matrimonial sacrament in the Elizabethan ethical system was something fixed by God in His Church and
supported by the law as a part of God's plan for governing the universe. Frankford is an authorized jus-
ticer. This gives a new sense to her famous words
(IV, v, 103):

> He cannot be so base as to forgive me.

She hates her sin and in the same motion hates Wendoll. Her death is her expiation. This too puts Frankford in another light. He is not a prig by nature, nor,
in the Elizabethan mind, by action. To us his kindness
possibly seems a refinement of cruelty, but in the
sense of the play he is the judge, the institution, in
quite natural human form. Wendoll too is repentant,
but in the modern view he gets off very lightly. In
the author's mind justice was apparently satisfied
when Anne died and does not require the imposition
of punishments on Wendoll. In Elizabethan eyes her
act was worse than his, and it does not matter that
he was the base instrument of her fall or that her fall
was inevitable to the frail nature of her womanhood.
She is the one who has something important to guard,
the sanctity and inviolability of the family, the honour and good name of her lord and master. The depth
of her humiliation illustrates the power of the Elizabethan *mores* to reinforce the torments of the individual conscience.

It will be seen that violence is done in this play
to the reasonable modern view of probabilities in both
character and act, not only by the application of a
false psychology, but by the intrusion of social and
ethical conventions such as we do not regularly en-
dorse. These things were destined to grow in Jacobean
drama, and one must always be on the lookout for

the latter as well as the former dislocation. Heywood, though here a man of genius, was just the formalist to betray these things. The rule with him was absolute, and the play we are considering has other examples still. The issue before Susan is that of Isabella in *Measure for Measure* and of Erona in the *Arcadia* (II, xiii, p. 232 ff.). Charles's reason for urging his sister to yield herself to Sir Francis is not the same as Claudio's. Claudio wishes Isabella to buy his freedom with her honour; Sir Charles wishes to discharge in this extremity his obligation to his enemy. This gives opportunity for code morals such as we find in the plays of Beaumont and Fletcher and their contemporaries. We are asked to see in the action of Sir Charles a very high type of honour. To pay such a debt by such a means and then to die is the demand of the code. Sir Francis, when he contemplates the sacrifice Sir Charles is prepared to make, is struck with wonder (V, i, 120-3):

> Was ever knowne, in any former age,
> Such honorable wrested courtesie?
> Lands, honors, life, and all the world foregoe,
> Rather than stand ingag'd to such a foe.

Susan exhibits the same 'wrested courtesie.' She will yield but destroy herself; her brother comments (V, i, 88-92):

> Observe her love; to sooth it to my sute,
> Her honor she will hazard (though not loose:)
> To bring me out of debt, her rigorous hand
> Will pierce her heart—Oh wonder! that will choose,
> Rather than staine her blood, her life to loose.

Sir Francis, not to be outdone in courtesy and, as the hearers know, engaged in his affection to Susan,

makes the transcendently noble proffer of matrimony.
We rarely admire the heroics of bygone ages, nor do
we put such a value upon matrimony; but the discovery of such disparities is inevitable in reading the
literature of other times. We can at least understand,
and in understanding sympathize. Such is the psychology of Heywood and such his formal ethical
code.

There is no point involved as to which was first
among a closely associated group of dramatists, such
as Chapman, Marston, and Jonson, all of whom were
following the same fashion, working the same lead;
but in the poetizing of metaphysics and the introduction of the poetry of passion into drama, one certainly
has to reckon with Chapman as among the most important. He is the psychological dramatist *par excellence*. He not only delights in depicting the psychological states of his characters in and for themselves,
but he makes poetry of them. With him psychological
states are fact, figure of speech, and the things suggested by figurative language. There are almost no
minor doctrines and distinctions that he does not know
familiarly; so much so that the doctrines of soul and
body are both a poetic subject and a poetic instrument
in his hands as a poet. This circumstance makes of
him one of the 'metaphysical' group of poets, whose
essential quality has just been defined; for, like Donne
and his followers, Chapman enters into the very centre
of the realm of mental and emotional life, making his
entry through the portals of what were to him the
sciences of psychology and ethics.

He goes furthest when he takes sides in the ancient
warfare between reason and the will. Nothing better
reveals the trend of Jacobean drama than Bussy's stand
for the indomitability of passion. In depicting Bussy's
rebellion sympathetically Chapman takes sides against

the ethics of the domination of reason. He was to be followed by other dramatists—Webster, Middleton and Ford—in thus espousing the cause of passion and thus sympathizing with the sinner against the moral law. The appearance of this attitude marks a turning point in Elizabethan tragedy. Consider the nature of the appeal in the following passage in which 'blood' and not reason is the hero (*Bussy D'Ambois*, V, iv, 78-85, 131-40): [22]

> *Bussy.*　　　　　Is my body, then,
> But penetrable flesh, and must my mind
> Follow my blood? Can my divine part adde
> No ayd to th'earthly in extremity?
> Then these divines are but for forme, not fact:
> Man is of two sweet courtly friends compact,
> A mistresse and a servant. Let my death
> Define life nothing but a courtier's breath...
>
> 　O, my heart is broken.
> Fate, nor these murtherers, Monsieur nor the Guise,
> Have any glory in my death, but this,
> This killing spectacle, this prodigie.
> My sunne is turn'd to blood, in whose red beams
> Pindus and Ossa (hid in drifts of snow
> Laid on my heart and liver), from their veines
> Melt, like two hungry torrents eating rocks,
> Into the ocean of all humane life,
> And make it bitter, only with my bloud.

Shakespeare, Heywood, Chapman, and other dramatists show at work in various ways in the art of literary depiction that particular science which in their times recorded and explained man's conception of his own nature. That that conception in its essential features was largely true, or at least adequate for the use of very great dramatists, the world's opinion seems to indicate. We have tried to show that in its particular doctrines and applications Elizabethan faculty psychology grew faulty, to some extent misrepresentative of human nature, when compared with an older less ambitious literary use of the subject and with our own later and broader knowledge of man's mental and physical constitution. Concomitant with the exploitation of various practical aspects of the old psychology at the end of the sixteenth and the beginning of the seventeenth centuries, and unmistakably reflective of this exploitation, was that great and vital series of plays—the Elizabethan and Jacobean drama. The dramatists drew rather alarming pictures of man, his situation, his character, and his fate. They were no doubt wrong in a good deal of their philosophizing on the subject, but the pictures they draw are so convincing as to cause us some uneasiness.

CHAPTER VI

THE WELL OF DEMOCRITUS

> If then it be true that Democritus said, *That the truth of nature lieth hid in certain deep mines and caves;* and if it be true likewise that the Alchemists do so much inculcate, that Vulcan is a second nature, and imitateth that dexterously and compendiously which nature worketh by ambages and length of time; it were good to divide natural philosophy into the mine and the furnace, and to make two professions or occupations of natural philosophers, some to be pioners and some smiths; some to dig, and some to refine and hammer.—Bacon, *The Advancement of Learning.*

THE MAIN emphasis in university study about the year 1570 can be seen in the following passage from Harrison: [1] 'And for the other lectures, as of philosophie, logike, rhetorike, and quadriuials, although the latter (I meane arethmetike, musike, and astronomie, and with them all skill in the perspectiues are now smallie regarded in either of them) the uniuersities themselues doo allow competent stipends to such as reade the same.' Notice the juxtaposition of rhetoric, logic, and philosophy (which it will be remembered included the sciences as well as philosophy). Roughly speaking, the first two years of the course for the bachelor's degree were devoted to logic and rhetoric, so that by the end of that period the student might become skilful in the art of disputation; the last two years were largely devoted to philosophy and to those disciplines in which subject-matter was the important element.

When it is realized that the Aristotelian doctrine

139

of entelechy, or realization of form-giving cause as distinguished from mere potentiality, was the prevailing intellectual principle of the age, it will be seen that there was much sound sense in the curriculum. If a man was in his life to achieve the practical, he must learn to realize it through the form. The Renaissance in general and the Elizabethan age in particular were bent on the achievement of the practical, on what we call success, and they believed with as keen a faith as ours that it is possible to achieve it.

A characteristic of logical and rhetorical study in the Renaissance not to be forgotten is its affiliation with the doctrine of success. Gabriel Harvey,[2] whose ambitious pantings are rendered audible by his vanity, continually reveals this chief popular academic ideal of the age. The following he quotes from 'Smith': 'Boldness, eloquence and winning manners lead to success.' And these are the superlatives he applies to his ideal: 'Cordatissimi; sui confidentissimi; audacissimi, et jmportunissimi; eloquentissimi, et ad dicendum potentissimi; ore, et vultu gratiotissimi; ad omnia dicta, facta; ingenio, sermone præsentissimi; omnium in omnibus adulantissimi, aut saltem placentissimi, apud summos, mediocres, infimos summe præualebunt, et omnium animos suffurabuntur.' Harvey believes in self-confidence coupled with policy: 'A grain of creditt with other; and A dramme of confidence jn yourself; is powerable to remooue mountaynes and states, and to work Miracles: being politiquely applied with reasonfull discretion.' Be serpent and dove, lamb and wolf, he says: '*Acta fidem faciant. Columbinus serpens: serpentina columba: Agnina vulpes: Vulpinus agnus. Sed agendum quamprimum aliquid Notabile, et famosum, publice prædicandum: quod vel a magno quouis viro possit procedere. Tum rei soli familari, omnibus uijs, et modis, appetentissime instandum, peritissime constandum. Nulla lucelli occasiuncula, aut circumstantiuncula omittenda.*' The following is what Harvey has to say about Bruno: '*Jordanus Neopolitanus, (Oxonij disputans cum Doctore Vnderhil) tam in Theologia, quam in philosophia, omnia reuocabat ad Locos Topicos, et axiomata Aristotelis; atque inde de quauis materia promptissime arguebat. Hopperii principia multo efficaciora in quouis Argumento forensi.*' Later he adds, 'Gallant Audacity, is neuer owt of countenance: But hath euer A Tongue, & A Hand at will.'

To Harvey, getting on in life was a matter of *audacia, eloquentia, et suavitas;* to Bacon and others, particularly Machiavelli, the successful conduct of life became the subject of a philosophy. Bacon [3] even goes so far in *The Advancement of Learning* and *De Augmentis Scientiarum* as to set down the *principia* of a science of Negotiation with rules for self-advancement drawn mainly from the Bible, but reflective of his own life experience. That man has not a right to become the architect of his own fortunes, that is, within his assigned status, never entered Bacon's head. Perhaps it never entered any Renaissance head unless Puritanism had first entered it, and even then it is doubtful. 'We must,' Bacon said, 'strive with all possible endeavour to render the mind obedient to occasions and opportunities, and to be noways obstinate and refractory towards them. For nothing hinders men's actions and fortunes so much as this, to remain the same, when the same is unbecoming...and nothing is more politic than to make the wheels of the mind concentric and voluble with the wheels of fortune.' We must, he teaches, study and watch our fellows, since occasions and opportunities come from the characters and actions of our fellow-men. The *Essays* are full of this doctrine of getting on. Critics usually dispose of this quality in Bacon by calling it Machiavellianism. To call it by that name is nothing more than to say that Machiavelli shared in a trait which was part and parcel of the age.

The subject of logic[4] was early expanded and corrected by additional works of Aristotle. The *Logica vetus,* made up of the *Categories,* the *Interpretation,* and Porphyry's *Isagoge* and based on the translations of Boethius, became in the twelfth century the *Logica nova,* which included the above works plus the *Prior* and *Posterior Analytics,* the *Topics,* the *Sophisms,* and the *Liber de Sex Principiis* of Gilbertus Porretanus. Without the *Analytics, Topics,* and *Fallacies* logic had hardly been a subject at all. It now became a power especially in the practical and comprehensive form of the *Summulae Logicales* of Petrus Hispanus (Pope John XXI. d. 1270), the first Aristotelian logic in complete instrumental form. The Renaissance therefore long contented itself, as in the important work of Melanchthon, with revising the *Organon* on Aristotelian lines. Ultimately came the anti-Aristotelian logic of Ramus and the still more subversive work of Bacon. Ramus recast Aristotle in order to make him more practical and in so doing made the *Organon* itself take on more serviceable forms. Ramist logic thus became one of the principal channels through which school learning manifested itself in literature. Ramist logic is an important subject for this reason. Rhetoric had abandoned in the Middle Ages its Aristotelian importance as the art of persuasion and had narrowed its ground to mere ornamentation. It had ceased to be responsible for ideas and had devoted itself to words and figures. The interesting thing to be observed, however, is that logic and rhetoric joined hands in the educational scheme of the Renaissance and, with the disputation as their instrument, gave such training in the practical art of thinking as the university was able to give.

In an active and enterprising age like the second half of the sixteenth century, when the stress was on disputation, when the whole subject of religion was debated by larger parts of the population than had ever debated any subject before, and when men in public life were successful in proportion to their polemical skill, it was inevitable that changes should occur in the matter and manner of debating itself. The body of knowledge at the beginning of the century was very largely in foreign languages, was the prerogative of classes of persons, and was rigidly bound up in the formalities of traditional bodies of methodology. Knowledge was indeed a mystery and a specialty, and though largely inaccessible was most desirable. The people of the early period had a simple and earnest confidence in learning in and for itself and as a means of solving the problems of the present world. With the Reformation and the doctrines of Calvin came the idea that learning was necessary for the hereafter as well as for the here and now. Men were suddenly made responsible for the achievement of their own salvation, not a salvation resting on virtue and obedience only, but resting also on comprehension. The task was difficult; though knowledge was forthcoming, it was misleading and, without the technique of knowledge, full of deceptions; hence the renewed importance of dialectic. The disputational game was an old one, but Protestantism gave it a new importance. The task and tendency of the century, as has been said, was to simplify, to explain, to interpret, and to apply. These tendencies we shall consider in the greatest master of the short-cut the world has ever known, the brilliant and pugnacious martyr of St. Bartholomew's, Petrus Ramus, who rewrote in

simplified form the trivium and most of the quadrivium. His method of procedure may be made clear
by describing what he did to the all-important subject of logic. To him, as to generations of both his
predecessors and his successors, logic was dialectic
or the art of reasoning according to rules and moods.
His desire was to sweep away everything in the subject of logic except dialectic. For Aristotle, logic had
been, almost certainly, not only an instrument for
demonstration, but also an encyclopædia and a science
of sciences, the organization and interpretation of
knowledge. This seems obvious in the categories themselves, since the categories of quantity and quality,
and to some extent the other categories, find in them a
place for every art and science. The *Prior* and the
Posterior Analytics are far more than merely dialectic
in their scope. But Ramus regarded logic as an instrument.[5] He defined the subject in terms of its end,
and said *Bene disserere finis logices*. He had startled
the academic world in his youth by his famous thesis
on the doors of the Collège de Navarre: *Quæcumque
ab Aristotele dicta essent, commentitia esse*, which
might be rendered colloquially, 'Aristotle is all wrong.'

Ramus [6] was a critic and not a scientist. He did not
question fundamentals. His was a mind which discriminated between the important practical things in
existing school subjects and the digressive and unes-
sential things. Perhaps he aspired to be a friend to
Aristotle. His logic is still Aristotelian but is reduced
to one-tenth of the bulk of the *Organon*. Ramus simplified the *Organon* and re-arranged it to meet the
practical purposes of dialectic, making of logic a tool
for demonstration rather than a science of human reason. He, therefore, omits the more discursive parts—
all rules and canons, the discussion of categories, definition as such, demonstration, and the solution of fal-

lacies. He starts with brief definitions and divisions of dialectic, then plunges at once into the ten places of Invention. The most surprising, and for us the most important thing is that Ramus draws his illustrations from literature, such authors as Ovid, Virgil, and Cæsar, and from the Scriptures. The order of general procedure is also surprising. Whereas the Aristotelians had treated Judgment or Disposition first, Ramus treats Invention first. In Aristotelian logic the machinery of Argumentation and Demonstration had been set forth and carefully explained before the application of the art to practise had been considered; whereas in Ramus all that was known about the making of arguments is taken up first, and such explanation of the dialectical machine as is necessary follows it. This second part is reduced to a minimum, and Invention, which in Aristotelian logics had been rather neglected, is in Ramus greatly expanded and emphasized. This re-arrangement suggests and exemplifies an assertion of the rights of the practical as opposed to the theoretical and points the way to Bacon and Descartes. As a general force in the direction of the advancement of science Ramist logic is, for the reason stated, of recognized importance.

But Ramus had nothing to add to the logic or methodology of Aristotle. He goes through his series of the ten places of Invention very simply and with illustrations brilliantly chosen from his poets. He explains the places somewhat as follows: 1. The cause efficient is that by whose force the thing exists, that matter being perfectly known whose cause is understood. The cause efficient may work by itself or by its accidents (including necessity and fortune). 2. Of the material cause Ramus, in his desire to avoid difficulty and controversy, merely says that matter is a cause why the thing is. 3. The formal cause is that by which a thing has its name and being. Man has his form by virtue of the possession of a reasonable soul, a triangle its form by virtue of its three-sidedness, and so forth. 4. The final cause is that for which the thing is made or done, e.g., the end of natural things is man; of man, God. The end of grammar is to speak correctly, of rhetoric to speak eloquently, and of logic to dispute well. 5. The effect is that which arises from the cause, as in the case of motion or change. 6. The subject is that which has something adjoining it, and the adjunct is that which is adjoined to the subject. 7. Differentia. 8. Contraria. 9. Relativa. 10. Comparison, both quantitative and qualitative. Since the last group is treated at greater length than the others, it is difficult to tell exactly what the ten logical places of Ramus really are. After this discussion of the places of logic come what are called the secondary arguments, really necessary concomitant explanations, such as Distribution of arguments, Definition, and Testimony. The first part is thus an independent logical machine of very simple structure. Commentators and Ramist logicians added a good deal to the simple dialectic of Ramus. Abraham Fraunce's *Lawiers Logike* (1588), for example, is very much more detailed. The definitions of Ramus are crude and no doubt needed amplification; they were, nevertheless, from the start usable by persons in the logic of schools. They became the recognizable jargon of controversy, as when Polonius[7] says, 'This effect defective comes by cause.' It is also true that one is frequently able to detect the preliminary gathering of arguments by the Ramist system by sequential reference to causes, effects, subjects, and adjuncts.

Wilson[8] introduces a somewhat similar machine into *The Rule of Reason*, which he also intended as a manual of the most practical utility. He arranges his book in the Aristotelian order, treating *Judicium* before he treats *Inventio*, but, like the Ramists, amplifying the latter when he comes to it. When a question comes into controversy, he says, go through the places with it, and examine every word by every several place. For example, in the examination of the question is it lawful for a priest to marry, first apply 'a priest' to all the places, then refer 'a wife' to all the places; then see wherein these two agree and disagree. By definition a preacher is a clerk or shepherd, instructed to set forth the Kingdom of God and desirous to live virtuously; by the general word he is a minister, a shepherd, a holy man, a gospeler, upright in living, faithful in bestowing the words of truth; by the kind it is found that Peter, Paul, and Chrysostom were secular men; by the proprium, the preacher is to teach in godly wise; by the whole, he must be completely instructed; by the parts he is to discover appropriate matter in the Scriptures, deck it out handsomely according to the principles of rhetoric, and utter his words, distinctly, plainly, and in a loud voice; yoked words are 'preacher' and 'preaching'; adjuncts are labour, diligence, and wit; *modus*, to feed Christ's flock; the container is the words of the Scripture; the thing contained, the word of God; the form is taken from the conversation and manner of living of the preacher; the efficient cause is God and the Scriptures; the effects are the sinners converted; the thing appointed is the searching of the Scriptures; the place is the pulpit; the annexum is the stipend; the other places do not apply. Next take up the word *uxor*, first by definition; as, a wife is a woman lawfully received into the fellowship of life for the increase of children and the avoidance of fornication, and so on. Having again gone through the long list of places, the author proceeds with his comparison for the construction of arguments. He finds in the definition that both the preacher and the wife desire to live virtuously. Whoever desires to live virtuously must marry a wife; every preacher desires to live virtuously: ergo every true preacher must marry a wife. If the adversary denies the proposition at large, called the major, you can do nothing with it unless you find confirmation in the definition of a wife. Marriage, he finds, is for the increase of children and for the avoidance of fornication; therefore, he constructs the following sorites: Whoever desires to live virtuously desires to avoid fornication. Whoever desires to avoid fornication desires marriage. Therefore, whoever desires to live virtuously desires marriage. Another argument may be based on the general word. Whatsoever is man may by God's ordinance marry a woman. Every preacher is a man, and so forth. Repugnancies may be modified as follows: if it is argued that women are often shrewish, neglectful of children, and so forth, you may argue that, since these qualities do not cause marriage, they shall not hinder marriage.

This example will illustrate not only the painful tediousness of the dialectical method but will show that even in the places of logic Ramus is simpler than the Aristotelians.

Let it be remembered that Ramus was himself a famous orator [9] and that his point of attack was the application of logic first of all to rhetoric and then to other studies. In his desire to show the excellence of the logical precepts and examples which found their use in every great work of the intellect, he joined the reading of the poets and orators to the study of academic subjects, approaching by this means the teaching of literature proper. This must be regarded as something of a discovery. It can hardly be questioned that Sidney,[10] who was a devoted Ramist, and other men trained in the university when Ramus was dominant had their attention directed to the logical aspect of literature and were encouraged in the embodiment of logical and rhetorical forms in their works by the precept and example of Ramus. Abraham Fraunce, for instance, drew the illustrations for his *Lawiers Logicke* from Spenser's *The Shepheardes Calender*.

The vogue of Ramism in England is connected with that earlier Sir William Temple (1555-1627), fellow of King's College, Cambridge, and tutor in logic (1576-85), secretary to Sir Philip Sidney (Sidney died in his arms at Arnheim), secretary to Essex, and in his later life a distinguished and efficient provost of Trinity College, Dublin. As tutor in logic, Temple, according to Anthony Wotton, 'laboured to fit his pupils for the true use of that art rather than for vain and idle speculations.'[11] In 1584 Temple issued an annotated edition of the *Dialectica* and, in the years following, was a controversialist of European note in behalf of Ramus against Aristotle. To say that Sir William Temple was a Ramist, or that Cambridge was a Ramist centre, means that this particularly practical and intimate method of study became familiar to the important generation of Cambridge men during the time when Temple was at Cambridge. This cannot but have increased the consciousness of rhetorical and logical forms in literature and caused these things to be prized for their excellence. Every literary man— Spenser, Greene, Harvey, and the others—who was at Cambridge during the period, seems to show a conscious use of these forms in his writings. Sidney's contacts with learning, both at home and abroad, were sufficiently numerous and intimate to account for his interest in Ramus.

The popularity of Ramus is not to be questioned.

This popularity becomes significant when it is remembered that the method of Ramus was easy to
employ and was intentionally directed toward literature. Some idea of the degree to which he associated
logic and rhetoric may be gained from the fact that,
during the time (about 1546) when he was enjoined
from teaching logic in the University of Paris, he
gave lectures in rhetoric, but used the occasion to
point out numerous examples of the use of logic in the
orators and poets whom he read. That Ramus meant
his work to go into the very heart of practicality appears, rather quaintly, in the publication (1554) of
five discourses by the pupils of Antoine Foquelin at
the Collège de Presles, of which Ramus was master.
The first of these discourses proves that a king has
no need to be a philosopher, the second proves the
opposite; the third discourse proves that a king need
not be a soldier, the fourth, the opposite; the fifth
concludes the series and shows the degree to which a
king must be both a soldier and a philosopher.

The Renaissance [12] set its heart on learning the art
of reasoning, and, in spite of what seems to us a cum-
bersome system, it produced within the limits of that
system its share of great methodical thinkers. In the
Middle Ages the art of dialectical thinking had acquired so great a perfection that it dominated the
schools; the Renaissance with its new controversial
needs was not disposed to reduce the importance of
the subject of logic. The popularization of dialectic,
particularly by means of the logic of Ramus, but also
by the simplification of all logic and its translation
into the vernacular languages, served to fill the world
with logic-choppers. Men of conservative cast who
believed in an established agency for the determination of learned, particularly theological, questions
were naturally disgusted by the spectacle; no small

part of the censure of Ramus by men like Hooker is due to their resentment at his spreading the plague of superficial and pretentious disputation.

The comic possibilities of the situation were not overlooked by Shakespeare [13] and the comic dramatists. We know from Hamlet that 'the age is grown so picked that the toe of the peasant comes so near the heel of the courtier, he galls his kibe.' Logic reinforces the dominance of the First Clown:

It must be 'se offendendo;' it cannot be else. For here lies the point: if I drown myself wittingly, it argues an act: and an act hath three branches; it is, to act, to do, and to perform: argal, she drowned herself wittingly.
Second Clown. Nay, but hear you, goodman delver,—
First Clown. Give me leave. Here lies the water; good: here stands the man; good: if the man go to this water, and drown himself, it is, will he, nill he, he goes,—mark you that; but if the water come to him and drown him, he drowns not himself: argal, he that is not guilty of his own death shortens not his own life.

Logic also sets off the pedantry of Polonius:

> Your noble son is mad:
> Mad call I it; for, to define true madness,
> What is't but to be nothing else but mad? ...
> Mad let us grant him, then: and now remains
> That we find out the cause of this effect,
> Or rather say, the cause of this defect,
> For this effect defective comes by cause:
> Thus it remains, and the remainder thus.
> Perpend.

A delightful passage between Falstaff and Prince Hal reflects the technique of disputation rather than pure logic. In the tavern scene that follows the robbery in *1 Henry IV*, Falstaff makes a triumphant refutation of the rather apparent charge of cowardice:

Why, thou knowest I am as valiant as Hercules: but beware instinct; the lion will not touch the true prince. Instinct is a great matter; I was now a coward on instinct. I shall think the better of myself and thee during my life: I for a valiant lion, and thou for a true prince.

Later in the same scene, it is announced that 'the sheriff and all the watch are at the door.' Falstaff, alluding to the recent denunciation of himself as 'a villainous and abominable misleader of youth,' says,—

Dost thou hear, Hal? never call a true piece of gold a counterfeit: thou art essentially mad, without seeming so.

To this Prince Hal replies,—

And thou a natural coward, without instinct.

Falstaff disposes of this with the statement,—

I deny your major: if you will deny the sheriff, so; if not, let him enter.

That is, Falstaff denies the major term of the *quæstio*, that he is a coward; he does not deny the minor term, that his courage is controlled by instinct.

Pedantry rejoiced in logical terminology, and blundering ignorance no doubt indulged in this ridiculous form of self-betrayal; but, nevertheless, proficiency in dialectic with its concomitant rhetoric was the most serious educational and cultural ideal of the age. There is a suggestion of the intellectual trend of the times even in a customary admonition with reference to speech. One must realize, in such a case, that the faculty of speech was dignified in Renaissance thinking as the chief accomplishment which God had chosen to bestow upon man, to distinguish him from the brute beasts; therefore, as a symbol of man's distinguishing quality, it was to be observed, respected, and cultivated. 'Be modest in each assembly,' says Sir Henry Sidney [14] in a letter to his son Philip, 'and rather be rebuked of light fellows for maidenlike shamefastness; than of your sad friends, for pert boldness. Think upon every word that you will speak, before you utter it: and remember how Nature hath rampered up, as it were, the tongue with teeth, lips, yea, and hair without the lips; and all betokening reins or bridles for the loose use of that member.' We have another version of the same thing in the advice of Polonius to Laertes: 'Give every man thy ear, but few thy voice.'

Renaissance books on serious subjects begin, according to logical practice, with careful definition. The definition often consists in the allocation of the subject to be treated in the grand scheme of the universe. Elyot [15] opens *The Gouernour* with a definition in 'compendious form' of the public weal. 'A publyke weale,' he says, 'is a body lyuyng, compacte or made of sondry astates and degrees of men, whiche is disposed by the ordre of equite and gouerned by the rule and moderation of reason.' Public weal he differentiates from common weal by the property of order or degree, which supplants the chaotic lack of order in a community. He illustrates his definition from the orders of the angels in heaven. Bacon [16] does the same thing in *The Advancement of Learning*, though his faith in the existence of the hierarchy is not complete. Hooker,[17] with the same purpose as Elyot's in mind, uses, with apparently complete belief, this same approach to the idea of order. Definition, which Milton describes as 'that which refines the pure essence of things from the circumstance,' was the primary and customary logical approach to all subjects to be treated.

An early and awkward stage of logic in literature,

wherein there was a disposition to drag logic in by
the ears, appears in the *Arcadia* [18] of Sir Philip Sidney,
with whom, as a Ramist, of course logic and rhetoric
go hand in hand. Note, for example, the general situation which arises when Musidorus discovers Pyrocles
dressed as an Amazon, and the manner in which
Sidney handles it. The situation has its peculiar importance in Renaissance thought. Pyrocles is doing
violence to nature by assuming the outward form of
the other sex. His situation is not only one of shame
but of danger. In thus doing violence to nature, what
injuries may he not suffer in his virtue? It is not the
shame of modesty which overtakes Pyrocles, it is the
shame of derogation from his station of prince and
gentleman: 'So that *Pyrocles* (who had as much
shame, as Musidorus had sorrow) rising to him, would
have formed a substantiall excuse; but his insinuation
being of blushinge, and his division of sighes, his
whole oration stood upon a short narration, what was
the causer of his Metamorphosis? But by that time
Musidorus had gathered his spirites together, and yet
casting a gastfull countenance upon him (as if he
would conjure some strange spirits) he thus spake
unto him.' In the address of Musidorus are these places
of Ramist logic: 'Remember what you are, what you
have bene, what you must be: if you consider what
it is, that moved you, or by what kinde of creature
you are moved, you shall finde the *cause* so small, the
effect so daungerous, your selfe so unworthie to runne
into the one, or to be driven by the other, that I
doubt not I shall quickly have occasion rather to
praise you for having conquered it, then to give you
further counsell, how to do it.'

Other features of this argument are that by assuming the dress and the behaviour of a woman Pyrocles
will endanger his mind. His behaviour cannot come

naturally (kindly) from him, but as 'the mind is pro-
portioned unto it.' As Pyrocles softens his heart to
receive the 'peevish affections of that sex,' he will be
making the first down-step to all wickedness. Musidorus compares, as *causes*, reason and love—love,
which Pyrocles has chosen, has inquietness, longings,
fond comforts, faint discomforts, hopes, jealousies,
ungrounded rages, and causeless yielding as *things
adjoined*. 'But that end how endlesse it runs to infinite evils, were fit inough for the matter we speake
of, but not for your eares, in whom indeed there is
much true disposition to virtue.' Musidorus can already see the *effects* in Pyrocles: (1) in reason giving
place to sense, (2) in the subversion of the course
of nature, since man has given place to woman, and
(3 and 4) in breaking the laws of hospitality to Kalendar and of friendship to Musidorus. In his answer,
Pyrocles, granting 'the good disposition nature hath
bestowed upon me' and that 'that disposition hath
been by bringing up confirmed,' attacks the moving
cause assigned: there is no degradation in assuming
the guise of a woman, since man has his origin and
nurture from her. Women are framed by nature to
the same exercise of virtue as men, as, for example,
the Amazons, who want neither wit, valour, nor fairness; and virtue and fairness should ever be joined.
He is not, therefore, degenerated by assuming the
guise of a woman. This answers the argument as to
reason and as to nature. As to Kalendar, he declares
himself more of a host than a guest; and, as to the violation of friendship, he would not be guilty of it,
though almost justified by Musidorus' hard treatment
of him. In the defence of his 'virtue' he resorts to a
dilemma: 'for if I be so weak, then can ye not with
reason stir me up as ye did, by remembrance of my
own vertue: or if indeed I be vertuous, then must ye

confesse, that love hath his working in a vertuous hart.' Then says Pyrocles, with complete confirmation of the author's intention, 'But these disputations are fitter for quiet schooles, then in my troubled braines, which are bent rather in deeds to performe, then in wordes to defende the noble desire which possesseth me.'

In writers later than Sidney the bare bones of logical disquisition are less in evidence, though the logic is still there. They never lose the stir of ideas, the inquisition of principles and special cases, and the zest for controversy that mark the earlier time. Elizabethan literature is alive with debate over issues drawn, issues of every sort and kind. It is no wonder that drama flourished, which is itself an art of contest, dialogue and debate, agreement and disagreement. The reason for this preoccupation with controversial utterance is already patent. It arises from the conception of logic (or rather dialectic) as an instrument for the discovery of truth,[19] and from the learned conception of truth itself. In a world in which the genetical principle of comprehension was not known, knowledge itself was viewed as a finished, though not always achievable, corpus. This was typically true of theology, and relatively true of medicine and all the sciences. There were many difficulties of charting and exploring, but the land of science was on a level. The points and principles known by self-evidence, revelation, and authority were the guides. The syllogism, supplemented by an acute knowledge of the fallacies, was the chosen and obvious instrument for the discovery of truth—by deduction and induction. One would not say that Renaissance thinkers were really successful, despite the widespread use of dialectic, in avoiding misleading arguments. It would be worth while to work out the common fallacies com-

mitted by the Elizabethans. They were certainly numerous. Logical instruments were used by everybody;
on the highest levels, with skill and distinction; on
lower levels, probably not.

Logic was, nevertheless, the key to truth and its de-
fender. Now, what does this situation reveal as to the
Renaissance conception of truth itself? It may be said
that it suspends truth, not between hypothesis and
verification, but between the affirmative and the negative in debate. In such circumstances truth becomes,
not a fixed proposition, but a shifting, elusive, debat-
able thing to be determined by dialectical acumen
before it shines forth in rhetorical clarity by its own
unassisted effulgence. It follows also that every question has two sides, and that the acutest minds would
habitually see both sides. Now, drama itself, as just
said, is debate, and the issues it loves to treat are de-
batable issues. Shakespeare, the acutest of Renaissance
thinkers, has a boasted breadth of mind, an ability to
see both sides of a question, and a sympathy with all
sorts and conditions of men. His picture of Shylock
the Jew is a perpetual surprise to those who know
Shakespeare's times. No one can tell whether Boling-
broke or Richard II is in the right. Is it not fair, then,
to regard Shakespeare as an exemplification of controversial broadmindedness in an age of advocacy? If
so, we probably have to do with an intuitive response
to the spirit of the age rather than with any sort of
formal learning and applying of logical processes.

The fact that logic had been for hundreds of years,
since the revival of Aristotle in the thirteenth century
or before, the principal subject in the higher schools
brought it about that the language of logic had made
its way into the vocabularies of all modern tongues.
In other words, since language and thought are merely
different aspects of the same phenomenon, logic had

taught men to think in the abstract. It had given them
the tools for thinking; that it had thus taught the
world to think, the words in the various languages
of Europe are a witness. So deeply had the language
of logic entered into the English vocabulary by
Shakespeare's time that usually one cannot tell
whether Shakespeare is aware of the logical denota-
tions, or connotations either, of his language or the
forms of his thought. Now and then he reveals un-
questionably that he was familiar with the logic of
the schools. But the technology of formal logic is not
a thing which ordinarily appears in pure literature. It
is plain enough in the controversial writings of ped-
ants like Harvey, fanatics like Stubbes, or youthful
humanistic enthusiasts like Sidney; but ordinarily the
skeleton of discourse ought not to protrude and in
Shakespeare does not. In depicting the vagaries of
logical pedantry, a subject of perpetual fun to comic
writers, technological bones are, of course, made to
protrude and to bear their labels. Nevertheless, when
one beholds the great enthusiasm for dialectic and the
respect in which it was held, and realizes, moreover,
that it was regarded as the most practical of all school
subjects, one would expect to find in Renaissance
literature deep and important influences and permea-
tions of logic. Since the outcroppings of logic are dis-
cernible over the face of the country, are not the deep
veins of concatenated thought also to be discovered?
To point to the wit, acumen, and clarity of Elizabethan literature, qualities very frequently associated
with external evidence, is no doubt justifiable. Hooker
was a teacher of logic, William Temple was Sidney's
friend and secretary, Milton wrote a Ramist logic, all
educated men studied it. It seems within the bounds
of reasonable probability that Elizabethan literature
was strongly influenced by both logic in general and

by dialectic. This would be manifest in the tragedies of Shakespeare and the comedies of Ben Jonson, sharpening the significance of both. One of the results of Elizabethan devotion to logical exercises, it might fairly be claimed, was the appearance in the age of a number of prose masterpieces whose merit is a logical merit, such as *Of the Laws of Ecclesiastical Polity*, *The Advancement of Learning*, and *The Anatomy of Melancholy*.

CHAPTER VII

THE ELOQUENCE OF PERSUASIONS

But in regard of the continual mutinies and seditions of
the affections,

Video meliora, proboque;
Deteriora sequor:

reason would become captive and servile, if Eloquence
of Persuasions did not practise and win the Imagination
from the Affection's part, and contract a confederacy
between the Reason and Imagination against the Affections.—Bacon, *The Advancement of Learning.*

WE HAVE seen that man prided himself during the Renaissance, as he still does, on reason
as his distinguishing gift; we have also seen
that he sought to use reason operatively. Now, since
speech in its various forms was the 'discourse of reason,' let us see how man sought to use speech in its
service; or, in Bacon's words, let us consider 'the application of reason to imagination.'

Professor J. M. Manly's description of the relation
between Chaucer and the medieval rhetoricians,[1]
within limits and with many at least partial exceptions,
holds good for the relations between the writers of
the later years of the reign of Queen Elizabeth and the
rhetoricians of that day. He regards Chaucer, not as
having proceeded in his literary workmanship from
crude native power to the mastery of style and
method, but as having proceeded by way of a gradual
release from the sophisticated methods of rhetorical
art to a relatively free exercise of creative imagination
based on the observation of life. Professor Manly does

not imply that Chaucer's rhetorical habits came to him solely from Geffroi de Vinsauf (*Nova Poetria*), whom Chaucer mentions, or from John de Garlandia, Matthieu de Vendôme, Cicero (*De inventione* and *De Oratore*), the Pseudo-Cicero (*De rhetorica ad Herennium*), or other rhetoricians whom he may have known, or were certainly formed by imitation of Dante, Petrarch, and Boccaccio, or from the French poets of the time; but only that these, or some of these, contributed forms for the expression of his rhetorical bent; these Chaucer gradually mastered and made organic. In somewhat the same way, as regards the work of individuals and, possibly also, as regards the progression of writers from 1579 to 1605, there is a similar rhetorical bent and a similar gradual growth in freedom. One need not contend that, except in certain cases, the bonds of these authors were as close as those of the later Middle Ages; nor would one think that complete emancipation from formal regulation was an end in view. It is rather that, as time went on, rhetorical fetters clanked less loudly. The works of the sonneteers and their contemporaries, Shakespeare's early work, for instance, are examples of heightened conventionality. As the period advances the writings of different men, sometimes as in Shakespeare's own case the same man, though at first bound by conventions, achieve an impression of complete freedom; but it is essentially a liberty within the law. Elizabethan literature remained rhetorical.

The three main divisions of rhetorical thought, as given by Professor Manly, serve also in the Renaissance as a rough test, although the subject of rhetoric had taken on certain new forms: (1) arrangement or organization (*dispositio*), (2) amplification and abbreviation, (3) style and its ornaments. The Elizabethans betray their rhetoricism in their methods of beginning and ending, in the development of their topics (by *sententiæ* and *exempla*), in their formal use of *prosecutio* in passing from introduction to body of discourse, by their amplification by means of *sententia, exemplum*, and *digressio*, and in their constant and apparently discriminating use of the figures of grammar and the figures of rhetoric (a distinction supplied by Quintilian) and of tropes and schemes.[2] The Elizabethans used the apostrophe (divided by rhetoricians into *exclamatio, conduplicatio, subjectio,* and *dubitatio*), *prosopopoeia* (a sort of pathetic fallacy), *periphrasis* or *circumlocutio* and its opposite *expolitio*, and, very commonly and with apparently deliberate intention, many of the ornaments of style: figures of words or colours of rhetoric, figures of thoughts, and tropes. Ornaments of style are divided by Professor Manly conveniently into (1) those in which 'human emotion and æsthetic feeling have always found utterance' (metaphor, simile, exclamation, rhetorical question, etc.) and (2) 'highly ingenious [and artificial] patterns of words and thought, such as using the same word at the end of a line and at the beginning, heaped-up rhymes, and alliteration.' It is of course the first class for which the evidences of conscious use are hardest to find, since formalism breaks down in that class into the natural practices of emotional speech. In the second class it is obvious at first glance that the Elizabethans used not only the stock patterns of the rhetorics but employed large numbers of rhetorical figures borrowed from both ancient and modern literature, as from the Petrarchists of France and Italy, from Seneca himself, and from the orator Isocrates,[3] a great favourite in the English Renaissance. Another remark of Professor Manly's which applies in general, though not so closely, to Renaissance literature is this: 'The elaborate system of technical devices was discussed [by rhetorical thinkers] only with reference to the form and structure of each device, never with reference to its emotional or æsthetic effects.'

All stories and, in a sense, all literary subjects (philosophical, scientific, historical, political, and literary) were theoretically old. The age was fond of the dictum, 'There is nothing new under the sun.' And authors definitely understood the literary task as the making the old seem new. To this end rhetoric was the authorized and only recognized means. Indeed, rhetoric was the art of making the old seem new.

It should also be said that, as a whole, Elizabethan writers entered more strongly than the writers of Chaucer's time into the rhetoric of public speaking, the oration and the declamation. Possibly their greatest interest was in oratory and its principles as applied to politics and theology;[4] these branches of rhetoric they reflect widely and constantly. Shakespeare introduces formal orations into *Julius Cæsar* and many set speeches before battle into the history plays. According to Stow, when the soldiers were within a mile of the town of Axel, on which (6 July 1586) they were about to make an attack, Sidney[5] addressed his troops after the ancient mode, and exhorted them to acquit themselves in the approaching battle like Englishmen, 'which oration of his did so link the minds of the people that they desired rather to die in that service than to live in the contrary.' The similar practice of Essex and other leaders is well known. It is not uncommon to have a man estimated in terms of rhetorical culture. Sir Henry Wotton[6] says of Essex:

The Earl was a very acute and sound speaker when he would intend it; and for his writings, they are beyond example, especially in his familiar letters and things of delight at court, when he would admit his serious habits, as may be yet seen in his impreses and inventions of entertainment, and above all in his darling piece of love, and self-love. His style was an elegant perspicuity, rich of phrase, but seldom any bold metaphors; and so far from tumour, that it rather wanted a little elevation.

With this one might compare Ben Jonson's famous description in *Timber*[7] of Bacon as an orator:

Dominus Verulamius.—One, though he be excellent and the chief, is not to be imitated alone; for never no imitator ever grew up to his author; likeness is always on this side truth. Yet there happened in my time one noble speaker who was full of gravity in his speaking; his language, where he could spare or pass by a jest, was nobly censorious. No man ever spake more neatly, more presly, more weightily, or suffered less emptiness, less idleness, in what he uttered. No member of his speech but consisted of his own graces. His hearers could not cough, or look aside from him, without loss. He commanded where he spoke, and had his judges angry and pleased at his devotion. No man had their affections more in his power. The fear of every man that heard him was lest he should make an end.

Sidney's *A Discourse to the Queenes Majesty touching hir Mariage with Monsieur*[8] seems consciously constructed in accordance with the principles of deliberative oratory. In his introduction Sidney humbles himself and begs a hearing on the ground of his love and loyalty. This is Insinuation. He says, 'Herein I will now but onely declare what be the reasons that make me thinke the mariage of Monsieur unprofitable for you. Then will I answere your objections of those feares which might procure so violent a refuge, the good or evill which might come unto you by it, must be considered, either according to your state or your person.' The Narration is practically omitted, the sentences just quoted giving the Proposition and its divisions. The Confutation occupies the greater part of the address: 'Now resteth to consider what be the motions of this soudaine change as I have heard you in most swete wordes deliver.' This sentence introduces Sidney's arguments against the marriage. The Conclusion takes the form of summary, one of the authorized types: 'Since then it is dangerous for your estate as well because it (by inward weaknesse principally caused by division) is fitt to receive harme, as because he both in will & power is like enough to doe harme, since to your person it can no wayes be comfortable (you not desiring mariage) & neither to person nor estate he is to bring any more good then any body, but more evill he may, since the causes that drive you to this are either feare of that which cannot happen, or by this meane cannot be prevented: I do with most humble hart say unto your majesty, etc.' The composition seems here and elsewhere to take the form of periods. In the part just quoted a *colon*, made up of three *commas*, ends with the word 'prevented.'

Such material is extremely common in Elizabethan literature, too common and often too skilfully used to be noticed. It is frequently difficult to tell whether it is being consciously employed, though many Elizabethan writers or printers notify the reader by means of a note on the margin that the text exemplifies some rhetorical grace. Very frequently the formality of use betrays a conscious purpose. The employment of the technical terminology of rhetoric is a good test, and frequently mere numbers are significant. One can be perfectly sure that Ascham, with his devotion to Cicero, is a rhetorical writer. Ascham builds his prose very often on the periodic principle. He uses much rhetorical terminology, such as *sentence*, *example*, *similitude*, and *matter*. An examination of *The Schole-master* reveals many formal digressions (some of them acknowledged at the start and then supplied with *redditus ad propositionem*), examples of *correctio*, *ante occupatio* (the imaginary objector), alliteration, balance, and heaping up of synonyms; many similes (seventeen used as proofs of propositions), at least thirteen *exempla* (mostly personal experiences), thirteen cases of apostrophe (one in which Cicero is addressed is particularly artificial).

Such crudities in the employment of formal rhetorical technique as we see in Ascham, Sidney, Greene, and other earlier writers grow less, as might be expected, as the careers of particular writers advance. In Shakespeare and his later contemporaries rhetoric is so naturally employed as almost to escape notice. There is no longer any creaking of the machine. We are not for that reason, however, to think that Elizabethan literature had forgotten or rejected rhetorical art. There is in the greatest of the Elizabethans a rhetoricism which, based solidly on the teachings of the schools, has been refined by practice and experience until nature and art are one, or, as Polixenes[9] puts it in *The Winter's Tale*, 'the art itself is nature.' Almost every degree of obviousness or of unobtrusiveness can be found.

The subject of rhetoric offered wide opportunity for study and invited every sort of literary, historical, and philosophical exploitation. It had during the sixteenth century not only its present connexion with literature but its ancient affiliations with law, preaching, and politics. However cramped and pedantical the subject-matter of rhetoric may seem to be and however shallow may seem the ends in view for which it was pursued, it is worth remembering that rhetoric is a subject with an honourable history and that it was in a preferred position in sixteenth-century education. Rhetoric was a fundamental undergraduate subject in universities and not unknown in grammar schools. It went hand in hand with dialectics in the production and criticism of disputations and assisted in the awakening of literary appreciation from the pages of Cicero, Isocrates, and Terence. Rhetoric must have been, because of its connexions with literature and because of its relation to public affairs, indeed because of its brightness in comparison with other subjects in the curriculum, a school discipline of great value when taught by cultured and judicious masters. In any case, it played a large part in the education of Sidney, Hooker, and Bacon.

The *Marginalia* of Gabriel Harvey [10] supply this witness: 'Wilsons Rhetorique & Logique, the dailie bread of owr common pleaders, & discoursers. With his dialogue of usurie, fine, & pleasant.' That the *Rhetorique* of Thomas Wilson was popular no one can doubt. The vigour, good sense, humour, and practicality of the work will account for its popularity in the presence of many rivals. Harvey's note perhaps implies that he considers himself, as no doubt he did, far beyond the use of so elementary a work in the vernacular. But, whether the rhetoric of the Elizabethans came from the learned authors known and used at the university or from other sources, nearly all the works of the time make use of rhetoric. To deny its use is to be convicted of careless observation.

One might think from the following sentence taken from 'Democritus to the Reader' [11] in Burton's *Anatomy of Melancholy*, that Robert Burton had produced his book *currente calamo*: 'I must... do my business myself, and was therefore enforced, as a Bear doth her whelps, to bring forth this confused lump,

I had not time to lick it into form, as she doth her young ones, but even so to publish it, as it was first written, *quicquid in buccam venit*, in an extemporean style, as I do commonly all other exercises, *effudi quicquid dictavit genius meus,* out of a confused company of notes, and writ with as small deliberation as I do ordinarily speak, without...terms, tropes, strong lines, that like *Acestes'* arrows caught fire as they flew, strains of wit, brave heats, elogies, hyperbolical exornations, elegancies, &c. which many so much affect...I am therefore in this point a professed disciple of *Apollonius* a scholar of *Socrates*, I neglect phrases, and labour wholly to inform my reader's understanding, not to please his ear; 'tis not my study or intent to compose neatly, which an Orator requires, but to express myself readily & plainly as it happens.' Burton then constructs an elaborate simile about a river. He is shamming, using a rhetorical trick to conceal rhetoric. The nature of his material and of the man himself call for the continual use of *exempla*, either case-studies, stories, or fables. 'Hyginus, Fab. 220, to this purpose hath a pleasant tale. Dame *Cura* by chance went over a brook, and, taking up some of the dirty slime, made an image of it; *Jupiter*, eftsoons coming by, put life to it, but *Cura* and *Jupiter* could not agree what name to give him, or who should own him. The matter was referred to *Saturn* as Judge, he gave this arbitrement; his name shall be *Homo ab humo, Cura eum possideat quam diu vivat*, Care shall have him whilst he lives; *Jupiter* his soul, and *Tellus* his body, when he dies.' Burton is noted for his frequent use (and great delight in) digressions. He marks them as well as his returns to the thread of his discourse. His figurative language is abundant and varied. There can be no doubt that he took pleasure in it. He likes the figure of the heaping up of words, repetition of various kinds, and interrogation: 'I know there be many base, impudent, brazen-faced rogues, that will *nulla pallescere culpa,* be moved with nothing, take no infamy or disgrace to heart, laugh at all; let them be proved perjured, stigmatized, convict rogues, thieves, traitors, lose their ears, be whipped, branded, carted, pointed at, hissed, reviled, and derided, with *Ballio* the Bawd in *Plautus,* they rejoice at it, *cantores probos; babae!* and *bombax!* what care they?' The following shows correspondence with the places of logic. 'Of these labours, exercises, and recreations, which are likewise included, some properly belong to the body, some to the mind, some more easy, some hard, some with delight, some without, some within doors, some natural, some are artificial.'

Finally, Ben Jonson is a man whose extensive knowledge of school learning has so united itself with the mind of the man that he is perfection as a rhetorician and at the same time seems only to be following the method of unaided naturalness. The following from *Timber,*[12] *De stilo, et optimo scribendi genere,* both expresses and exemplifies what, with men like Jonson, Bacon, and Hooker, had become the rhetorical habit: 'For a man to write well, there are required three necessaries—to read the best authors, observe the best speakers, and much exercise of his own style. In style, to consider what ought to be written, and after what manner, he must first think and excogitate his matter, then choose his words, and examine the weight of either. Then take care, in placing and ranking both matter and words, that the composition be comely; and to do this with diligence and often. No matter how slow the style be at first, so it be labored and accurate; seek the best, and be not glad of the forward conceits, or first words, that offer themselves to us; but judge of what we invent, and order

what we approve. Repeat often what we have for-
merly written; which beside that it helps the consequence, and makes the juncture better, it quickens
the heat of imagination, that often cools in the time
of setting down, and gives it new strength, as if it
grew lustier by the going back...So did the best
writers in their beginnings; they imposed upon themselves care and industry; they did nothing rashly: they
obtained first to write well, and then custom made it
easy and a habit...So that the sum of all is, ready
writing makes not good writing; but good writing
brings on ready writing.'

It is, however, possible to get a somewhat profounder view of the significance of Renaissance devotion to rhetoric. It is Aristotle and the Aristotelian
spirit which offer a better explanation of this enthusiasm than the vaguely described exuberance of the
age, which is usually adduced as a reason. Aristotle's
rhetoric is political. Sidney and Shakespeare and
Bacon and many other Elizabethans were also political
in their thinking. Next to theology politics was the
most engrossing subject of Renaissance thought, and
even theology had its political colouring.

'Rhetoric,' says Aristotle,[13] 'is the counterpart of
Dialectic. Both alike are concerned with such things
as come, more or less, within the general ken of all
men and belong to no definite science. Accordingly,
all men make use, more or less, of both; for to a certain extent all men attempt to discuss statements and
to maintain them, to defend themselves and to attack
others.'

Aristotle's teachings are fraught with practice and
arise out of a knowledge of the subject; and, although
he was probably never understood completely, he sets
a tone which echoed in the Renaissance. The fact
that Sidney actually translated Aristotle's *Rhetoric* is

preserved for us in the manuscript of a treatise on the figures of rhetoric, *Direccions for Speech and Style* by John Hoskins,[14] who, in the passage where he says that he has lately seen Sidney's translation of two books of the *Rhetoric* in the hands of the noble and studious Henry Wotton, declares that Aristotle's work is 'the directest means of skill to describe, to move, to appease, or to prevent any mood whatsoever. Whereunto, whosoever can fit his speech shall be truly eloquent.'

The system that Aristotle laid down was forgotten, but its parts remained. He had said that proofs from psychology were two: the character of the orator (hence the *Institutes* of Quintilian) and the disposition to be brought about in the audience (hence his own study of the passions and affections in the *Rhetoric*); and that proofs from logic were one (hence the *Topics* of Aristotle and Cicero). 'The purpose of this treatise,' says Aristotle[15] in the *Topics* (I, i-xiii), 'is to find a method which will qualify us as disputants in regard to every kind of subject, where the start of the inference is from probable judgments, and which will instruct us how to avoid stultifying ourselves when we ourselves sustain an argument... We call probable what appears to all men, or to the majority, or to the wise, and, among the wise, to all, to the greater number, or to the most distinguished and authoritative.' The sources from which he would draw materials for syllogisms and inductions are collections of opinion from various sources, resolution of ambiguities in meaning, discrimination between accidents, species and genera, assimilation of things to each other in their own likenesses or in their relation to other things.

The gist of the matter is there. The Elizabethans very much wished to dispute successfully, and it is

the parts of the ancient art and science of oratory
which, like the fragments of truth in the fable of
Osiris, they gather as best they can. Aristotle, in so
far as he covers the subject of rhetoric, is a marvel of
clearness. A speech has two parts. You must state
your case, and you must prove it. The only necessary
parts of a speech are the statement and the argument,
and it cannot, in any case, have more than introduction, statement, argument, and epilogue. Refutation
of the opponent is part of the argument; so is the comparison of the opponent's case with your own. The
introduction of political oratory will be made out of
the same materials as those of the forensic kind,
though the nature of political oratory makes intro-
ductions very rare. The subject is known already, and
therefore the facts of the case need no introduction;
but you may have to say something on account of
yourself or your opponents; or those present may be
inclined to treat the matter either more or less seriously than you wish them to do. You may accordingly have to excite or dispel some prejudices, or to
make the matter under discussion seem more or less
important than before. In political speeches you may
maintain that a proposal is impracticable; or that,
though practicable, it is unjust, or will do no good, or
is not so important as its proposer thinks. Argument
by 'example' is highly suitable for political oratory,
argument by 'enthymeme' better suits the forensic.
Political oratory deals with future events, with reference to which it can do no more than quote past
events as examples. Forensic oratory deals with what
is or is not now true, which can be better demon-
strated, because not contingent—there is no contin-
gency in what has already happened. Parts of the
Rhetorica ad Alexandrum deal extensively with political science—governmental policies and alliances.

How much knowledge of the actual Aristotle the Elizabethans had one does not know; but one feels that the Aristotelian ideal of rhetoric as an instrument in the service of reason, operating upon the passions of men in order to make prevail the wisdom of their superiors, is exactly the Elizabethan conception and desire.

Plutarch [16] in his life of Pericles greatly praises him for his knowledge and practice of rhetoric. Plutarch lays stress on persuasion in the following terms:

For as it falleth out commonly unto people that enjoye so great an empire: many times misfortunes doe chaunce, that fill them full of sundrie passions, the which Pericles alone could finely steere and governe with two principall rudders, feare, and hope: brideling with the one, the fierce and insolent rashnes of the common people in prosperitie, and with the other comforting their grief and discoragement in adversitie. Wherein he manife̱tly proved, that rethorike and eloquence (as Plato sayeth) is an arte which quickeneth mens spirites at her pleasure, and her chiefest skill is, to knowe howe to move passions and affections throughly, which are as stoppes and soundes of the soule, that would be played upon with a fine fingered hand of a conning master. All which, not the force of his eloquence only brought to passe, as Thucydides witnesseth: but the reputation of his life, and the opinion and confidence they had of his great worthines.

There are many other passages in Plutarch to the same effect as regards rhetoric. The power of persuasion and the political function of the orator may be said to be the subject of *De Oratore* of Cicero. The point of view of Plutarch, Cicero, Quintilian, and probably the Greek and Roman historians, about the statesman and the orator was certainly maintained during the Renaissance; perhaps the works of the men just mentioned are the primary channels for the diffusion of the Aristotelian idea of rhetoric, perhaps more important than the works of Aristotle himself.

Bacon,[17] as usual, sees the situation with great clarity; he always discovers or re-discovers the truth. 'The duty and office of rhetoric, is,' he says, '*to apply Reason to Imagination* for the better moving of the will.' He reprehends Plato for the low opinion of rhetoric he expresses in the *Gorgias*, and contends that in perfection of idea 'if a man should speak of the same thing to several persons, he should speak to them all respectively and several ways.' Bacon, convinced of the social importance of rhetoric, recommends further study and investigation of the political part of the subject. In another place, he says that invention in rhetoric is not a true invention but a '*Remembrance* or *Suggestion*, with an application.' To procure the ready use of knowledge demands preparation, which is scarcely a part of knowledge, but is useful. Ancient writers on rhetoric, Bacon says, recommend that speakers should have certain marks or places which may excite their minds to return to and reproduce such knowledge as they need. The purpose of this is not merely to aid us in disputing with others, but 'to minister unto our judgment to conclude aright within ourselves.' These 'places,' he says perspicaciously, also direct our inquiry. 'For a faculty of wise interrogating is half knowledge.' He is speaking of that part of invention which is called Topics and sees in the subject a new profundity: 'The larger your anticipation is the more direct and compendious is your search.'

The persuasive function of rhetoric may also be copiously illustrated from drama, which may be said to be made up very largely of argument and persuasion. Let us choose an illustration from Dekker.[18] Both *The Honest Whore* and *The Second Part of the*

Honest Whore turn on the belief that persuasion, the truth having once been put home in the mind of the hearer, is absolutely compelling and irresistible. In the *The Honest Whore* Hippolito's address directed toward the conversion of the prostitute Bellafront is in the form of the forensic declamations such as were written in schools and universities. The force of persuasion establishes remorse of conscience in her heart by presenting to her a true picture of her trade, and her conversion follows as a matter of necessity. Even more interesting is the combat of words on which the action of the second part turns. Hippolito, now seeking to undo the good he has accomplished in the first part, engages with Bellafront in a disputation. They take sides with the understanding that the one advancing the better arguments is to be adjudged the victor, not only in controversy but in deed. The continuance of Bellafront's virtuous state is to depend solely on the force of rhetoric:

Hip. Your hand, Ile offer you faire play: When first
We met i'th Lists together, you remember
You were a common Rebell; with one parlee
I won you to come in.
Bel. You did.
Hip. Ile try
If now I can beate down this Chastity
With the same Ordnance: will you yeeld this Fort,
If with the power of Argument now (as then)
I get of you the conquest: as before
I turnd you honest, now to turne you whore,
By force of strong perswasion?
Bel. If you can, I yeeld.

Hippolito announces his major proposition:

To be a Harlot, that you stand vpon,
The very name's a charme to make you one.

He proceeds to argue this and then announces his minor:

> Thus for the name; for the profession, this,
> Who liues in bondage, liues lac'd, the chiefe blisse
> This world below can yield, is liberty:
> And who, (than whores), with looser wings dare flie?

This also he argues by syllogistic and sophistical method. Bellafront avoids the danger, not by plain denial or objections but by what Wilson[19] calls 're-bounding againe of reasons made.' She bases her argument on this thesis:

> To proue a woman should not be a whore,
> When she was made, she had one man, no more.

At the conclusion of the argument they both claim victory and Bellafront saves herself by flight.

It is evident in Dekker's treatment that Bellafront is a victim both of the psychological theory that woman's substance is weak and changeable and of that which makes conversion a matter of the access of spirits to the heart and renders hesitation and deliberation impossible. She distrusts herself; and yet Dekker allows her to escape, thus showing more than the customary faith in the integrity of woman. Certainly, nothing could be more completely formalized, beyond the range of modern poetic faith, than the use of both psychology and rhetoric in these two plays. Such issues to be decided by such means and such considerations!

Psychologists, modern psychologists, tell us that language and thought[20] are not different things within the human mind but are merely different aspects of the same mental activity. Thought is, one might say, the obverse and language the reverse of a medal.

With language must be included, of course, all expressive acts—gesture, posture, all symbols assumed
to express rank and class, and style in vocal and written expression with all its devices. It follows by a
natural amplification of this idea that Elizabethan rhetoric bears the same relation, roughly speaking, to
logic and subject-matter that all language bears to all
thought; that is, the one is merely the manifestation
in written word of the other. One may, for example,
see in the formal features of Elizabethan literature the
qualities of Elizabethan thought. This is obvious in
the fondness of Elizabethan authors for figures of
speech based on analogy, such as the simile and the
metaphor, in a sort of contentious use of antitheses,
in an endless confusion and variety in vocabulary,
and, in general, in a hortatory quality which betokens
deadly earnestness and vigorous interest in living
and thinking. Finally, one may see in Elizabethan literature as literature a factitious and inconsistent conventionality, almost cosmological in its proportions,
which lends conformity to individual writers and to
the group as a whole; one may say that never did a
group of writers stand out more clearly as a group,
than do the writers of the age of Elizabeth. If this
theory is true, one should be able to find many pal-
pable evidences of what might be called Elizabethan
expressiveness.[21] Many such are to be found.

The characters in Marston's *Antonio and Mellida*,[22]
for example, are much preoccupied with grief, which
they often express in physiological terms. Antonio, the
son of Andrugio and therefore the hereditary enemy
of Piero Sforza, enters at the beginning of Part I
(I, i, 1 ff.), and says:

Heart, wilt thou not break? and thou abhorrèd life,
Wilt thou still breathe in my enragèd blood?

Veins, sinews, arteries, why crack ye not,
Burst and divulst ith anguish of my grief?
Can man by no means creep out of himself,
And leave the slough of viperous grief behind? ...
Have I felt anguish pour'd into my heart,
Burning like balsamum in tender wounds!
And yet dost live! ...
O, rugged mischief, how thou grat'st my heart!—
Take spirit, blood. . . .

Observe also the remarkable scene (IV, i, 281 ff.) where Antonio is nonplussed in presence of the urgency of his father. Antonio says his 'panting heart scuds round about' his bosom 'to get out, dreading the assailant, horrid passion.' He stands motionless and unable to speak until his father bids him heat his blood and 'be not froze up with grief.' In Part II grief becomes a still greater obsession. Antonio has a new occasion in the death of his father and the defamation of his beloved. To one who counsels him to be patient ("'Tis reason's glory to command affects') he says (I, ii, 280-2):

Are thy moist entrails crumpled up with grief
Of parching mischiefs? Tell me, does thy heart
With punching anguish spur thy gallèd ribs?

His heart will 'burst all covert' (II, ii, 5-6), his brain will melt in tears (Part II, V, ii, 154-5), and so on; but it is poor Mellida who actually dies of grief (Part II, IV, i, 284 ff.). Antonio fills much of Part I and still more of Part II with his ravings of grief or revengeful anger, and the expression of these passions is strikingly physiological as the quotations have shown. Antonio grovels on the earth a good deal, and, one gathers, flings his arms about, knits his brow, groans, and otherwise makes visible signs of his feelings. An actor who wished to play the part of Antonio in the way Marston seems to have indicated would give the impression of stepping directly out of one of those books on the feelings where the symptoms of a known passion are described; such as Wright, La Primaudaye, Charron, or Coeffeteau.

No aspect of Chapman's philosophy [23] is more significant than its doctrine of expressiveness. Indeed, it seems a clue to the Renaissance love for drama and all expressive arts. Poets and artists heard the voice of all the world speaking to them, saw a universe written full of messages, and gave to speech itself a special significance. These things Chapman exploits. He wished to find all the meaning to be had in a world which itself was a message from God. In *Ovid's Banquet of Sense* Chapman describes the power of the eye to inflame the heart and the power of the ear to appeal to the higher emotions. Perfumes and sounds, we are told, appeal to finer tempers only, and both air and odours feed love. It may be that there is also a doctrine of transfer of impressions between the senses. We are told that, when a picture is done exceedingly to the life, the eye takes such strong heed of it that it cannot contain it alone; the ear shares the impression. To Chapman physiognomy is of immense practical importance. The signs of character are always visible and can be read by one skilled in the art of reading signs. By reading character one also foretells the future; for, if one knows men, one knows what they will do. By remembering that each natural agent works but to the end of making what it works on like itself, one comprehends Chapman's important doctrine of persuasion. Rhetoric does not work persuasion, but is a means to make it work.

Emotion in the subject arises in proportion as it chimes in with the raiser's spirit. Byron is past meas-

ure glorious (boastful), and that humour feeds his
spirits, especially when men blow it up with praise
of his perfections. He can thus be confirmed in any
error. If the air contained in our ears be not quiet but
troubles our hearing with offensive sounds, the ear
can faithfully receive no other voice. It follows that
Byron's emotion (ambition) is not a disease bred in
himself but whispered in by others who have swelled
his veins with empty hope. Thus does Chapman develop a science of social manipulation. Words are
great matters. By words one may vent the fiery impressions which otherwise nature could not live to
contain, for they would break ribs of steel. To unpack
one's heart affords relief. Byron's words are also
potent. Like music, they almost ravish La Fin's soul
from death. Byron knows that his oratory has convinced the Chancellor because he observes a blush
upon the Chancellor's cheek. Byron will not have
his ear blown into flame by the reading aloud of his
doom. Words plant opinion, and opinion, like medicine, works upon man's blood and changes it. On the
other hand, good counsel feeds the heart with sweet
hope, and philosophy sweeps passion from thought: it
is the soul's broom. The face is the great index of the
soul. In *The Conspiracy of Charles, Duke of Byron*
the ambassador is instructed to penetrate the heart and
marrow of the king's designs, to observe the countenance of discontented persons about the court. The
courtiers read Byron's character in his picture: a face
of excellent presentment, not so amorous with pure
red and white, but the whole proportion is singular.
It has good lines and tracts drawn through it, the
'purfle' (adornment) is rare. In it is nothing which any
of the rules of physiognomy regard as a blemish. But
it is like a tree late blossomed when all the frosts are
past, on which one may discern what fruits will grow.

The carriage of the neck is something stooping, the eyes have a voluble and mild radiance, the aspect is masculine, the instinct lion-like. Similarly in *The Tragedy of Charles, Duke of Byron* the king claims that he is able to read La Fin's mind in his face. In *Monsieur D'Olive* we learn that the visible signs of the shrewish nature are a dull eye and a sharp nose; a dry hand is the sign of dissipation. Since everywhere throughout the plays of Chapman there is evidence that gesture and facial expression are the means of reading character, one wonders to what extent the principles of physiognomy were to be found in the actors' art. Still more important, it seems, is the stress on expressiveness. It suggests a sort of watchfulness in all human life foreign to the modern world.

Let us consider for a moment, in this age of ours, characterized by so abundant expression with so little attention paid to it, what life would be like in another sort of age, when the spoken or the written word was, in universal belief, an irresistible force through the power of persuasion. What an importance must have been attached to political utterance which might by its mere impact on the ears of the people shake the king upon his throne or surround him with loving subjects; and what a weight of earnestness must have rested upon the preacher of the Word, who was veritably a dispenser of the bread of life! Those who heard would inherit eternal life, and those who did not hear would suffer eternal torment. Now, those into whose ears the truth had passed had no choice, if they were normal human beings, but to obey that truth. Those who heard the established truth and did not thereupon profess it, were condemned on the doctrine of persuasion as children of the devil. It was just and right that such persons should be led to the stake and burned.

CHAPTER VIII

THE WINDOW OF MOMUS

> First therefore, the precept which I conceive to be most
> summary towards the prevailing in fortune, is to obtain
> that window which Momus did require, who seeing in
> the frame of man's heart such angles and recesses, found
> fault there was not a window to look into them.—Bacon,
> *The Advancement of Learning.*

A N ATTEMPT has been made to present an exposition of the more strictly formal aspects of Renaissance thought in so far as that seemed necessary in order to show the nature of its impact on literature, and also in order to discover how, and where, and to what extent in literature Renaissance learning functioned. Our purpose in this chapter is to discuss Renaissance attitudes of mind [1] and thus prepare ourselves to understand the characteristic behaviour of that mind. Such discussion may ultimately explain certain important opinions and characteristic notions of Renaissance people. For example, one would like to know whether or not the wide currency and popularity of Ramist logic had anything to do with the headlong way in which Elizabethan men acted first and theorized afterwards. It may be that the practical directness of the Ramist system, the belief which it engendered in the naturalness of short-cuts, gave in some instances encouragement to Elizabethan precipitancy, though in general one would conclude that Ramist logic and Elizabethan directness are merely concomitant manifestations of the same spirit of the age. This probably means that the many manifestations of the influence of theology, philosophy, and science on Renaissance literature are of a precisely similar kind. The Elizabethans no doubt chose only those things from the field of learning which suited their own natures and ends; the things chosen were neither inert nor merely corroborative. Elizabethan life is the soil out of which grew both the impulse to express and the choice of form for expression; but, once chosen, forms, facts, and congenial ideas wrought effects of their own of increasing importance.

In the type of literary study suggested in this chapter attention is to be directed to the nature of the responses to Renaissance learning which literature and history make manifest, the subjects of study themselves entering as discriminable factors into the intellectual life of the time. Renaissance learning expresses certain distinctive ideas and calls other ideas into being, although probably the expressive function is usually greater than the generative function. But discrimination is not easy within the field. Mediæval and classical learning blend with each other, and both of them blend with new matters and native traditions; so that a complex appears in history, biography, and literature. The research demanded for the determination of relatively simple facts in such a study is most extensive, since almost no object of study stands alone as a result of simple causes. The importance of such research arises from the truth of opinions and points of view one may be able to arrive at by means of it, and the value of results depends even more on reflection than on research.

Renaissance literature in the broad sense in which the term is here used is a reflection of the Renaissance mind. Since the Renaissance mind was a complex of many elements, the task of seeing that mind through literature alone with anything approaching adequacy and completeness is probably impossible. It is not, on the other hand, possible to revivify the literature without a knowledge of the mind that produced it. It may be that the study of an organized cultural element like the academic corpus would throw light on literature by illuminating the minds of the producers of literature, particularly since in the period chosen for study the curriculum of schools and colleges was eagerly resorted to for literary guidance. We must endeavour to learn how the Elizabethans looked at learning and what they thought they saw in it. We must not imagine them looking with our eyes at our body of learning. Neither the eyes nor the learning are the same. Such an attempt as this ought to be supplemented by an extensive and catholic study of history as well as literature, although it is of course here necessary to present the literary study in a more or less isolated form, without claiming too much for such a study. At every turn our task is conditioned by factors other than those of education and formal culture; and, in order that borderlines may be made clear, we must now devote some space to various social and intellectual features of life in the Renaissance. We shall have to content ourselves with indicating, mainly through questions, various unexplored territories into which at this time we cannot hope to penetrate. Now that we have had something to say about the differences between Renaissance learning and modern learning, we should like to say something also about the differences between Renaissance minds and modern minds.

It is difficult to tell what the Renaissance in England really meant when its fashion dictated, irrespective of existent circumstance. a particular answer to a particular question. The literature of the age is, for example, full of denunciations of the life of the court and of praises of the life of the shepherd or the simple rustic man. Bacon and Essex threaten to withdraw from the turmoil of the court to the society of their books in simple, servantless existence. No doubt this was in part a reaction against the subtleties of a disputatious age with its discussions of love, politics, science, and the *modus vivendi*. Was it more than a parade of humanism? There was entering in at the time a classical thread, stoical as well as pastoral. As a manner of thought, pastoralism [2] has immense importance in Elizabethan literature. With Sidney and Greene it became a doctrine. Shakespeare entered into it with all apparent sincerity and built at least two plays about the theme of the simple life; but perplexity arises if one asks, for example, 'Is there in the lyricists, in those who are something more than merely pastoral, indeed in Shakespeare himself, a genuine sentiment for nature in Elizabethan poetry?' Perhaps all that the Elizabethan poets had was a simple and direct appreciation of nature,[3] which might be assumed as a mere pastoral fashion or might, being seriously considered, lead to something profounder and more deeply reasoned. Montaigne [4] went to nature realistically, and, according to Ben Jonson, 'all our English writers will deign to steal...from Montaigne.'

The romantic ideal [5] is also a masquerader in its embodiments. It is pretty well agreed that life borrows ideals and motives from literature and that literature also copies life.[6] Therefore, one finds the ideals of an age both reflected and reinforced in the forms of art. The fact that a man like Sidney applied to his own activities a formalized ethical system, mainly from Aristotle, is extremely interesting. Sidney's deliberate effort to make of himself a model courtier was evidently recognized as successful by his contemporaries,

who called him 'the president of chivalry.' One may
go further and say that that sort of conscious application of the principles and doctrines of the new learning is a striking and significant characteristic of the
whole period. To what extent then did important
persons of the Renaissance attempt to live up to the
literary ideals of the time; to that, for example, of the
perfect prince or courtier, the philosopher, the sage,
the saint, or the martyr? Bacon certainly aspires to be
a new and greater Aristotle. In the realm of literature
what, one asks, were the new romantic types? Spenser
and Sidney seem to give us back the heroes of chivalry recostumed in Aristotelianism, the same that
Boiardo, Tasso, and Ariosto had tended to caricature.
The earlier romantic type was at its very end, and
before the turn of the century the dramatists had begun to study their heroes psychologically and thus
break down the type into the individual.

One would not over-simplify and so render the
minds of Elizabethans elementary, but a knowledge of
the subjects they talked about and of the backgrounds
of their ideas does not remove all difficulties. Their
minds were of course as mature, often as exploratory,
as those of any age; the point of differentiation between their age and ours is that there are at our
command many devices of thought,[7] mainly technical, and many points of view which had not then
been discovered. Behind the difficulties of sixteenth-
century English, a less well developed instrument than
recent English, behind the obscurities of a forgotten
Renaissance culture we shall find that poets and
thinkers were then as now struggling to shove forward
the bounds and limits of language and thought and to
express what had hitherto remained unexpressed.
Donne seems reluctant to associate form and language
with ideas like that of God and the spirit. Milton

when he attempts to express ideas of space, silence, eternity, and the void abyss reveals a conscious struggle to enlarge the bounds of normal comprehension. Marlowe says in *Tamburlaine* (V, ii, 98-110),

> If all the pens that ever poets held
> Had fed the feeling of their masters' thoughts, ...
> If these had made one poem's period,
> And all combined in beauty's worthiness,
> Yet should there hover in their restless heads,
> One thought, one grace, one wonder at the least,
> Which into words no virtue can digest.

Shakespeare often confronts the ultimate in passion and suffering and sometimes breaks down speech into exclamation and incoherence. But, generally speaking, the difficulties we encounter are not with language but with the machine of knowledge, age-old, into whose extended parts had entered elements which increased its complexity. To follow completely the thought of Shakespeare, Milton, and Richard Hooker is to have mastered a great system of intellectual and moral culture differing much from ours and now in large part forgotten, but not simpler than ours or from a logical point of view less adequate. Meantime the history of literature occupies itself with story, poem, drama, and essay, sometimes as if these things had come into being like individuals in a series of plants or animals; whereas the users of these forms did not understand them as we do, and literature rarely talked about itself. In literature the Elizabethans seem to have had relatively little self-consciousness along with their almost incredible activity.

Among all the traits and qualities of the Elizabethans one must not fail to notice their energy and enterprise. A will to achieve seems to have been general in the age. One finds encouragement for it in

Aristotelian ethics, in Calvinistic theology, in the circumstances of a new world discovered and waiting to be explored. The Elizabethans preached the strenuous life as earnestly as do our own contemporaries, and yet of course with appropriate differences. Work with us has become a democratic manifestation. With the Elizabethans it was probably an aristocratic ideal, whose kinds were sharply discriminated. School learning held up to the prince and the courtier the ideal of a superior existence which was to be achieved by effort—gentlemanly pursuits, study, dress, bearing. The prizes of life, now theoretically at least open to all, were the reward of their labour. Some few lowly things, borrowed from the ancients, about agriculture, trades, and handicrafts, are repeated in the books; but the chances are that the lower classes, like modern organized labour, were more orthodox and regarded work as a curse. The tendency would be to keep sports alive as a mitigation of the hardships of toil. Certainly the life of the time was full of hardships. The houses of all classes were relatively very poor. Means for storing food and protecting wealth were inadequate. Medical science was at so low an ebb that recovery from disease seemed (and was) a matter of chance or divine favour. Ignorance of economic fact and the instability of the medium of exchange caused failures or successes in business to be regarded rather as the results of fortune than of prudence. It was natural that hardship should be regarded as inevitable; escape as difficult or impossible; and comfort, security, and wealth as divine favour or mere good fortune. There was, however, impinging upon the sense of hazard and chance an authorized attitude which regarded all misfortune and bereavement as divine punishment for sin; so that the uncertainties and misfor-

tunes of their lives may be said to have thrown the
Elizabethans into the lap of religion.

In no part of the social fabric are the differences
between the Elizabethan age and the modern world
more striking than in the field of religion. We know,
from instances in our own world and from abundant
records in the sixteenth century, the suddenness and
violence of religious conversion and the quality of its
sincerity, which carried it into the smallest details of
thought and conduct. Probably, an undeliberative intensity on the one side and an intellectual confusion on
the other are the keys to the religious life of the age.
Something must be believed and promptly and un-
waveringly acted upon, but just what it was was a
matter of the utmost diversity of opinion. One sees
something of this in the Renaissance saints and men
of God—Ignatius Loyola, Francis Xavier, Charles
Borromeo, Aloysius Gonzaga, and their Protestant
counterparts, as also in the mystics. The lives of these
men have much to tell us of their age; we usually hear
a story of concentrated and consecrated partisanship.
In no age perhaps has religion had such effective and
such narrow leaders. What seem to us essential things
were rarely at issue. Cartwright and Whitgift battled
over investiture. The attack on mysticism took the
form of advocacy of the doctrine of individual salvation as against the idea, closely akin to Platonism, that
the soul may be absorbed in God. Roger Williams [8]
and John Cotton debate, not for and against religious
toleration, but, like many of their predecessors, on
the proper exegesis of the parable of the tares in the
wheat. The battle seems always to have been fought
at the barriers, but it was unceasing; and no subject
so coloured and controlled men's thoughts in the age
as did religion. Now, a battle at the barriers is a battle

of logic rather than of reason over issues to be adjudi-
cated, not investigated or arbitrated.

We have declared that literature cannot be divorced
from the minds and hearts of those that produced it,
specifically that it is impossible that sixteenth-century
literature should not be concerned with religion. We
now say that politics is also important. In the works
of Sidney and Spenser, in the historical plays of Shakespeare, in the life and work of Bacon and Hooker, and
in many other places, a knowledge of current theories
of the state is of fundamental significance. One must
know what orders of society were valid and important in Elizabethan England and claimed to have divine
sanction. There was democratic thinking [9] in Beza,
Hotman, Mornay, and Buchanan; there may have
been considerable quantities of it in the England of
Sidney's youth, but aside from that there is very little,
or none at all, to be found in England in the latter
half of the sixteenth century. Probably, most of the
statesmen of the Renaissance believed in reform, since
institutions, although divinely created, might grow
corrupt or completely evil through the wickedness
of men, and therefore need to be restored to primitive
perfection, but institutions could not and should not
be revolutionized or recreated. There was thus no very
clear idea of political progress [10] as we in the modern
world conceive of it. The political programmes, even
of Bacon, who wrote mainly in the reign of James I,
looked toward the past rather than the future.

Bacon, whose opinions are illuminating, saw, because of the breadth of his knowledge of history and
politics, the propriety, even the necessity, of change
and adaptation. His belief in the continuance of evil
and the degeneration of good makes him a reformer.
In his essay 'Of Innovations' he says,

For Ill, to man's nature as it stands perverted, hath a natural motion, strongest in continuance; but Good has a forced motion, strongest at first. Surely every medicine is an innovation; and he that will not apply new remedies must expect new evils; for time is the greatest innovator; and if time of course alter things to the worse, and wisdom and counsel shall not alter them to the better, what shall be the end? ... All this is true, if time stood still; which contrariwise moveth so round, that a froward retention of custom is as turbulent a thing as an innovation; and they that reverence too much old times, are but a scorn to the new.

In 'Of Seditions and Troubles' he cites the following causes:

The Causes and Motives of seditions are, innovation in religion; taxes; alteration of laws and customs; breaking of privileges; general oppression; advancement of unworthy persons; strangers; dearths; disbanded soldiers; factions grown desperate; and whatsoever, in offending people, joineth and knitteth them in a common cause.

Everything in the list is amenable to reform. That his view is static is perfectly clear from the last sentence in 'Of Innovations':

And lastly, that the novelty, though it be not rejected, yet be held for a suspect; and, as the Scripture saith, *that we make a stand upon the ancient way, and then look about us, and discover what is the straight and right way, and so to walk in it.*

Absolutism and capitalism had developed late in the Middle Ages, and both were dogmatically and blindly protecting themselves with shreds of theory snatched from the garments of the ancient world, and, in prac-

tice, by assumption, injustice, and violence. A theory
of the rule of the saints, the Puritan theocracy, was
growing in men's minds, and, particularly in its pres-
byterial forms, had in it the rudiments, but none of
the spirit, of the democratic system. Meantime, feu-
dalism and chivalry were still dominant in tradition
and lent themselves to the interests of the ruling
classes.

Political stability was in part achieved by the en-
forcement of social classification. It must be apparent to any reader of Elizabethan literature that
it attaches great value to the nobility and the integrity
of that class. The cruel snobbery with which Malvolio
is treated in *Twelfth Night* is perhaps a commonplace
reflection of the general attitude toward the man who
aspired to rise above his station. Elizabethan literature
usually also undervalues the common people.[11] The
common people were allowed the function of tilling
the soil and providing by work and trade the material necessities on which society should live. Bacon
has a finer and fairer view of them, as he shows in his
essay 'Of the True Greatness of Kingdoms and Estates'
and elsewhere. But there is little kindness towards
them in literature. They were expected to be content
with the position to which Providence had assigned
them, to be diligent, docile, humble, and obedient;
and the ambition to rise above their social status must
have been regarded as subversive and dangerous,
actually sinful. But the common people were certainly
feared in Elizabethan times, and there must have been
among them a growing class-consciousness. Puritanism
must have been working subversively upon them. In
point of fact, the lower classes did improve their
position in larger numbers than ever before. There
was in theory no recognized distinction between the
bourgeois poor and the bourgeois rich, but there must

have been in practice; privilege [12] must then as now have gone to the rich and conformity must then as now have been the ticket of admission to the society of the upper classes. There are, however, many matters still in doubt, matters reflected in a puzzling way in literature.

What shall we say, for example, of the influence of economics on literature? The facts are these. The importation of gold and silver from America into Europe in the sixteenth century brought about a period of prosperity, a great inflation of trade, and a great betterment of material and social conditions. By actual capture, by trade with Spain and Portugal directly, and indirectly by trade with France and the Low Countries much of the new metal found its way into England and there produced an era of good times. Queen Elizabeth and her ministers, like various modern governments, got credit for a set of conditions with which they had almost nothing to do and which they did not understand. Indeed, nobody knew what was happening or why or had knowledge sufficient to describe it. The age is thus silent about what was perhaps the very greatest factor in the production of its own greatness. In studying the literature of the time one can only apprehend the presence of a great force which was making men active, comfortable, and domineering, raising the standard of living, revolutionizing institutions, and giving the lie to what was often only a doctrinal pessimism. Behind the formal elements we study was this great unknown power. We should not, however, minimize the importance of ideas, since they furnished the forms for literary expression in the Renaissance, as always.

Granted that rulers, such as Henri IV and Elizabeth, sought to embody in their households new ideals of noble living, to what extent were their efforts mere sham or barbarous failure? One would think them mere pretence in view of the crudity and selfishness of courtly life—bad fare, foul lodgings, riotous crowding, swearing, gambling, quarrelling, duelling, jealousy, intrigue, and licentiousness. Surely Elizabethan drama has bases of this sort. It may be that Middleton is less of a satirist and more of a realist than we think him. Noisy manifestations of sorrow were good form in the best circles, and back of all these publicities lies, of course, the primitive practice of finding consolation in the objectification and ritualization of the unpleasant. The Elizabethans certainly had the habit of cutting the Gordian knot of their complexes more summarily than we do, but it may be that we can perceive vaguely others of their methods of freeing themselves from their troubles. Privilege is in some sense the answer to the question, the privilege of wearing certain colours and garments, of liveries, of precedence, of access to the royal person, of titles, honours, money, and the opportunity of making it easily. Over against a life of ignorance and want there was a spectacle (partly barbarous show) of romantic and regal brilliance which must have helped to make life endurable, even interesting. Back of the royal progresses there seems to have been a definite intention to build up a feeling of allegiance in order to establish credit and public confidence. The propriety of doing this is in Machiavelli. One gets the idea that Elizabeth and her nobility were cold-blooded in their political policy to the point of disingenuousness. Bacon was completely practical, and there are not as many tears in Shakespeare, as in Galsworthy, over the miseries of the poor. The commiseration of poverty was perhaps a more or less stereotyped thing, for the rights of man was not yet a living doctrine. The common man had grown less rather than more important since the days of *Utopia*. Italianate books on education and courtesy never failed to say that virtue is the only basis of nobility, but the peasant outcry of John Ball had secured no constitutional recognition. An idea of equality is also implicit in Latin writers, explicit in Cicero and Seneca; but in Shakespeare's time the debate between patrician and plebeian was revived to the disadvantage of the latter. It would be difficult to find any writer of the Renaissance treating the subject who fails to describe the Gracchi as traitors. The ancient idea of the rights of man and the Gregorian idea of one flesh meant no more than that all men were equal before death and chance. One would not, however, forget that the idea of Robin Hood and the rustic hero still had vitality and that Deloney, Dekker, and to a limited extent Heywood glorified yeomen and artisans. The doctrine of the validity of social classes was unquestioned and the proletariat found little voice; but, in view of the happenings of the next age, one must believe that, in the minds of stubborn nonconformists and elsewhere, revolutionary tendencies were at work. We are probably, however, justified in concluding that in politics as in religion we are usually confronted with dogma and not with a rational consideration of social conditions and human rights.

To say how ancient ideas entered into and affected the existent complex is very difficult. They probably entered more slowly and had a smaller total effect than we imagine, for the Renaissance seems to have treated the classics selectively, choosing mainly those things which reinforced its own desires and tendencies; just as, for example, the Renaissance popularity of Isocrates must be due in some measure at least to the congeniality of his ideas to those which underlay Tudor absolutism. Indeed, there is much to commend the belief that the Renaissance was in large part a modified mediævalism. The Renaissance possibly admired the Platonic academy [13] as much because of its own zeal for cliques, sects, guilds, and political bodies, as because it longed for opportunity to discuss philosophy and art. The history of such institutions would no doubt reveal ancient tastes and customs with Italian modifications. Each group probably had its own special body of doctrines grounded in its appropriate philosophy, and tradition simply became more intelligent rather than less. Such a change seems to have taken place in orders of knighthood and chivalry, which, though outworn, were never more highly regarded. Vows of brotherhood and heroism, often recurrent in Elizabethan literature, were strengthened by the cult of friendship. The oath and the curse retained much of their traditional power and were reinforced by religion. Belief in magic in one form or other was prevalent and found in the Cabala and ancient writings much to support it. Even outworn delusions and doctrines and practices for centuries under the ban of the church found things in the new learning to revive them. A study of code morals and the ethics of the caste [14] would be most valuable in showing the old not weakened but strengthened by the new. Many now discredited ideals of conduct which had come down from the Middle Ages seem to have been upheld vigorously in Elizabethan England. The duty of revenge was probably both traditional in England and part of the heritage from the ancients. It was vigorously assailed by Christianity, but, for literary employment at least, it emerged strengthened by Seneca. Indeed it may have been for generations living on in the community in the face of the most solemn religious prohibition.

The Elizabethans still professed the ideal of the rescue of the Holy Sepulchre. They had the ideal of

the brotherhood of kings, the belief in the efficacy of
the royal touch, and the institution of judicial combat. There were demonological possessions, witchcraft, evil spirits (often under human control), and
ghosts of the departed dead—all denied by the Church.
These things were not merely from the Middle Ages
and the darkening past. Some of them are from the
literature of the ancient world and from the Bible
itself. It happens that many of these extraordinary
things, both superstitions and social beliefs, became the
stock-in-trade of Elizabethan drama and other Elizabethan literature, and one cannot help wondering to
what extent they were regarded as valid human experiences and to what extent they were merely imaginatively endorsed. Had the Elizabethans made any
progress towards conquering their belief in Lady Fortune and Fortune's wheel? Certainly there was the
keenest interest in the examples of those who had been
the victims or the beneficiaries of Fortune's fickle-
ness.

Some clue to the puzzle of the Elizabethan mind
might come from inquiring how the thought of death
manifested itself in the English Renaissance. The later
Middle Ages produced the Dance of Death. The basis
of treatment is fear, the spectacle of death used to produce repentance and preparation. The writers of the
Middle Ages thought of death in terms of skeletons,
corpses, bones, and charnel houses. Their themes were
the *Ubi sunt*, the decay of beauty, the certainty of
death. Do not these themes persist in the Renaissance,
and what is the nature of its *ars moriendi* literature? [15]
Certainly there are new elements, such as the Stoicism
one finds in Mornay and Cardan and *Hamlet*; as also
Plutarch's attitude toward death, strangely coloured
in Montaigne. Protestantism might be expected to
have personalized the note of Christian resignation and

rendered more pronounced the jubilation over the fact of salvation, but one hears little of it. The elegiac idea, the note of pure pity, seems also strangely silent in the age.

Of all the difficult and obscure questions we have been forced to ask in this chapter the one we now approach is the hardest. Is it possible at this distance and with the materials at our disposal to determine the nature of the Renaissance mind and to state it in terms of the thought-habits of the current modern world? If we can find an answer to this question, we shall have found an answer to most of the others.

We might begin with the query, 'What did the Renaissance do with the scholasticism of the Middle Ages and with the general habit of analogical thinking?' The Middle Ages had built up a perfect system of the phenomenal and epiphenomenal worlds, so that deductive logic became an instrument of certainty. Symbolism was more than symbolism; it was general correspondence. To what extent were the intellectual operations of the Renaissance of the same order and kind as those of the Middle Ages? The 'realism' of the schoolmen was anthropomorphic. Man belonged to nature and the universe and corresponded to it in his mind and his body. By means of symbolism and personification realism worked out its sets of agreements and effected short-cuts in thinking. An elaborate system of co-ordination and subordination, together with a rigid principle of obedience to authority, assisted to the same ends. The greater part of Renaissance thinking is probably of this kind. The Scriptures themselves when elevated into the ultimate guide of life were used as a substitute for thinking things out either causally or genetically, indeed as a substitute for investigation. The Scriptures [16] as variously interpreted sometimes served as an inhibition to the free exercise of mind on the part of the religious and caused them to forbid others to use their minds, since it was believed that, if the Scriptures had spoken, ultimate truth was at hand. To question them was to question God. The Renaissance mind inherited or adopted generalized simplifications, formulæ, for the applications of its ethical, religious, and scientific systems. It could not consider, or at least was not in the habit of considering, observed data apart from these generalizations.

Perhaps this principle can be best understood in its operation in the field of ethics. The educated people of the Renaissance knew in some respects more about ethics than the people of our time, but in other respects they did not. They had the articulated system of Aristotle as it had been variously modified. This system had arisen from observation and reflection on the ways of human life; but it was Socrates, Aristotle, Epicurus, the Stoics, and various Christian moralists who had done the reflecting and observing. The Renaissance received the ethics pretty much as a pupil receives his lesson. The conceptual elements grew at the expense of rational elements, such as suspension of judgment and particularity of choice. The Renaissance adopted the findings or principles of ancient ethics and neglected its methods. Aristotle says in effect, 'If a man wishes to live a happy and successful life as a citizen, it is evident that these are the ways in which he must do it.' And he argues his principles in the light of situations. The Renaissance habitually adopts the principles of Aristotle and says, 'Be wise. Be just. Be temperate. Be courageous. And hold to these qualities for the reasons stated.' The Renaissance uses precept as a basis of instruction, and the moral philosophies of the past move into the realm of the Ten Commandments. The Renaissance was well schooled in the principle of obedience to authority by its past, and the instruction continued. Instead of a questioning and reasonable philosopher Aristotle becomes a lawgiver, and his ethical principles, which were once reasoned ideals, become precepts; and precepts so authenticated called, by social habit, loudly for action, whether rejection or adoption. There was no room left for thought. Spenser turns Aristotle's virtues, themselves often so shading into one another that they cannot be wholly distinguished, into 'twelve private moral virtues.' In Spenser's hands the virtues are patterns of action, symbols of conduct. This kind of thought is habitual in the age. Mythology yielded its set of symbols. Many poems and dramas use mythology [17] (along with aphoristic and exemplary wisdom) formally as a means of expressing ideas, pointing lines of action, and criticizing conduct.

The Renaissance also joined in the search for similitude, for its faith in analogy was unshaken. The writers of the time have the habit of citing all scriptural cases and enumerating all examples from history or tradition. They fill out and complete their patterns. There must, for example, be names provided for all the demons as a parallel series to those of the angels. It was a feature of Cardan's empirical system that he should not suffer himself to be convinced by a single sign; he was careful and an advanced thinker and yet that circumstance did not prevent him from being a victim to false analogy. Note Shylock's casuistry about Jacob's and Laban's flocks and the insistence of Laertes that his vengeance was subject to adjudication to determine under what conditions it might be satisfied in nature. Instances of mechanistic crudity in Renaissance thought betray the faultiness of its system, a system which led the thinkers of the time to subsume variety under a single proverb, to generalize

over-hastily, to give adherence to suppository final
causes when they had the weight of authority back of
them, as the idea, for example, that everything has
a use, every poison an antidote, every disease a cure.
The theology of sixteenth-century Protestants does
not seem to have been less dogmatic than that of the
Catholics, being equally authoritarian though possibly
less formalized. No doubt Protestantism was slowly
rejecting much of the religious machinery of the past;
but in the first instance Protestantism merely substituted with reinforced persistence an equally formal
system, biblical instead of Catholic, which seems to
have made few changes in manner of thought and
method of procedure.

The serious thinking of the time, usually starting
with a principle, always regards an abstract, or the
application of an abstract, as the ultimate goal of
thought. The established method of the thinking was
to fit the particular objects of thought into their places
in a pre-arranged scheme. In such a system every class,
each trade and occupation, has its proper position and
its formula,—the lunatic, the lover and the poet, and
man in his seven ages. Science in such a scheme becomes mere numbering and recording, though of
course science was always subject to the correction
by the common sense of the scientist. This kind of
thinking caused the wide adoption of the (Platonic)
idea that a beautiful body must contain a beautiful
soul, ('There's nothing ill can dwell in such a temple,'
says Miranda[18] of Ferdinand), and that felony results from a physical corruption of the blood; also
that bastards are morally perverse and natural enemies
to the social order. Psychologically such conceptions
arise almost solely from imagination, and neither invite nor allow any exercise of rational thought. In so
far as such conceptions are new they indicate a break-

ing down of formalism in the intellectual *schemata* of the Renaissance. Yet formalism was still prevalent. It still compelled attention to times and seasons, to anniversaries, lucky and unlucky days, festivals and saints' days. Protestant theology, though active in its negations, was perfectly formal (logical rather than symbolic) in its operations. Puritanism as a social force had its basis in the dictum that worldly occupations and amusements are the efficient cause of sin.

It may be perhaps agreed upon that the mind of the Renaissance moved habitually on a conceptual rather than a rational level. It was in the habit of adopting and applying generalizations made by others. It could make generalizations of its own, but Bacon at least distrusted them because they were likely to be made without proper reflection and exploration. The age seems to have been trained in no inductive habit of mind by means of which it could observe significant differences and thereby avoid over-hasty generalization. Bacon [19] seems to imply that his age tended to see similarities more readily than it did differences. For example, he says that one of the *desiderata* of his time was a new ethic, based upon the observation of life as it was lived then. He says that a knowledge of men's vicious practices in their various trades and professions is as necessary as a knowledge of their duties. His point is that one needs to be fully informed in order to draw any conclusions as to what one ought to do. 'So that we are much beholden to Machiavel and others, that write what men do and not what they ought to do... Nay, an honest man can do no good upon those that are wicked to reclaim them, without the help of the knowledge of evil.' This principle accounts for the downfall of Brutus. Bacon finds it exceedingly strange that moral philosophy has not been reduced to written inquiry, and he proceeds to enumerate what is needed: 'to set down sound and true distributions and descriptions of the several characters and tempers of men's natures and dispositions.' In another place he says significantly that good exemplars carrying the portraitures of good, virtue, duty, felicity have been made, but 'how to attain these excellent marks, and how to frame and subdue the will of man to become true and conformable to these pursuits, they pass it over altogether, or slightly and unprofitably.'

Now, this vagueness in the realm of ideals and rational actions to which Bacon calls attention is duly compensated for by a proper sharpness of outline in the realm of the perceptual and the conceptual. It must have required great vividness of conception, imagination operating under heat, to produce the statutes for the burning of heretics and papists. Such an unthinking clarity of mind on the lower level would account in some measure for the surprising ferocity of the Renaissance, a ferocity of the fanatic and the dogmatist, far worse than anything recorded from the Middle Ages. Note the vindictiveness of punishments and the cruelty of judges.[20] It would be interesting to inquire to what extent religious persecutions were also political, or personal, or due to economic jealousy, for such circumstances would have increased their cruelty; but here one may remark, on the basis of current experience in our own time, that the cruelties of that age seem characteristic enough of its cocksure mentality. But a still more important question to be asked in connexion with Renaissance mentality is this: does not a state of mind which arises from such mental habits eventuate in crises? If convictions are deep and imaginative conceptions unjustifiably clear, tragedy, as in the case of Othello, stalks upon the stage. Strong feeling, superficial thinking, and the error of over-hasty generalization were the bases of tragedy, then as now; and one asks if the Renaissance, in its exaggerations (the customary resort of unreflective minds), does not provide the chief occasions for human tragedy; indeed, if it does not become the tragic age *par excellence.*

As a concomitant to the mentality of crisis just described, one might observe that life in the Renaissance seems to have been more clearly marked externally than is modern life, as if it carried with it its symbols of action and classification. Curiosity in private life seems to have been less restrained as one observes it in the attitude towards the unfortunate and the grotesque, the insane and the physically deformed. Clear marking, as if for identification, seems to have been demanded. Liveries and class costumes were universal. The significance of colours in dress, of hatchments and insignia, made things easily recognizable. Indeed, we perhaps miss much of the political significance of Elizabethan plays because we have lost this form of communication. Gossip and slander were common and were not so easily controlled as in our time by the devices of concealment and privacy. There seems to have been a greater intimacy between master and servant than in the modern world. Did not people live in streets thick with beggars and noisy with cries and clanging bells? Such conditions would account for and render more realistic the sentimentalized publicity, the posing presented as the natural thing, that characterize Elizabethan drama. The world was full of signs which, like military commands, might institute prompt and appropriate actions.

If then one grants that along with vagueness and inconsistency in ideals, the result of confused thinking or of no thinking at all or of hasty generalization, there was in the Renaissance great clarity in individual

concepts, great proclivity for action, and an almost
universal doctrine of obedience to tenet, so that action
assumed the forms of individual impulse, mob violence, or bitter partisanship, one will find features
in the life of the time ready to initiate action. If the
mind of the age, collectively and individually, was like
a loaded cannon, there were plenty of things in the
age to touch it off. At a distance the age presents the
spectacle of a series of disasters and fulminations. Certainly this vividness of existence, these contrasts of
daily life, sudden joy and sorrow, hope and despair,
friendship and hatred, are part of the general temper
of the time, which was indeed a time of enduring
conflicts, fierce duels, impossible conspiracies, and sudden killings in the heat of passion. There was rage in
the general attitude towards torture and the punishment of malefactors. Faith in the spoken word even-
tuated in fiery oratory, and loud laughter was as easy
a resort as tears. All in all, it seems that life in Elizabethan England was, relatively to our own, more
hectic in religion, politics, the family, love, and friendship. This generalization is no doubt valid and will be
admitted, but, because the matter is important to us,
we should like to have more information, better authenticated. There are well authenticated stories of
what men did out of pure excitability under one
passion or another, such as that of Sir John Davies,[21]
who broke a cudgel over Richard Martin's head while
Martin was seated at the barristers' table in the hall
of the Middle Temple. No political motive would be
more readily understood than vengeance and personal
hatred. What are the records of feuds between families, how are they justified and interpreted, and what
forms did they take? We need information of this
character to serve as a background for understanding
and appreciating Elizabethan drama. What, one asks,

were the chief public dreads of the time and how intimately were they felt? The Turks? The Spaniards? The Papists? Or the outbreaks of the populace? What were the chief dreads of private life? The fear of Hell? The plague? Robbery and murder? Witchcraft? We know that all of these things were operative and that there was a widespread feeling of insecurity,—a superb background against which to throw a drama of love, like *Romeo and Juliet,* or of hate, like *The Revenger's Tragedy.*

To a world like this the renaissance of ancient culture had brought many ameliorating doctrines, together with a renewal of Christian hope and the beauty and satisfying power of Christian charity. It brought an attractive world of pagan things besides. The schools could point out the desirability of worldly power, the pleasure of a correctly regulated life in court or city, as well as military glory, self-realization, politeness, the enlightened practice of love and friendship, and the benefit and propriety of allegiance. Indeed, it must not be thought that the theory we have propounded with reference to the Elizabethan mind would be true except in a very general sense. It would be absurd to apply too rigidly such a doctrine to Bacon, Shakespeare, Hooker, and many other of the greater minds of the age. One would recall, too, with full consciousness of its importance the argumentative quality of Elizabethan discourse and point out that a custom of that sort carries with it a habit, not only of seeing two sides of every question, but of searching them out and exploiting them. One would merely claim that the practice of conceptual thinking and over-hasty action was strongly characteristic of ordinary Renaissance minds and that it was fostered by a widely held doctrine of obedience and respect for authority, and by a belief that the fulness of knowledge was in the past rather than in the future. One might claim, also, that the situation bred in the Elizabethans a habit of emancipating themselves from their complexes by the ready application of what were believed to be the maxims of immutable traditional and revealed truth.

If then the culture of the Elizabethan age was built on a foundation of still powerful mediævalism—formalism of thought, inability to originate ideas, multiplicity of aim, mechanistic linking of conception and action—and if the Elizabethan was a man whose nature propelled him to activity, what were the salutary and congenial patterns of action? Certainly Renaissance learning supplied many which stirred the ambition of the individual. In the literature of the upperclasses, and practically all Elizabethan literature is the literature of the upper-classes, satire, irony, and raillery are alleviating forces. Lyly does not take himself so very seriously, and there is a lightness of touch in Sidney and Spenser, reflective of More and Castiglione. There is much raillery in Shakespeare and Dekker and an approach to objectivity in Jonson. Satire awoke anew about the year 1600. The age took comfort in traditional culture and in action, to a greater degree than in reflection and investigation.

It will therefore be seen at a glance that the thesis that the Elizabethans were prevailingly conceptual rather than rational explains neatly both the creative tendency of the Elizabethans and their somewhat deficient critical power. Satire, although it appeared at the end of the sixteenth century, is not one of the greater contributions of the reign of Queen Elizabeth. Burlesque and parody on a grand scale, both of which rely on deliberate perception of incongruity (for example, between style and subject or between matter and manner), are special manifestations of the satiric spirit. They are in Shakespeare's Falstaff and Cervantes' Don Quixote; but they are not, generally speaking, forms in which the English Renaissance excels. Real sophistication and real cynicism would come with the influx of rationality. What we have called the conceptual habit of mind on the part of the Elizabethans seems also to tell us why the scientific spirit was developed *later* and to show us what enemies it had to encounter when it entered the field.

By and large, the world of Lyly, Sidney, Spenser, and Shakespeare was a progressive world in the matter of thought; but it was following a brave fashion of putting its best foot forward. Because the Elizabethans often forgot their troubles or because they bore them valiantly, it is not to be thought that they had no troubles. Indeed, one would like to question and possibly modify the accepted opinion that the English Renaissance was a period during which for once the *joie de vivre* was universal. One does not get that impression from the reading of Bacon's letters, the pamphleteers, or the minor authors in general. Was it the Puritans only who spoiled the paradise by insisting on the sadness and hopelessness of worldly life? By no means. The world stood condemned by the very highest court as well as by its own particular miseries; it could never have been proper to praise the world, nor do Elizabethan authors generally praise it. The optimism of the Renaissance has been exaggerated. The happiness of the time was strictly limited by time and class. A flood of pessimism overwhelms the literature of the reign of King James. The truth of the matter seems to be that, in the finer years of Queen Elizabeth, even when writers were conventionally professing disgust with the world and professing pleasure only in the contemplation of Heaven, they were really deceived by the new learning and the new prosperity and saw a golden age about to come upon them. It made them temporarily jubilant. The low casual tones seem to come from men who had difficulty in seeing hope in a world of so much danger and destitution and in forgetting even momentarily the weight of gloomy doctrine past and present. Theory was against a renaissance. Children were born in filth, disgrace, and sin. Destined to a life of misery, they were a trouble and a recurrent and inevitable disappointment to their parents. If children were deformed, their deformity was of soul as well as body. Old age, though its theory had collected a few bits from a more generous antiquity, was mainly misery, helplessness, and subjection to ridicule. Marriage had its theoretical as well as its practical ills, both much dwelt upon. It meant penury, drunkenness, scolding women, cuckoldry, the afflictions of pregnancy and childbirth, the sadness of widowhood, and the ingratitude of children. These things are part and parcel of the teachings of the age with reference to life on earth.

Immediately, a man's best chance would seem to lie in ignorance and non-participation; ultimately, in learning, applying, doubting, and rejecting. But that is the story of later centuries, after men had taken to heart Bacon's aphorism that man should be the servant and interpreter of nature. Our concern is with a people disposed to obey rather precipitantly and at any cost a vast body of ready-made statutes, which they did not and could not understand as we understand them.

CHAPTER IX

INTERPRETATIONS OF TIMES

> For all knowledge is either delivered by teachers, or
> attained by men's proper endeavours: and therefore as
> the principal part of tradition of knowledge concerneth
> chiefly writing of books, so the relative part thereof con-
> cerneth reading of books. Whereunto appertain incidently
> these considerations. The first is concerning the true cor-
> rection and edition of authors; wherein nevertheless rash
> diligence hath done great prejudice...
>
> The second is concerning the exposition and explica-
> tion of authors, which resteth in annotations and com-
> mentaries; wherein it is over usual to blanch the obscure
> places, and discourse upon the plain.
>
> The third is concerning the times, which in many cases
> give great light to true interpretations.
>
> The fourth is concerning some brief censure and judg-
> ment of the authors; that men thereby may make some
> election unto themselves what books to read.
>
> The fifth is concerning the syntax and disposition of
> studies; that men may know in what order or pursuit to
> read.—Bacon, *The Advancement of Learning*.

WE HAVE had the temerity to inquire into
the characteristic behaviour of the Elizabethan mind. It is, therefore, proper that we
should call attention to the difficulties which beset
those who would truly interpret Elizabethan literature, which is the expression of that mind.

Bacon and many other writers of the Renaissance
were keenly aware of the advancement [1] of their own
beyond other ages and had the same rather crude idea
of progress which today prevails. This idea of human
progress they stated, much as we do, in terms of
material progress. 'Oh, if you knew,' says Campanella,
'what our astrologers say of the coming age, and of

our age, that has in it more history within a hundred
years than all the world had in four thousand years
before! Of the wonderful invention of printing and
guns, and the use of the magnet, and how it all comes
of Mercury, Mars, the Moon, and the Scorpion!' The
distinctions drawn between various ages in the world's
history do not seem, however, to have proceeded far
beyond the distinction between better and worse.
Most qualitative differences among ages and peoples
remained unknown. We are much like the Elizabethans in this matter, with far less excuse. We too
have been born into an age whose importance to us
makes other ages inconsiderable. We have, moreover,
adopted widely the very questionable doctrine, that
the greatest literature is secure from the ravages of
time. The result of these two opinions is that we have
said to the writers of earlier times, 'We will listen to
you only in so far as you talk to us about ourselves
and will hear you only if you are able to divert us
from our preoccupations.' But not all of us are like
this, or completely so. The spirit of our age makes us
want the truth and gives fact significance to us, to
such a degree that we are seeing more and more
clearly what it was that the Elizabethan writers said
and perhaps are learning to care more for their meanings than for other meanings attached to their works
by persons who have read into them thoughts that
the Elizabethans never uttered or feelings which they
could never have entertained. One would not question
the right of every age—indeed it would be absurd to
do so—to re-read the classics, including Shakespeare,
anew in the light of the view of human existence
entertained in that age. Nevertheless, we may express
the belief that Shakespeare's meaning,[2] in so far as one
can recapture it, is the greatest of all meanings and
that, by thinking as far as possible as Shakespeare

thought and feeling as he felt, one may appreciate his work more truly, deeply, and profitably than by any other critical approach whatever.

Another circumstance which throws difficulty in the way of understanding the age of Queen Elizabeth is our own changing conception [3] of it. We can see that even a generation or two ago rather simple and romantic ideas about 'the spacious times of great Elizabeth' were customary, and we know that they linger on, infecting thought and opinion and preventing the truth as we see it from becoming manifest. The literature of the English Renaissance has tended to brighten the age with a false lustre. The chroniclers, particularly Harrison and Stow, and the religious controversialists, such as Foxe and Cartwright, must be used to correct the pictures drawn from poets and dramatists. Our picture of the English Renaissance shifts continually, and it does not make the matter simpler to realize that what the Renaissance thought of itself was a similarly shifting thing.

Yet in one respect the Elizabethans were more stable than we are, undesirably stable, in that the writers of the age seem to have been almost completely anachronistic, whereas we have a stronger perception of historical perspective. They felt fewer differences than we do between Roman times and the modern world. They accepted the Romans almost as brothers and frankly pictured them in terms of Elizabethan life. They were not alone in this. The ancients and the men of the Middle Ages had done the same thing. Plutarch himself had made, so far as externals and issues were concerned, no allowance for a difference in time between Coriolanus and Julius Cæsar, and Shakespeare is not to be blamed for receiving them both on equal terms into his own age. The Elizabethans made friends with the ancients and amplified

their own society by admitting to it on equal terms
the great men of old. Indeed, the literary intelligence
of the Elizabethans is largely due to their hospitality.
Of course associations of literary and otherwise cultivated persons in the court, the Inns of Court, the
universities, and elsewhere must have served in some
measure to disseminate classical culture and give
it currency. The actual ideas in Lyly's and Shakespeare's comedies seem to presuppose much familiarity
with literary thought in the minds of audiences. As
has been said, literary ideas were also moral, but the
English Renaissance took its moralistic instruction
in a gay fashion and relatively without asceticism; if
its æsthetic was moral, its morality was also in some
measure æsthetic. It was slow to believe that beauty
was condemned by religion. Even in their moralistic
fashion of thinking the men of the time did something
to ennoble beauty. They understood and approved the
Greek idea of all-round development for the individual and admired physical perfection, dress, dignities, and personal accomplishments. They admired
leisure, wealth, courtesy, beauty, frankness, wit,
gaiety, and ceremony; and they espoused in their politics the institutions which gave security to these
things. Amusements and diversions were provided for
and sanctioned in all books of education. No doubt
the teachings of Plato, Aristotle, and the Stoics reinforced in England, as in Italy, these characteristic
Renaissance ideals, for the task of comprehending and
absorbing ancient culture was relatively easy in an
age when popularization had proceeded so far.

Nevertheless, the classicism of the Renaissance is a
very mixed thing. The learning of antiquity did not
supplant but blended with mediæval learning. The
classics supplied forms, interpretations, and ultimately
materials,—materials, however, which had often been

mediævalized, sometimes debased, before they were used. And yet they seemed to the Renaissance precisely as 'classical' as if they were fresh from the pages of an ancient. Perhaps there was no current idea of the original and the derived versions of a story. To treat Shakespeare's *Troilus and Cressida* as if he had had a free choice in narrating the events and depicting the characters of the story and might if he chose have given it a Homeric atmosphere is to forget Lydgate and Caxton and all that had been done to the Troy legend. Greek romance, written by the dispersed and Latinized Greeks of the Roman Empire, was to the Elizabethans precisely as Greek as Herodotus or Euripides. In point of fact, this degenerate romance suited Elizabethan taste rather better than greater earlier Greek literature. Petrarch himself wrote on mediæval subjects, as did most authors of the Renaissance. It follows that humanism is not so much theme or story as form and style. In order to write like a humanist the thing needed was proficiency in the use of mythology and ancient history and philosophy. There are speeches in the manner of Livy in the works of Renaissance historians, even of English chroniclers. These appeared no doubt as mere imitations, but they served to dignify history and to restore the noble Aristotelian idea of rhetoric as the instrument for persuasion. Of course genuine contributions from classicism continued to make their way into common use as important direct influences in even the later Renaissance. Humanism did not die out. Along with pseudo-classic trash, such as that which clings to dedications and addresses, the greatness of ancient literature continued to instruct the Renaissance. This is perhaps particularly true in England, where the classics were slow in operating, for the English seem to have kept for generations, along with truer ones, the mediæval

conceptions of the ancient world. There was, however, a genuine revival of interest in the classics in the
time of Spenser and Shakespeare. It must be remembered also that in England we have to do not only
with an imperfect and mixed classicism but mainly
with a Latin classicism. Such classical culture as the
English Renaissance had and could understand was,
relative to mediæval culture, simple and exact in conception, easy and natural in thought. The English
Renaissance was, moreover, interested in classical depictions of men and the ways of men. In this connexion one thinks of the bright pages of Virgil, Ovid,
Seneca, and Cicero as those which exercised the greatest degree of direct influence. The period of the
assimilation of the classics, lasting well through the
sixteenth century, was in England, to some extent, a
period of awkwardness. The superficial was mistaken
for the essential, for the English were not good scholars. In the study of the classicism of the Renaissance
what we need to know is the ancient authors, not in
their purified modern forms with archeological and
textual addenda, but these authors, plus their *spuria*,[4]
as printed and glossed in the sixteenth century and
particularly as translated in the careless, anachronistic
way of Elizabethan translators.[5]

In seeking to determine essential differences between literature in our own time and that of the
Renaissance, one is at once confronted with the bar-
rier to one's appreciation offered by the greater hospitality of that age to practical, scientific, and moral
subjects[6] for literary treatment. Gabriel Harvey presents the point of view of the connexion between
science, particularly cosmography, and the poets in
a series of extraordinary marginal notes:

Other commend Chawcer, & Lidgate for their witt,
pleasant veine, varietie of poetical discourse, & all

humanitie: I specially note their Astronomie, philosophie, & other parts of profound or cunning art. Wherein few of their time were more exactly learned. It is not sufficient for poets, to be superficial humanists: but they must be exquisite artists, & curious vniuersal schollers.

M. Digges hath the whole Aquarius of Palingenius bie hart: & takes mutch delight to repeate it often.

M. Spenser conceiues the like pleasure in the fourth day of the first Weeke of Bartas. Which he esteemes as the proper profession of Urania.

Axiophilus makes the like account of the Columnes, and the Colonies of Bartas. Which he commonly addes to the Spheare of Buchanan. Diuine, & heroicall works: and excellent Cantiques for a mathematicall witt.

Excellent Doctor Gesner made as singular account of the most learned Zodiacus of Palingenius Stellatus, as owre worthie Mr. Thomas Digges. Who esteemes him aboove all moderne poets, for a pregnant introduction to Astronomie, & both philosophies. With a fine touch of the philosophers stone itself. the quintessence of nature, & art sublimed.

After further praise of the poets for their astronomical lore, Harvey adds this sorrowful statement: 'Pudet ipsum Spenserum, etsi Sphæræ, astrolabijque non plane ignarum; suae in astronomici Canonibus, tabulis, instrumentisque imperitiae.'

But, as an offset to this prosaic conception, there is the strong and doctrinal sense of form possessed by Renaissance thinkers. Elizabethan authors are generally able to give to underlying ideas an adequate form, however inferior to classical models. The poets of the age of Elizabeth seem to have comprehended a relation between content and purpose, on the one hand, and form, on the other. They made themselves clear on the subject in hundreds of places. Jonson says, for example, in *Timber*,'

Poesis et pictura.—Poetry and picture are arts of a like nature, and both are busy about imitation. It was excellently said of Plutarch, poetry was a speaking picture, and picture a mute poesy. For they both invent, feign, and devise many things, and accommodate all they invent to the use and service of Nature. Yet of the two the pen is the more noble than the pencil; for that can speak to the understanding, the other but to the sense. They both behold pleasure and profit as their common object; but should abstain from all base pleasures, lest they should err from their end, and, while they seek to better men's minds, destroy their manners. They both are born artificers, not made. Nature is more powerful in them than study.

A neglected passage of even greater significance is the conversation between the Poet and the Painter[8] in *Timon of Athens:*

Poet. Our poesy is as a gum, which oozes
From whence 'tis nourish'd: the fire i'the flint
Shows not till it be struck; our gentle flame
Provokes itself and like the current flies
Each bound it chafes. What have you there?
    Painter. A picture, sir. When comes your book forth?
    Poet. Upon the heels of my presentment, sir.
Let's see your piece.
    Painter.   'Tis a good piece.
    Poet. So 'tis: this comes off well and excellent.
    Painter. Indifferent.
    Poet. Admirable: how this grace
Speaks his own standing! what a mental power
This eye shoots forth! how big imagination
Moves in this lip! to the dumbness of the gesture
One might interpret.
    Painter. It is a pretty mocking of the life.
Here is a touch: is't good?
    Poet.   I will say of it,
It tutors nature: artificial strife
Lives in these touches, livelier than life.

There is evidence of intelligence about the principles of art in these passages. We may take it for
granted that modes of expression in arts of all kinds
are defining agents in the study of the Renaissance;
also that, in the conception of the age, literature is
about life and that as a whole literature was expected
to speak truth about life. But in so far as literary art
is conventional it is not a very reliable record of life,
unless we understand the conventions which it sets
up for its procedure and allow for them in our own
conclusions. We need, therefore, to know something
about the conventions of literature in order to judge
how much we must qualify our interpretation of it
as a revelation of Renaissance thought. The subject
of literary convention in its relation to the interpretation of literature has been long neglected and is not
yet set in order. Criticism as applied to the Elizabethans has usually looked at them as if they were
contemporary with itself and has even now not fully
admitted in theory that we may if we will, and if our
minds are sufficiently well-informed, sympathetic and
flexible, in some measure defy time and bring to life
literary enjoyments long deceased. After all, Hamlet's players were the 'abstract and brief chronicles of
the time.' Criticism has said that literature must stand
the test of time as if it were a blessing and not a calamity that time should be the victor.

We know much about literary art, particularly
dramatic art, in the Renaissance in England, less about
the other arts; if other arts were studied along with
literature, we should find the same principles applying
to the heightening of appreciation and the revelation
of the Renaissance mind. To what extent, one asks,
was art still closely connected with ordinary life and
subservient to its uses, there being no hard and fast
line between fine art and utilitarian art? It is ordi-

narily thought that a taste for art for its own sake
awoke first in the Renaissance, but in what ways or
to what extent is not known. Costume was probably
less barbaric than it had been, though still far more
ornate, symbolic, and conventionally expressive than
anything in the modern world. The baroque was in-
truding on the merely ornamental, and art was probably being used in costume and elsewhere to make life
splendid rather than individual or beautiful. One
would like to enter some extremely conservative circle
and ask, for example, the extent to which funeral
effigies were still used and what their current forms
were; or enter some traditional area and learn more
about the vitality of folk festivals and what their nov-
elties were. There is no doubt that conventions in art
were breaking down in favour of a franker individual-
ism of expression, but just how far this had proceeded,
for example during Shakespeare's busy years from
1595 to 1602, is not known, nor what were the points
and occasions of attack. We do not know the extent
to which Elizabethan art was conventional rather than
freely inventive. No doubt its freedom was greater
when it was serving courtly circles than the common
people. The conventions of literary art are our chief
concern, but light might come from a knowledge of
all the arts. The impression that literature was relatively freer from traditional forms and practices than
were other forms of art, may be due rather to our
blindness than to the absence of conventional forms.

Our chief concern in our search for truth in literary interpretation is with the extent to which we are
to take seriously means of expression definitely literary. For example, nothing gives more trouble than the
relation between the actual in Elizabethan social life
and the various amatory and other conventions [9] of
literature. Elizabethan literature is full to overflowing

with the clap-trap of social convention in courtship, love, and marriage—colours, dress, *demandes d'amour*, courtly casuistry, love psychology, and the ideals of natural honour. Rabelais laughed at many of these things. Shakespeare laughs too at 'the numbers that Petrarch flowed in,' though he knows these amatory forms and uses them often significantly. It is hard to believe that even so conventional a form as the sonnet[10] has not much serious importance in the expression of individual feeling. It is also hard to penetrate below the surface and ascertain what poets and dramatists regarded as truth about the courtships and marriages they present for our consideration. Whether a woman should marry with one she loved or permit her hand to be disposed of by her parents was a lively enough issue to bring the subject prominently into Elizabethan drama. Vives and all those who write on ethics for women[11] are emphatic in their belief that the woman should submit her will to her parents. Ascham, not a narrow thinker, is convinced that she should. The arguments are all against liberty of choice, and a passage from the Old Testament[12] declaring that a virgin may be absolved from a vow made without her father's permission is often quoted. Was it, one asks, an open question with Shakespeare, or are Juliet and Desdemona possibly guilty of tragic fault in marrying against their fathers' will? Certainly Jessica pays no penalty, but in that case the father is an unbeliever and for Jessica to marry a Christian was to achieve salvation. It may be that the elements in the various conceptions of love one finds in Elizabethan literature are mixed. There are traces of the ideal of chivalry[13] and extensive appearances of the doctrines of the *Romance of the Rose* and of courtly love. There are also native and classical elements, less self-conscious and more spontaneous. Per-

haps the stories of Hero and Leander and even of
Romeo and Juliet have no meaning except the simple
one that successful love is happiness and unsuccessful
love mere tragedy. An unlovely native element in the
jig, the lewd jest, the indecent publicity of the marriage bed, and even of lyings-in, is close at hand,
although the new culture of the Renaissance undoubtedly felt the need, as all cultures must, of shrouding
in form and ceremony the manifestations of sexual
love; even courtship must be something besides itself.
As regards these refinements in the relations of the
sexes we are mainly concerned with Platonism, which
ran strongly through the age from Hoby's translation
of *The Courtier* to the end of the period. The natural
way in which Shakespeare embodies the theory ,of
Platonic love [14] in *The Merchant of Venice, Twelfth
Night*, and other plays, the popularity of Spenser and
Sidney, both avowed Platonists, and the frequency
with which Platonic love is alluded to and praised
give one the impression that the doctrine was taken
very much to heart. Finally, there is the doctrine of
female honour, traditional and vastly reinforced by
religious teachings based on the early fathers of the
Church, such as St. Augustine, St. Ambrose, and St.
Jerome, which lies at the root of plays like *A Woman
Killed with Kindness, The Honest Whore*, Part II,
and *Measure for Measure*, a doctrine supported by the
elemental theory of woman's nature. It is, nevertheless, surprising how much of the compendious material
on the subject of love from the *Romance of the Rose*
and its successors is to be found in Shakespeare's pages.
The Elizabethan nobility was, moreover, so well up
on the *ars amandi* that one wonders how much sincerity is to be attributed to the attitudinizing of
Lyly's and Sidney's heroes.

Let us illustrate the intrusion of conventionality

from another field. The art of writing history was
taught the English in a practical way by Polydore
Vergil.[15] He saw the disorder of the English chronicles and the necessity of resorting to documentary
verification. But he believed in something more. He
believed in making history tell a story and conform to
certain Greek and Roman and Renaissance conceptions of political life and its leaders. To do this he
found it necessary not only to verify traditional history, but to shape it to an end, to subject it to the
processes of selection with proper attention to the
principles of emphasis and subordination. In this kind
of history writing one's own best political and philosophic conceptions become the purposes of God, and
one proceeds to make them stand out in the medley
of human events. Plutarch had reshaped, actually
paired off according to fancied resemblance, his subjects in his *Lives of the Noble Grecians and Romans*.
The conceptions of Greek tragedy as to the lives and
fates of heroes were part and parcel of ancient thought
about public life, and Plutarch made his heroes conform to this definite pattern. The Greek conception
of the lives of the great served as a way of organizing
life, which the Renaissance eagerly adopted, not only
in its tragedy and its 'Mirrors for magistrates,' but in
its writing of history. Polydore Vergil, in the interest
of his own views as humanist and in the interest of the
Tudor kings, who favoured the Lancastrians, forced
this world of ancient ideas about life down upon English history. Polydore's conception of the significance
of history was adopted by subsequent Elizabethan
chroniclers, who were not, however, willing to forego,
as the Italian was, Brute and his British progeny. The
resulting interpretation of English history is popularly
felt to this day, a situation which comes about mainly
through Shakespeare, who gave eternal currency to

Polydore Vergil's figments. The point is that fact is something or nothing in literature, but that what Shakespeare regarded as fact (and truth) is a matter of importance. One would not, however, depreciate too much the conceptions of Renaissance historians, which were certainly a great improvement on anything the world had then and have persisted for centuries.

There are also difficulties in the way of a correct interpretation of the literature of the Renaissance which arise from the Elizabethan conception of the literary art. One is confronted in Elizabethan literature by a surprising lack of individualized criticism.[16] The habit of expressing personal impressions had not yet been formed and its technique was unknown, though occasional highly prized bits, like Sidney's confession of his liking for the old song of Percy and Douglas, are indeed to be met with. When the English found it necessary to write critically, as they did in their defences of poetry, they resorted, not to individual impressions or observations or to philosophy, but to the ready-made criticism of the Italians, itself a cento of the utterances of classical masters. Beyond that there was no technology of criticism, no language in which to express appreciation, perhaps no conception of literary art as such. There are many exceptions,[17] some of which have been noted above. Art itself was possibly only a thing, or a part of a thing, at best a manifestation of the logical formal cause. When Michael Angelo[18] criticized Flemish painting on the ground that it lost itself in details and appealed to crude people by subject-matter only, he was really striking at the principle of multiplicity in art in behalf of the principle of unity. He is really recommending a supersession of the principle of multiplicity by the principle of unity, substituting one kind of art for another. Michael Angelo also sees that uncultivated popular taste always misses the larger unities and interests itself in detail or, as we say, in the sensational. It is not in Flemish painting and tapestry only that one finds the mediæval insistence on exactness of detail, a sort of careful prolixity, coupled with an obliviousness to considerations of time, place, and relative importance. Elizabethan dramatists did not disregard the principle of the three unities so much because they did not know them as because they knew another kind of art. Elizabethan dramatists and storytellers are genuinely vague about time and place and about what are the more important actions in a group of actions. They were in point of fact slowly surrendering, under classical and Italian influence, the habit and technique of multiplicity in art in favour of the principles of unity. One wonders to what extent the dramatists learned the new art by experience and as an accident of subject rather than from theory, as they might have done from the hectoring Aristotelians. May it not be that certain subjects, such as that of Faustus or Romeo and Juliet, compelled a unity in their very telling and thus taught as a practical principle the unity they had thrust upon the drama?

This makes it inevitable that one should ask why the Renaissance did not or could not invent plots.[19] The answer is that, since there was so much material new to the audience, the idea of plot-making had not yet come to them. The requirement that the fiction-maker shall be able to invent plots is a new one. The writers of Shakespeare's time had not yet felt the necessity of inventing plots. Shakespeare goes as far as any of them, and yet he usually contents himself with reshaping imaginatively old plots. Throughout the sixteenth century men of learning, in science and philosophy as well as literature, engaged themselves in reshaping, amplifying, explaining, and rendering available older learning; and their riches were such that they performed their tasks in a joyous way as if they did not dream that what they had was less than the sum total. The situation with reference to old subjects in fiction and the drama is merely that which prevailed throughout. There were new ideas in the age, but most activity went into the retouching of old ideas.

So it is also perhaps with reference to characterization in fiction and the drama. Authors inherited a group of persons from ancient literature and history. To these still other persons had been added from more recent literature and history. Both groups they accepted factually. They had besides certain purely fictional characters, mainly types, traditional or borrowed. Other characters, probably factually regarded, came with the stories freely supplied from France and Italy. All of these the dramatists were at liberty to reinterpret and amplify. In this rehandling Shakespeare advances into the realm of creation, and yet the more or less accidental and factual element enters into some of Shakespeare's greatest creations. Falstaff is an evolution, —Sir John Oldcastle, a slandered Lollard, put down in Eastcheap and set talking. Shylock is not merely the usurious Jew of *Il Pecorone;* he has been amplified with the agonies of Lopez. So far as Richard III is concerned, he is merely Sir Thomas More's egregious villain made vocal. Of course, Benedick and Beatrice, Dogberry, Sir Toby, Iago, Othello and others are so far from any known source that one grants to Shakespeare an unasked-for independence. But one sees no evidence in the field of knowledge of the art of characterization as it is known in modern criticism. The art of characterization, as distinguished from simple biographical narrative, was there, but often not as a conscious factor. Indeed, the conception of human character as set down in formal psychology, and often evident in literature, taught instability in the natures of men, taught that there was no such thing as consistency of character, except in so far as it might result from 'complexion' or be super-induced by training. This circumstance seems to indicate that there are limits to be placed on our applications to the Elizabethan drama of an Aristotelian technique or to the criticism of Elizabethan literature of a modern technique of prose fiction.

It can be proved, however, that faculty psychology was consciously applied to the problem of characterization. Let us take the case of Webster's *The Duchess of Malfy*.

There is scarcely a trace of psychological characterization in the tale in Painter's *Palace of Pleasure*. As Painter tells it, it is a story of some great people who underwent misfortunes, committed crimes, and fell from their high estate. The Duchess is blamed for everything. Being a woman, she was sensual and wanted a husband; in marrying without the consent of her brothers she sinned in not maintaining the dignity of her rank. In the source Antonio is a praiseworthy enough figure to begin with, but is corrupted by love and ambition. Webster has seen in the Duchess the possibility of a more complex character. Her situation is one in which the choice of tragic deed is intelligible and human. But for our purposes the significant thing is that Webster, in order to achieve his purpose, has had to create all the characters. The original author of the tale and the Elizabethans in Painter's day did not conceive of character as Webster did; they had not yet learned how. They had not realized the implications of a philosophy which taught that everyone is liable to succumb to the onslaught of the passions. Webster shows us that he had learned this thing. In the case before us the effect of it was to make psychology a chief means in the literary art of characterization. Webster changes the story, though he sometimes makes the mistake of following Painter too closely; but he is no longer merely telling a story by means of the stage, an earlier phase in the history of drama. Webster sought to give the characters life and to interpret them credibly from the point of view of what was known and taught about the human heart and mind and soul. The characters form a series of psychological studies; not so mechanically labelled as in Chapman, but marked sufficiently to betray Webster's purpose to any honest mind. Character as character simply does not exist in Painter. In Webster a developed attitude is seen, his people being interpreted fully according to certain psychological doctrines. There is room in that psychology for alterations of character so abrupt that they do not seem to us plausible; but, all in all, the gain is enormous. One is tempted to draw other illustrations of this use of psychology and its concomitant ethics from Webster, Tourneur, Beaumont and Fletcher and others, for they all reveal the stage of conscious art just described. Possibly also one must recognize that, whether consciously or unconsciously, the art of characterization in Elizabethan drama was promoted by the controversial qualities of the age, its love of contrast, and its habit of seeing two sides to every question. These qualities would have tended to sharpen Elizabethan minds for the perception of issues.

Literary results are not always greatly affected, or literary practice, by a conscious technique of art; but the solution of our problem demands that we should make it clear that the Renaissance had not fully discovered itself, and, as we have seen, had no adequate criticism. Art was very seldom considered on purely æsthetic grounds, so that there are only faint traces of what must have been, then as now, a universal moving fact, namely, that pleasure in literature is taken for granted. Sidney in the *Apologie* and Spenser in the letter to Ralegh prefixed to the *Faerie Queene* say in effect that the story of a noble person gives more pleasure than a book of moral philosophy and is therefore more effective. More effective for what? For the teaching of morals. The element of æsthetic pleasure is recognized but is not conceived of apart from morals. The basis of Sidney's comparison is the assumption that literature must teach morals, and his work of criticism becomes the discovery of the relative moral effectiveness of history, philosophy, and poetry. But pleasure was concomitant to morals, and Sidney seems to have been keenly appreciative of Chaucer, Spenser, Sackville, and others. His rational processes take little account of the artistic aspect of his responses. Again, his feeling is right when he points out the absurdities of the rambling episodic plays which he had witnessed on the popular stage; but his reason is a mere mechanical acceptance of the doctrine of the unities, that the events of so many years and of so many places could not be imagined as having taken place within two hours on the narrow confines of a stage. In the history of Shakespearean criticism [20] one sees that one hundred and fifty years passed before critics and interpreters freely admitted that Shakespeare in spite of his faults did actually give pleasure to his readers and auditors. We must realize that doctrines *qua* doctrines do not operate in the world until they have been worked out and stated, although the facts on which they are based may long have been in existence.

The controversy over the stage may be recalled

here. The objections of the Puritans—Gosson, Stubbes, Prynne—are entirely on moral and religious grounds; and the defenders of the stage—Lodge and the others —meet the attack on the same level and consequently have a hard time of it. The defenders say over and over again that the deeds of evil-doers have to be displayed as a warning to all who would do evil. The strange thing is that a great part of the Elizabethan drama in its actual structure and content betrays only slight intention on the part of its authors to teach moral lessons. Perhaps no accepted way of embodying morals had yet been worked out. There is of course, particularly in the earlier plays, a large element of didacticism, usually merely overlaying a story interesting in and for itself. However free dramatists were to tell stories for the joy of telling them (as in *Tamburlaine*), no evidence that we possess shows any critical friend of the drama willing to let that artistic activity speak for itself when justification was called for. We get little bits of superimposed moralizing on situations which strike us as false because the author suddenly twists his story round in order to introduce the proper moral touch. Alice Arden's piety is much in evidence as she is about to be hanged, and the file of prostitutes in *The Honest Whore*, Part II, are soundly rebuked. In other words, in literature as in life, the Elizabethans habitually mistook the moralistic for the moral.

The mind of the Renaissance seems simply not to have moved into the realm of æsthetics; it has discovered a liberal type of formalized ethics, and this it has made do service to art as well as to the conduct of life. The suggestion may be hazarded that this is not unnatural. It takes immature thinkers to this day much longer to become articulate about æsthetics than about ethics; for in matters of taste formulæ, easily grasped and applied, will not serve. For one to become discriminative about similarities and differences in the realm of emotional shades and of form imposed by language, one has first to become sensitive enough and intelligent enough to perceive them; and then, even a more difficult thing, one must gain an awareness of self in relation to emotional effect.

In saying that Renaissance poets, such as Shakespeare and Spenser, lacked a theory of response to beauty in art it is not implied that they lacked either a knowledge of art or an interest in beauty. It is obvious that both Shakespeare and Spenser knew the principles not only of the art they practised but of painting and music as well. Professor Manly has said [21] that Shakespeare's description of the Siege of Troy in *The Rape of Lucrece* suggests 'the attitude of one who knew the feeling of the brush in his hand'; he adds this significant comment: 'This is far from saying that Shakespeare was an artist or ever had any technical training; but it is in keeping with the fact—especially characteristic of the Renaissance—that a richly endowed nature often finds expression through all the kindred arts of music, poetry, and painting.' No age ever had a greater passion for beauty than had the Renaissance, and no age without a passion for beauty could have created so much beauty. The Elizabethans felt as yet slight need to question ancient tenets, then universally accepted, as to the uses of poetry. They had neither the weariness with the ordinary that made the seventeenth century resort to extravagance nor the overgrown intellectualism which made a still later time resort to critical theory. It may also be said that in the glass of the universal into which they looked there was slight need for a divorce between ethics and æsthetics.

There is no doubt as to the moral purpose of Tudor drama, except possibly *Tamburlaine* and a few other plays, but it is hardly such a moral purpose as we should entertain. It differs in this, that the moral is part of the structure of all formal thinking, but is rarely recognized as moral except when it is an addendum, that is, a formal precept or exemplum.

Gorboduc, Damon and Pithias, Selimus, The Misfortunes of Arthur, and scores of other plays have the tone and purpose of *The Mirror for Magistrates.* People must be taught how to behave according to ethical patterns. Particularly, kings and their counsellors must know how to conduct a well-ordered state. Instruction by example was the favourite method of instruction, preferable, according to Sidney and Spenser, to instruction by precept. Both laudable and execrable examples are to be shown, all examples being accompanied by enough treatise-like comment to make them and their places in the moral system intelligible. The result is that characters in the early tragedies often seem to be merely mouth-pieces for sentiment. Ethical purposes are revealed, and human behaviour is condemned or justified in formal ethical terms. Marlowe [22] exhibits a good deal of formal psychological and ethical knowledge but takes the first step forward, in that his plays make a definite use of the principle of individuality. Some of his figures are, however, constructed much to pattern. One of the ways in which Elizabethan drama became more realistic and convincing was in outgrowing didactic formalism. The same natural, mental, and moral philosophy lies behind the actions of later as of earlier characters, and the terminology remains; but the best plays at least are genuine human documents. To interpret the actions of human beings through the medium of a familiar learned terminology and to allocate them in a familiar ethical system of philosophy is a different thing from thinking about the system and its

ideals first and then constructing the characters to fit
the principles. This, it may be said, the later Elizabethans rarely if ever did.

The moral significance grows in intensity and am-
plitude with Elizabethan drama. The play of *Macbeth*
echoes and trembles with fears, mostly natural fears,
fears of conscience and damnation, punishment and
retribution. His fears humanize Macbeth; they are
usually the fears of a good and even a great man. One
could select many passages from the moral treatises
of the day which explain ethically and psychologically
the situation Shakespeare sought to depict in *Macbeth*.
An illustration from the play can be found for almost
every phrase of La Primaudaye's [23] account of fear,
which is here quoted in abridged form: Cowards, he
says, are not only afraid 'of men, of the hazards of
warres, of troubles & seditions, . . . of the losse of their
goods, of diseases, of dolors, yea, of the least discom-
modities and aduersities that can befall men: the euent
of all which, causeth them vsually to forget all reason
and dutie, but they are also frighted with dreames,
they tremble at sights and visions, they credite false
abusing spirits, and with a forlorne feare they stand in
awe of the celestiall signes. Briefly, upon the least occasions that may be, and such as are unwoorthie the
care of a prudent and valiant mind, they fall oftentimes into such vexation of spirite, that they loose it
altogither, and become mad and inraged. . . [they] flie
from temporall death as much as may be, as also
from griefe, which they feare in such sort, that com-
temning all vertue and iustice, they labour for nothing
more, than to preserue their liues togither with their
carnall commodities. . . I might here mention sundry
vices, which . . . are nourished of cowardlines and pusil-
lanimitie, as namely, crueltie, treason, breach of prom-

ise,   impatience,... idlenesse,   slouth,   couetousnes, enuie, backbiting, and all iniustice.'

We might use this example to elucidate one aspect of the criticism of Elizabethan literature, neglected until recently, which lays claim to great importance in the appreciation of the literature of the age. This aspect is the 'metaphysical' or psychological obsession of, particularly, the later Elizabethans. The psychology held by the Elizabethans was a confused and inconsistent congeries of many beliefs, in which doctrines of many ages jostled each other indiscriminately. The subject was completely familiar to educated persons and had become an inevitable way of feeling and describing mental situations. It seems probable that, after its popular revival toward the end of the sixteenth century, psychology was used functionally by the principal writers of the English Renaissance, and that, largely under the influence of Stoical writers, there arose in the latest period a very dominant philosophy of life which permeates a great deal of the most important literature of that period. If these things are true, namely, that poets and dramatists used their knowledge of current psychology and ethics for essential parts of their literary art, as material or as instrument, then this philosophy, though often erroneous, becomes something more than a mere subject of curious interest. If to the writers of the earlier years of the seventeenth century, life became, under stress of domineering psychological and ethical doctrines, a new type of force, one would expect literary emphasis on those characteristics of the mind of man which have to do with the outward movement of the faculties—with appetite, desire, the passions, and the will; for from these things have always been derived human achievement and human tragedy. One does find in the dramatists an appropriate mode of treating the problem of conduct.

The application of Shakespeare's own ethics and psychology to his greater studies of character [24] is most illuminating. His tragic heroes yield to passion, their reason is dethroned, and they are caught in the toils of disaster. Coriolanus falls through pride, Antony through the infatuation of love, Othello through jealousy, Lear through anger, Macbeth through ambition. Coriolanus sins against his country and the woman who had borne him; Antony betrays his wisdom and his soldiership; Othello takes vengeance into his own hands and slays his innocent love; Lear wrecks a kingdom; Macbeth suffers the agonies of a guilty conscience and becomes an embodiment of fear. Various psychological constitutions have been given Hamlet. Interesting and significant as these determinations are, we ought not to accept any one of them as a complete solution. To do so would necessitate our believing that Shakespeare consciously constructed his dramas around certain predetermined principles. It is impossible to believe that he did this. The compulsion of the profounder psychological, ethical, and religious ideas of the age affected Shakespeare in writing the plays and assisted him to write them. These ideas also helped the spectators to understand and appreciate them. We must believe that to Shakespeare psychology, ethics, and religion furnished a way of thinking and talking about people. His characters are representations of people; there are no definite explanatory solutions and interpretations to be discovered and uttered; to put it in the words of Mr. T. S. Eliot: [25]

> *Qua* work of art, the work of art cannot be interpreted; there is nothing to interpret; we can only criticize it according to standards, in comparison to other works of art; and for 'interpretation' the chief task is the

presentation of relevant historical fact which the reader is not assumed to know.

If Shakespeare wrote under the restraints of a conscious theory, his freedom would depend in some measure on the extent to which the learning he seems to display was common property; and, if one judges by the extensive reflection of philosophic knowledge in all kinds of literature in the age, it was common knowledge. But the idea that he did so is refuted by his universality. To find a solution in one aspect, however illuminating, is to overstress that element. Mr. Eliot would say that the work of art as such is directly apprehended. The process is certainly more nearly akin to synthesis than to analysis. Innumerable things, all the experiences of a lifetime, went into the making of Shakespeare's plays. His art is the expression of his comprehension of life as well as his experience as a living man, and to seize by abstraction on certain formal features of his philosophy, a philosophy very general in his time and not absent from ours, and to make these abstractions the explanations of his plays is to render the plays smaller than they are and less true.

It is obvious that the group of doctrines relating to man's intellectual and moral nature and based upon man's supposed position in the material and spiritual universe had wide currency in the early years of the seventeenth century. One effect of these doctrines was to destroy mediævalism, another to corrupt the Renaissance. Let us consider this in connection with Ben Jonson and his school. Jonson's culture was largely acquired by his own reading and study, not from the university. He had possibly a greater respect for school learning as such than he might have had if he had spent his four or seven years at Oxford or Cambridge. His interest is literary, and yet he knows all three philosophies. It comes about, however, that his learning is less formal than that of many of his learned contemporaries. It is derived from an extensive group of authors and is critical rather than didactic. His *Conversations with Drummond* reveal a wide range of reading both ancient and contemporary. It is significant that he put Donne at the head of all poets and that he seems to have approved of Chapman. Both of these men were more ingenious in the use of what they knew than was Jonson himself, and yet his mind ran towards what Dr. Samuel Johnson called 'metaphysical' poetry. The term 'metaphysical' for the poetry of the school of Jonson and Donne is not always understood, or rather the reason it was applied to this particular group of poets is not understood. 'Metaphysics' did not mean ontology and epistemology only; but, because of the vague states of these sciences, it was a wide term for the trans-natural. It was very generally applied to what we should call psychology. The soul of man was outside of nature, and what dealt with the soul, and with the instruments of the soul, was 'metaphysical.' Jonson, Chapman, and Donne were poets of mind, mental life, the spirits of life, indeed of that great branch of psychological and theological learning which was called rational philosophy. It is the exploitation of that realm which, becoming a fashion, gave us, one may say roughly, the characteristic qualities of Jacobean lyric and dramatic poetry.

In the following passages Jonson [26] seems to be thinking about this region as if it were a land to be explored:

Ingeniorum discrimina. . . . There are no fewer forms of minds than of bodies amongst us. The variety is incredible, and therefore we must search. Some are fit to make divines, some poets, some lawyers, some physicians; some to be sent to the plough and trades. There is no doctrine will do good where nature is wanting. Some wits are swelling and high; others low and still: some hot and fiery; others cold and dull; one must have a bridle, the other a spur.

Scientia. Knowledge is the action of the soul, and is perfect without the senses, as having the seeds of all science and virtue in itself; but not without the service of the senses; by those organs the soul works: she is a perpetual agent, prompt and subtle: but often flexible, and erring, intangling herself like a silkworm, but her reason is a weapon with two edges, and cuts through. In her indogations oft-times new scents put by her, and she takes in errors into her by the same conduits she doth truths.

In order then to synthesize in accordance with truth our findings in Elizabethan literature we should seek to become aware of differences between our own age, which is our standard of judgment, and the age of Elizabeth. But in estimating the prevailing trends of that age we should not give undue weight to special findings in special fields, but rather strive for a realization of the fact that we are dealing with reflections of all human life lived under different conditions.

Bacon saw that the 'times' might 'in many cases give great light to true interpretations.' He does not explain how this is to come about. It is obvious that 'true interpretations' of so great an age as that of Queen Elizabeth are most desirable; also that the age has already grown remote. We have discussed, as well as we could from the Elizabethan point of view and from ours, many of the obscurities and difficulties of true interpretations. We closed with the latest and possibly the most perplexing aspect that the age assumed. Perhaps this subject as discussed is what Bacon meant by interpretation of times.

CHAPTER X

DISCLOSING AND EXPOUNDING OF MEN

But the soundest disclosing and expounding of men is by their natures and ends; wherein the weakest sort of men are best interpreted by their natures, and the wisest by their ends.—Bacon, *The Advancement of Learning.*

WHAT do we, when speaking of literature, mean by background? It must be something which we perceive with our minds and feel with our emotions as a living part of the literature of the past. It cannot be just detail, or even bodies of separate details attached as notes to particular passages or grouped together by community of subject as we see in H. W. Seager's *Natural History in Shakespeare's Time* (London, 1896) or Cumberland Clark's *Shakespeare and Science* (Birmingham, 1929). Many books of this kind, besides innumerable annotated editions, have been prepared for the purpose of supplying us, as students of Elizabethan literature, with more or less necessary and significant pieces of information explicatory of the literature of the period. It may be said that scholarship itself is almost universally so employed, and that there are even those who question unconsciously the right of scholarship to employ itself with any other process. It has been left quite naturally for those of us who are readers and students to make use of the information supplied by others or acquired by our own researches in the building of our conceptions of Elizabethan literature.

This formation of a picture of Elizabethan literature is a synthetic process,[1] and it is not only entirely legitimate but necessary for scholarship to concern itself with synthesis as well as analysis. Indeed it would be pretty generally admitted that there is at all times a very great need for scholarship to build things as distinguished from gathering the materials for building, for the difference between the odd bit of information or fact and the completed picture is the same as that between those fragments of the pedamental sculptures of the Parthenon while they lay for centuries beside the temple and those same fragments after they had been combined with other fragments to re-form statues. It was entirely proper to gather and study fragments, but the object of so doing was to restore them to life by putting them in their places, so that they helped to reveal the conceptions of Phidias. Likewise, no background can be very significant for literature so long as it remains fragmentary, so long as it is not truly restored to life; this can be done usually only with those parts of background which entered imaginatively into the creation of that literature. Opinions, beliefs, ideals, and emotions are therefore more significant than fact, record, and cultural history, although these matters are essentials in the operations of imaginative realization. It does little good to learn the kinds of houses the Elizabethans inhabited unless we can somehow ascertain how people thought and felt while they were living in those houses; or the date or authorship of a play if the play is to remain an inert and insignificant thing. Much of our study has been so persistently analytical that we have sometimes forgotten that unless, in our hand or other hands, it becomes synthetical we can never realize its object.

The analytical method of approaching the culture of a past age is essentially to describe various parts of the field as separate constituent units, and relate them in such a way as to form one plan. A plan is not a synthesis. One really looks at a map, such as the following, on which the various qualitative constituents of learned culture are laid out on a flat surface, without realizing that it is a conventional diagram:

Theology	Cosmology	Natural Philosophy
Mathematics		Psychology
Cosmography		Ethics
Astronomy		Politics
Music		Law
Grammar	Logic	Rhetoric

In such a diagram it is not possible to indicate overlappings or to show relationships by contiguity, because it renders too definite what Bacon calls the 'lines and veins in the partitions of knowledge'; but it will serve to illustrate the analytical method of approach. In such case the observer puts before him the map and looks at any part he chooses or at all of it. But the total picture he sees is after all only his abstraction; it is not the concrete reality of things as they are—or were. If the abstractions are drawn from the same level, they will, as Ramus saw, be valid. The trouble is that these bird's-eye views are often not recognized as being abstractions at all but are thought of as furnishing concrete pictures of reality; whereas their usefulness is of another sort. Actually the aspects of the field are not segregated spatially. Each is within the whole field and cannot be withdrawn into any portion of it. It follows that no aspect is discrete or separable (except in abstraction) from any other aspect. We forget that what we call mind and matter, time and space, are simply aspects of an event abstractly conceived.

To represent diagrammatically the synthetic approach would be more difficult, for one has, so to speak, entered the field of solid geometry. The observer must always observe the whole field, or at least be so placed that he may at any moment be impressed by any object within the whole field. We will suppose that he looks at the whole unsegregated area from a series of observing posts outside of it. The field will each time present to his eyes a somewhat different shape; and each time the focal point will be in a different place. What was, in the first diagram, an area in the field has become an observing post, such as history, school learning, or æsthetics. If the surface of the field is conceived of as being curved instead of flat, the possibilities of variation will be even greater, and greater still if one supposes that light from an outside source (what Bacon called an image for 'the light of understanding' of the observer) is diffused unequally over the surface. One would perhaps approach still nearer to a suggestion of the problem of synthesis if one substituted a sphere for a curved surface, for it is not possible to see the whole surface of the sphere at once, although it actually and perhaps actively exists. A transparent sphere might be better still, although we should then, like our ancestors, be troubled with the problem of the Antipodes. This speculation may at any rate be suggestive of a synthetical as distinguished from an analytical approach to the culture of a bygone age.

By the principle of synthesis as applied to the literature of the past we usually mean the unification which occurs in the mind of the critic or scholar or that

which is embodied in the individual human life of
the man who lived and wrote in the age in question.
We sometimes mean also the complete comprehension
of the work of art or the general picture of the art
of the age. More particularly, we have in mind at this
time the various organizations of the world of an
earlier time which may be made on the basis of studies.
Organizations from special points of view, such as
the psychological dwelt upon in an earlier chapter,
have the fault of the narrowness of abstraction. Although few minds are adequate to grasp the multitude
of details in relation to each other and to larger factors necessary for effective synthesis, even from a
single significant aspect, the fact remains that synthesis is legitimate and needful. The best syntheses
we have of the Elizabethan age seem to be those
formed by gradual and natural process in the minds
of great scholars. We need not make the matter un-
necessarily difficult, and may say, for practical purposes, that the synthesis we seek is expressed in the
art of making the literature of the past come to life
(with its own life). The situation always offers the
possibility of the analysis of literature on the basis of
the ideas which produced it and the synthetic depiction of the literary situation in terms of itself. It might,
for example, be possible for us as scholars and critics
of Elizabethan literature to interpret that literature in
such a way that no word said would be unintelligible
to the writer we seek to interpret. Such criticism
would be synthetic and might in the range of experience be effective.

We have spent some time in discussing the great
positive intellectual factors of Renaissance literature
in terms of ancient, mediæval, and contemporary
European culture in the accepted partitions of human
learning. We have also had something to say about

the possible nature of the Elizabethan, giving some attention, on the negative side, to the effects of such matters as authoritarianism and tradition, inhibition and the spirit of the age. We should like now to put forward a suggestion for synthetic study based on a combination of these main aspects. From a sort of necessity and still more from lack of space, we resort to the mystical, content with saying that human life is the typical synthesis. Shakespeare's works suggest that that relatively unaccountable combination of qualities they possess reflects one of the greatest of all syntheses—the mind and heart of the author. The works of other men reflect other syntheses. We might, therefore, make our suggestion in these terms: the book culture of an individual writer like Shakespeare may become a known factor; the characteristic bent and the inevitable limitations of the age in which he lived, another factor, may also be known; the third element, the responses of the man himself to his culture and to his age and to things special to him, is at once the most important thing to know and the most difficult. Research, observation, and reflection may reveal with more or less adequacy the first and second of these states. The suggestion here made is that the qualities of the individual would become more manifest by virtue of definite knowledge of the first two factors. A synthesis of personality, which is the important synthesis, would then become more nearly achievable.

The outlines of the problem and some of its difficulties may be made clear by a brief consideration of the spectacle offered by two of the most famous men of the age. The two men, Robert Burton and Francis Bacon, were almost exact contemporaries, men of essentially the same cultural background, though apparently as widely different as two men could well be.

Paradoxical though it may seem, they were much more alike than one would at first think and both absolutely characteristic products of the age in which they lived. Their differences, however, are striking.

Robert Burton was far from untouched by the spirit of intellectual unrest that characterized his age. We may see in him many contradictory aspects of the thought current in the learned world when he wrote his book. We may see the subterfuges to which he resorted under pressure of a curious and honest mind, on the one side, and an inherited respect for tradition, authority, and law and order, on the other. Burton's method, which is very different from Bacon's, is this: after he has made a critical encyclopædia of his subject, he presents all authorities—all of the arguments on one side of a question and then all of the arguments on the other side. If at such points he had used his mind to make decisions, even on the basis of authority only, he would have been truly sceptical and, in a sense, scientific; but he does not do this. To have done so would not have been in accordance with the best thought of his age, since the questions he is considering are usually not questions for human beings to decide. It has been said that Burton is never dogmatic. We may go further and say that Burton never expresses an opinion unless it represents a mean between two extremes and, as a rule, unless he has authority for such a compromise. In this respect he is merely typical of the best thinkers of the Renaissance, even, to a considerable degree, of Montaigne and Bacon.

Burton, believing essentially the same things that Bacon believed, makes, according to his own less fortunate method, an honest attempt to arrive at the truth about things in general. Indeed, it may be said that *The Anatomy of Melancholy* is an 'advancement of learning.' Burton is more superstitious than Bacon, but scarcely more credulous, and he is likewise perfectly sincere. Such current statements as the following seem slightly misleading. In connexion with Burton's discussion of diet, it is remarked by a recent writer,[2] 'Here it is pretty evident that Burton wrote with his tongue in his cheek, for the juxtaposition of such extreme contradictions is too obviously amusing to pass the notice of even our English theologian.' No one would deny Burton the possession of a vigorous common sense and a fairly keen perception of the false and the absurd, but these qualities do not often manifest themselves when he is engaged in the writing of science. He is usually completely grave and sincere.

No part of the *Anatomy*[3] will illustrate better for us Burton's disposition, shared liberally with the men of his age, to believe in practice what he rejects in theory than his famous 'Digression of the Nature of Spirits' (Pt. I. Sect. II. Mem. I. Subs. II.). He makes a sceptical statement of the doctrine of spirits as follows: 'How far the power of Spirits and Devils doth extend, and whether they can cause this [melancholy], or any other disease, is a serious question, and worthy to be considered: for the better understanding of which, I will make a brief digression of the nature of Spirits.' Then comes an echo of the Alexandrist-Averroistic controversy over the interpretation of Aristotle which points to Galen as an age-long authority against belief in the potency of spirits. This is followed by a passage which reveals a consciousness of Gassendi and the modern Epicureans and their scientific realism. Whatever else Burton was, he was certainly one of the most widely read men of his time. His decisions may be wrong or inconsistent; they are not prejudiced and ill-informed: 'In former times, as we read *Acts* 23 [8], the *Sadducees* denied that there

were any such Spirits, Devils, or Angels. So did Galen
the Physician, the *Peripateticks*, even *Aristotle himself*, as *Pomponatius* stoutly maintains, and *Scaliger* in
some sort grants; though *Dandinus* the Jesuit *com. in
lib.* 2 *de anima*, stiffly denies it. . . *Epicures* and *Athe-
ists* are of the same mind in general, because they
never saw them. *Plato, Plotinus, Porphyrius, Iam-
blicus, Proclus*, insisting in the steps of *Trismegistus,
Pythagoras* and *Socrates*, make no doubt of it: nor
Stoicks, but that there are such spirits, though much
erring from truth. . . There is a foolish opinion, which
some hold, that they are the souls of men departed,
good and more noble were deified, the baser grovelled
on the ground, or in the lower parts, and were devils;
the which, with *Tertullian, Porphyrius* the Philosopher, *M. Tyrius, ser.* 27, maintains.' Burton gives a
summary of the great controversy on the existence
of spirits, siding usually with those who are against
spirits. A half-hearted orthodoxy is his test, though
he apparently sympathizes with those who have given
the spirit world a local habitation and a name. Maximus Tyrius is undoubtedly wrong in maintaining that
spirits are the souls of men departed; Proclus confutes
him 'at large in his book *de Anima & daemone.*' Psellus, 'a great observer of the nature of Devils,' held that
spirits are corporeal and mortal, feed, have excre-
ments, and feel pain when hurt. Cardan supports
Psellus, but Scaliger 'justly laughs him to scorn' for it.
But Socrates and Plotinus had their good demons, and
we Christians, on excellent authority, have our assist-
ing angels. Spirits probably are corporeal as Bodin and
David Crusius prove by several arguments; Bodin
shows that they are 'absolutely round, like Sun and
Moon, because that is the most perfect form.' There
is a lot of good testimony to the effect that spirits
have most interesting powers of locomotion, transpor-

tation, illusion, prophecy, and transformation of themselves and others 'into cats, dogs, hares, crows, &c.' But there are the incredulous. 'Many will not believe they can be seen, and if any shall say, swear, and stiffly maintain, though he be discreet and wise, judicious and learned, that he hath seen them, they account him a timorous fool, a melancholy dizzard, a weak fellow, a dreamer, a sick or a mad man, they contemn him, laugh him to scorn, and yet *Marcus* of his credit told *Psellus* that he had often seen them.' Then an array of testimony—Paracelsus, Lavater, Wierus, Cardan—from persons who have seen spirits. Cardan declares that some spirits are 'desirous of men's company, very affable, & familiar with them, as dogs are.' Then comes further testimony as to the mortality of spirits; but in spite of the plausibility of the subject Burton, the reluctant modernist, has to admit: 'But these paradoxes of their power, corporeity, mortality, taking of shapes, transposing bodies, and carnal copulations, are sufficiently confuted by *Zanch. c.* 10. *l.* 4, Pererius, in his comment, and Tostatus, questions on the sixth of *Gen.*, *Th. Aquin.*, *S. Austin*, *Wierus*, *Th. Erastus*, *Delrio*, *tom.* 2. *l.* 2. *quæst.* 29: *Sebastian Michaelis*, *cap* 2. *de spiritibus*, *D. Reinolds*, *Lect.* 47.'

Burton's mind was encyclopædic and very suggestible, profoundly, elaborately curious. He was obviously intelligent beyond almost any man of his age. There is scarcely a scientific, philosophical, or theological controversy of the Renaissance that he does not echo. He is shrewd, too, abundant in common sense and not lacking in courage. When we account for his failure to find out more of the truth about the subject, or rather the vast body of subjects, which he undertook to investigate, shall we say that he was superstitious and tied securely by tradition? He did have a liking for the lore of superstition, and no man of the age so exalted and magnified the importance of authority, since he makes of it his prevailing basis of decision; and yet he was keenly aware of arguments pro and con and of points at issue. He can, moreover, be convinced against his inclinations. The tenets of orthodoxy he adheres to closely whenever he is clear about them, although well aware of the contradictions and inconsistencies of theological tradition. Indeed, he is more than usually industrious about the task of showing how religious as well as secular authorities differ among themselves. His mind was not primarily logical or philosophic, and was yet capable of understanding these subjects. Possibly one might say that Burton, an authoritarian, suffered because he was not genuinely faithful to any authority.

Had he been a better Aristotelian, he would have produced a more consistent book. Aristotle is for ever in his mind, Pomponatius he had read effectually, Bodin is a favourite, he knows Telesio, who though nominally an anti-Aristotelian, followed an essential Aristotle in his scientific and philosophic work. Burton fastens the Aristotelian rubrics of the four causes, the predicaments (usually in the form of the places of logic), and predicables (with the machinery of definition and division) securely down upon his vast subject; so that no work, not even *Summa Theologica*, is objectively more Aristotelian than *The Anatomy of Melancholy*. Yet no work is subjectively more alien to the spirit of Aristotle. If such a thing is true, one can see how far afield from the master the teachings of an Aristotelian culture had wandered. If Burton had followed Ramus and borne the three laws in mind, or if he had followed the *Posterior Analytics* and what Aristotle has to say about induction, he could not have been so completely unscientific. Ramus had seen the truth of the principles that every scientific axiom must be true and universal, that it must be homogeneous with the object of the science, and that it must be expressed under its proper form, genus treated as genus and species as species. Burton had no inkling of these principles. He shows some knowledge of Bacon's Essays [4] and quotes a mistaken statement about the 'refrigeration of spirits' from *De Vita et Morte*. *The Advancement of Learning* and the later scientific works with their determined enunciation of principles of reform in science Burton either does not know or disregards as unimportant.

Yet when Bacon [5] speaks he seems to have scientific writers like Burton in mind. In Burton the human understanding is indeed prone to abstractions and to give substance and reality to things which are fleeting, and in him likewise there is a perfect case of one who sought his science in the reading of books and in his own lesser world. Poor Burton was also a devotee of the Idols of the Marketplace, for in him words plainly force and overrule the understanding, leading him 'away from truth into numberless empty controversies and idle fancies'; and, as for those Idols of the Theatre, Burton was the victim of a system, or rather of several different systems, and took up his substance too often from things 'accepted by tradition, credulity and negligence.' 'All,' says Bacon, 'has been left either to the mist of tradition, or the whirl and eddy of argument, or the fluctuations and mazes of chance and of vague and ill-digested experience.' Burton shows that deficiency of 'principles and chief axioms,' that 'admiration of antiquity, authority, and consent,... and of men for knowledge and arts' of which Bacon complained. Burton had only the most moderate idea that anything new might be discovered. He held rather that, by critical consideration and more careful treatment, the existing truth might be made more apparent and be re-apparelled more attractively. 'It may,' says Bacon, 'be thought a strange and a harsh thing that we should at once and with one blow set aside all sciences and all authors; and that too without calling in any of the ancients to our aid and support, but relying on our own strength.' Bacon's course and method were, 'not to extract works from works or experiments from experiments (as an empiric), but from works and experiments to extract causes and axioms, and again from those causes and axioms new works and experiments, as a legitimate interpreter of nature.'

Burton falls under denunciation in all three of Bacon's classes of false philosophy—'the Sophistical, the Empirical, and the Superstitious.' His strongest leanings were toward Neo-Platonism, but, as Bacon says of Aristotle's relations to natural science, Burton corrupted his Platonism by his logic. He was vastly interested in matters which Bacon would call empirical. It therefore follows that Burton was, first of all, a Neo-Platonist—Bacon's superstitious class—but that he was conscious of all phenomena and doctrine and completely eclectic, eclectic too in a fashion which dispensed with consistency. 'For my part,' says Bacon, 'I do not trouble myself with any such speculative and withal unprofitable matters.' Now, it happens that 'speculative and withal unprofitable matters' were just the things which interested Burton most, and it cannot be said that Bacon has it all his own way by any means. The popular approach to science, now and always, is Burton's approach, and is the approach of literature. Burton, therefore, concerns us much, for he epitomizes the learning of the Renaissance, reflects the catholicity of the time in the breadth of his interests, and exemplifies the often unmethodical habits of general readers in all ages. In the study of the thought of that age, and perhaps of all ages, one must be prepared for contrasts between contemporaries, intelligent men, as violent as that between Burton and Bacon (one would be at a loss to find a greater). Other men of the time reflect almost every agreement and disagreement between the mental attitudes of these two. They themselves present the case of two persons, not widely different in their learned culture, who were widely different in their individual reactions to it. Knowledge of the corpus of their learning enables us to discriminate more sharply between them. If this is true, the history of learned culture takes on renewed importance for literary study.

A good deal of the best spirit of the early humanists lived on in England [6] throughout the sixteenth century in the form of scholarship and in what is more important for our purpose, a feeling of profound admiration for the ancient classics. Ascham's [7] enthusiasm must have been common enough:

Athens, by this discipline and good ordering of youth, did breed up, within the circuit of that one city, within the compass of one hundred year, within the memory of one man's life, so many notable captains in war, for worthiness, wisdom and learning, as be scarce matchable; no, not in the state of Rome, in the compass of those seven hundred years, when it flourished most. . . .

And beside nobility in war, for excellent and matchless masters in all manner of learning, in that one city, in memory of one age, were more learned men, and that in a manner all together, than all time doth remember, than all place doth afford, than all other tongues do contain. And I do not mean of those authors, which, by injury of time, by negligence of men, by cruelty of fire and sword, be lost, but even of those which, by God's grace, are left unto us: of which, I thank God, even my poor study lacketh not one. As, in philosophy, Plato, Aristotle, Xenophon, Euclid, and Theophrast; in eloquence and civil law, Demosthenes, Æschines, Lycurgus, Dinarchus, Demades, Isocrates, Isæus, Lysias, Antisthenes, Andocides; in histories, Herodotus, Thucydides, Xenophon, and which we lack, to our great loss, Theopompus and Euphorus; in poetry, Æschylus, Sophocles, Euripides, Aristophanes, and somewhat of Menander, Demosthenes' sister's son.

Now, let Italian, and Latin itself, Spanish, French, Dutch, and English bring forth their learning, and recite their authors, Cicero only excepted, and one or two more in Latin, they be all patched clouts and rags, in comparison of fair woven broad cloths. And truly, if there be any good in them, it is either learned, borrowed, or stolen, from some one of those worthy wits of Athens.

A passage of the same warmth but kindlier spirit is to be found in Montaigne: [8]

I award, and I think with good reason, the palm to Jacques Amyot over all our French writers, not only for the simplicity and purity of his language, wherein he excels all others, nor for his perseverance in a work of such length, nor for the profundity of his learning, which enabled him to interpret so happily an author so stiff and thorny (they may tell me what they please about it, for I know no Greek; but I find throughout his translation so beautiful, so well-connected and sustained a meaning, that certainly he has either fathomed the real thoughts of the author, or, having, by such long intercourse with him, deeply implanted in his mind a general idea of Plutarch's mind, he has at least attributed to him nothing that belies or contradicts him); but above everything I owe him gratitude for having had the judgement to pick out and choose so worthy and appropriate a book to present to his country. We other ignoramuses had been lost if this book had not lifted us out of the quagmire; thanks to him, we dare now to speak and write,

and the ladies may lecture on him to the school-masters;
he is our breviary.

From the point of view of intelligent appreciation
there never was a better humanist than Jonson or
Camden. The special studies of both these men were
devoted to authors largely unknown to the groups
who admired Cicero, Quintilian, and Isocrates, and
who read Virgil and Ovid with an earlier freshness.
The spirit of these later humanists was equally interpretative and deferential with the earlier group, and
was, besides, more critical, for these were the days
when England as well as France had learned the bearings of the *Politics* and the *Poetics* of Aristotle as well
as of the *Ethics* and the *De Anima*. It may be said that
in one group, an earlier group, the school authors
were the principal objects of attention and imitation.
But from the beginning of the sixteenth century there
were the humanists who read the more difficult Latin
authors and some at least of the Greeks. Finally, these
humanists—Italian, French, and English—were translators and expositors and adapters and became in their
turn sources of classical ideas and forms. Greene,
Lyly, Marlowe, Shakespeare, Nashe, as well as Sidney
and Spenser, knew and felt the influence of grammar
school authors, with greater or less additions from the
second group. Jonson, Chapman, Marston, and Donne
knew the second as well as the first group and added
much from a third still more learned group. The
division between the simpler school authors and
the less available and more difficult groups marks
a distinction in time; for example, between what
was current in 1585 to 1590 and what was current in
1600 to 1605. There is perceptible, in other words, an
advance in scientific, philosophic, and cultural background throughout the period. Such an advance does

not need to be marked out in careful detail; in fact it
would be difficult to do so in view of literary lives
that extend over the whole period under consideration; but it needs to be recognized because it makes
itself felt collectively in the forms, tone, knowledge,
and purposes of literature. One can get a typical view
of the progression in mind by considering Jonson's
advocacy of Aristotelian principles for tragedy and
comedy, an advanced and critical idea struggling for
recognition against a method of composition already
established on a basis of imitation and experiment.

It comes about that the culture of almost every
writer of the period at the end of the sixteenth century and the beginning of the seventeenth century
becomes more definable when looked at in the mirror
of ancient literature and learning. One can usually
talk about the subject only vaguely, but the idea and
device are none the less sound. The writers of the
whole period were imitative, frankly so. So far as one
can see, they were all imitative and all betrayed themselves. Of course, no one cares whether they were
imitative or not except in so far as knowledge of their
affiliations with the classics and with current foreign
and domestic literature may make their meaning, both
denotative and connotative, clearer and more important. Strange to say, their imitative habits have little
to do with their originality, which was of a sort not
affected by the process of borrowing ideas, plots, and
forms from other authors; for their theory—and it is
surprising how successfully it worked in their hands—
was one which made them, on the authority of Quintilian and the great Italians, believe in absorbing into
themselves the merits of the greatest and best writers
of antiquity and the modern world in somewhat the
same way as a cannibal chief might increase his own
prowess by devouring his worthier enemies. Renais-

sance writers were pragmatical in their borrowings. Jonson's *Timber* presents a sort of paradox. His editor, M. Castelain,[9] added greatly to the number of passages known to have been copied outright from various mostly Latin authors. He says hopefully in his book that further research will probably result in finding sources for the rest of Jonson's *Timber*. Whether he is right or not, one does not dispose of *Timber* by pointing out that it is a book of excerpts. It is indeed a book of excerpts and yet is remarkably original. Although Jonson's description of Bacon as an orator has been found to be an adaptation of an ancient author, that description has nevertheless received the endorsement of Jonson, has passed like the rest of the book through his temperament, has been sanctioned by his knowledge and his taste, and is convincing, is, therefore, paradoxically speaking, absolutely original though borrowed outright.

In those cases in which an Elizabethan author, such as Lyly[10] or Nashe, has been subjected to a sufficiently careful examination, so that his sources have become known with accuracy and in their extent, a type and kind of critical information of very great value exists. Let us take, as a test case in the preliminary study of an individual writer, Thomas Dekker's[11] use of school learning. There is little evidence bearing on the subject of Dekker's education. It has seemed unlikely that he attended a university. There is even some question as to the thoroughness of his grammar school education, although in that respect the works themselves offer interesting testimony. Dekker shows abundant knowledge of classical mythology, which came mainly from the school authors, and evidently knew Latin, since he employs a good deal of Latin in his works and since he undertook to translate Dedekind's *Grobianus*. According to

Grosart, there are traces of scholarly culture even in Dekker's most hasty productions. Dekker shows a knowledge of the form of Latin scholastic disputations in *The Whore of Babylon* (1607); in *Satiromastix* (1607) he employs formal rhetoric for comic effect in presenting the characters of Horace, Sir Rees ap Vaughan, and Sir Quintilian Shorthose. Crispinus speaks a paradox in the latter play (, 238-40) not unlike Iago's paradox in *Othello* (II, i, 149-61). There is also a good deal of simple rhetoricism in *The King's Entertainment* (1604), and *Dekker his Dreame* (1620) is crowded with similes and other figures of speech—sometimes marked as such in the margin of the printed page, but all rather awkwardly applied. *Newes from Hell*—'The Deuils Answer to Pierce Pennylesse'—is good controversy, but, compared to Nashe, Harvey and Greene, singularly untechnical. *The Dead Tearme* (1608) is, however, most forensic—complaints, answers, dissensions, and invectives—but legalistic rather than academical in its quality. In *The Bel-man of London* (1608) Dekker puts into the mouth of the chief of the beggars a formal oration in praise of beggary in which Insinuation, Confirmation, and Conclusion are clearly in evidence. Dekker also produced that odd work called *A Strange Horse Race* (1603), in which the material of school subjects is presented under the scheme of a series of races. Astronomy appears as races of the heavenly bodies, physiology as a race of humours and spirits within the body, physics as a race among the four elements. Among the metals lead strives to overtake tin, tin silver, and silver gold. The virtues and vices also race with one another.

On the other hand, school learning in Dekker is not ingrained and permeative as in most other Elizabethan writers. His prayer for the two universities in *Foure*

Birds of Noahs Arke (1608) has unmistakably the point of view of an outsider: '... And seeing that these two Starres of Learning are to giue Comfort, or to fill with darkenesse this our whole Kingdome, bestow vpon them (O Lord) such beames of Heauenly light, that euen forraine countreyes, as well as our owne, may be glorified in their splendor. Direct all the studies of those that liue vpon the foode of the soule there, (which is wisedome) to a holy end. Make them to loue as brethren & to liue as Christians: suffer not vaine glorie to ingender pride amongst them, nor phantasticknesse of wit, to drowne them in ridiculous and apish folly. But so mould both their minds & bodies, that they may enter into those sanctified temples as thy children, & come from thence as seruants of thy ministerie. Amen.' The famous passage in *The Whore of Babylon*[12] on the life of the poverty-stricken scholar lays claim to the possession of learning, but suggests that the learning has been gained in no regular or easy way:

The Dragons that keep learnings golden tree,
As you now haue, I fought with, conquered them,
Got to the highest bough, eat of the fruit,
And gathered of the seauen-fold leaues of Art,
What I desir'd; and yet for all the Moones
That I haue seene waxe olde, and pine for anger,
I had outwatched them: and for all the candles
I wasted out on long and frozen nights,
To thaw them into day; I fild my head
With books, but scarce could fil my mouth with bread:
I had the Muses smile, but moneyes frowne,
And neuer could get out of such a gowne.

Dekker does indeed possess learning of a sort, as his allusions abundantly testify--to Horace, Virgil, Ovid, Martial, Seneca, Pliny, Suetonius, Tacitus, Plutarch, Paracelsus, and the Church Fathers. He uses a good many Greek names, alludes in one place to Homer, Hesiod, Euripides and 'some other mad Greeks,' and in *The Wonderful Year* he repeats what Aristophanes said 'in his Frog.' Dekker knew French and apparently Dutch and was well read in English literature.

Aside from a little rhetoric and logic, Dekker's works reveal but a small amount of school learning, in spite of the fact that he makes in at least two instances, as stated in an earlier chapter, a functional use of a rhetorical tenet of great importance, since both *The Honest Whore* and *The Second Part of the Honest Whore* actually turn on the doctrine of persuasion; that is, that the truth, being once brought home to the mind of the hearer, was absolutely valid and irresistible. The very naïveté of this use would indicate that Dekker was not a man of extensive learned culture. He writes like one who did not know how to use the academical tools he is employing, as in several other places where he brings in the current doctrine of the supremacy of passion over reason. This crudity appears, for example, in *The Second Part* (IV, i) in Hippolito's infatuation for Bellafront at the point where he quotes from the *Œdipus* of Seneca. Generally speaking, Dekker's use of psychology, formal ethics, and rhetoric is relatively to other authors of the time small in quantity and unskilful. The final impression of Dekker's academical culture is that his grammar school education was not a very thorough one, that he had not studied advanced subjects at the university, and that, as his words in *The Whore of Babylon* seem to imply, he had done most of his serious study in solitude.

Christopher Marlowe shows in his first play, *Tamburlaine*, and in all of his plays, an interes in university subjects, a knowledge of quadrivial subjects, of cosmography, and, particularly, of psychology and its ethical aspects. His learned culture is in academical form, as if it had come straight from the university. He had perhaps added very little to it by general reading, but he understood what his learning signified. Sidney was an Aristotelian and, aside from certain borrowings from the French and Italian writers on the nature and function of poetry and much of the matters of romance and chivalry, reveals hardly anything else but academical culture, which, however, is revealed fully and convincingly. He shows school learning in its applications to the problems of his work—of the trivium (grammar, rhetoric, and logic), of the quadrivium (which included music), and of the three philosophies. He, like Marlowe, knows the practical bearings of what he has learned, but it stands almost without supplementation in his intellectual culture. Somewhat the same thing can be said about Spenser, although in his case there was a much larger additional element of general Renaissance culture, more native elements, more religious culture.

Perhaps the most interesting case that can be cited is that of Thomas Nashe.[13] The great edition of Nashe's works by Dr. R. B. McKerrow makes procedure in Nashe's case a matter of far greater certainty than in the cases of many others. This much may at least be hazarded as an interpretation of Nashe's culture on the basis of Dr. McKerrow's findings: Nashe was evidently a poor student at the university, not nearly so good a student as either Greene or Marlowe. Nashe attended the university and no doubt knew in a certain fashion what was going on, but he never learned the subjects set for study, while he was at the university or later. After he left the university, however, or, for all we know, in part while

he was still at the university, he became a good deal
of a general reader. He read in a somewhat narrow
territory. He knew Cornelius Agrippa best, and
Agrippa was a writer of very great learning. If one
compares Nashe with Greene the contrast is striking.
Greene was evidently an excellent student at the university. He was well grounded in school learning.
The trivium, the quadrivium, Aristotelianism, and
Neo-Platonism (there was probably little true Platonism to be had) became familiar to him. When he
began to write he drew on his academical learning and
applied it to his tasks, made it into works; but Greene
never learned much else, except about the ways of
rogues and vagabonds. The circumstances of his
career may account for this fact.

We know a good deal about Shakespeare [14] from the
somewhat casual application of the principle we are
now considering. We know, for example (without
Ben Jonson's help), that Shakespeare was probably no
great Greek scholar, but that he knew and appre-
ciated many ancient classics; that he was a man of
very broad literary sympathies and of very considerable knowledge of science and philosophy. We know
that he could probably read Latin, certainly that he
read it in grammar school, and that he handled it in
an elementary form with ease. We know also that
he knew French and possibly Italian, but we know
that he used translations for his rather extended employment of foreign sources. The one place where
the classics enter in their originals into Shakespeare's
horizon is just where one would expect it to be,
namely, in his early work in which the simple grammar school authors, such as Ovid, Plautus, and possibly Seneca and Virgil, make themselves felt. He had
absorbed them in their essence, and they become part
of him in his more youthful work. We can be reason-

ably certain that Shakespeare did not go to the university, since he shows only a popular knowledge of the subjects of the university curriculum. We can be certain that he read extensively in the manuals of science and philosophy and courtesy circulated in great numbers during his working years. He seems also to have learned much from the books he used as sources for his plays and from general reading, such as Montaigne's *Essays*. His pages are not larded with Aristotelian terms and distinctions like those of Sidney and Spenser or with Stoical matters like those of Marston and Chapman. Shakespeare's learning is not of a formal cast; it may nevertheless be described as superior. His grasp of the essence of Renaissance learned culture is nothing short of grand. In the light of what we know of his career Shakespeare's cultural background is just what it ought to be, just what his life experience ought to have produced. Let it be remembered that he not only wrote plays but acted in many plays by men of culture and learning.

The case of Jonson is like that of Shakespeare, but with most significant differences. We know that he did not attend either of the universities but that he chose to make a scholar of himself by his own efforts; he succeeded amazingly. When the fabric of his culture is examined, it turns out that he shows little knowledge of the quadrivial subjects and that his philosophy is not of the academical kind, such as that manifested in writers who were university trained. Jonson [15] knew the simpler school classics and made in addition special studies of Seneca, Cicero, Quintilian, and the Roman Historians. In general, he advanced into a wide realm of learned literature, ancient and modern, a realm explored by but few men in his age. His favourite authors, in whose exploitation he took great pride (*'Tanquam Explorator'*), are a less well-known group than those of the school and the university. The manner in which he acquired his culture or scholarship made him critical; he read the works of other men as an equal; he maintained his own independence.

One would not be too positive about diagnoses such as the foregoing, which if carried through on the basis of present knowledge, or any basis other than long, thoughtful, and sympathetic study, would often be erroneous; but what has been said will at least suggest a point of view in the study of literary history, a method by means of which our comprehension of the syntheses presented in the lives and works of various Elizabethan authors may be improved. Fulness of comprehension may lead to imaginative restoration.

The method of study here suggested, though perhaps too time-consuming and too extensive in its demands to be made very readily into an instrument for the determination of fact—authorship or chronology— may yet lead ultimately to a fruitful comprehension of Renaissance literature. Indeed, thoroughness and intelligent method constitute the only true—though strait and narrow—road to the great objective. The field of study is so varied and so extensive that it will not yield to negligent precipitancy. Bacon tells us in one of his Apothegms that 'Sir Amice Pawlet, when he saw too much haste made in any matter, was wont to say, "Stay a while that we may end the sooner."' The Elizabethan field is not unknown even popularly, but, being known mainly from relatively few works and authors and to some degree from anachronistic commentators, it needs what Bacon calls 'minds nimble and versatile enough to catch the resemblances of things (which is the main point), and at the same time steady enough to fix and distinguish their subtler differences.' Resemblances in the Elizabethan literary field are, in spite of Bacon's implication, almost subtler than differences. Resemblances exist between such obviously contrasted pairs as Spenser and Cervantes, Milton and Montaigne, Bacon and Burton, Shakespeare and Jonson, Sidney and Donne, and, it may be, between Rabelais and Richard Hooker, resemblances within the normal range of the learning and the ideals of the Renaissance. These two things, the learning and the ideals, have seemed to us important because of the faith the men of the Renaissance had in the wisdom of the philosophers and the poets, a faith which was justified by their own works. How defective that wisdom was is almost too obvious. We have nevertheless tried to defend it against wholesale condemnation and neglect, tried to show that in many ways it was as good as our own. We have even suggested that in some very important ways it was better than ours. Whether this is true or not, the fact remains that the faith of the Renaissance justified its doctrines. Men believed in the best wisdom of the ages and dared to try to put it in practice. Their tools, though by no means perfect, were adequate for the very greatest purposes in written expression. What has been said is a sort of 'image in a crossway that may point out the way,' even if, as Bacon adds, 'it cannot go it.'

In this book we have had something to say of the situation of the man of the age of Shakespeare and Bacon with reference to the doctrines of man's relation to God and the created world, something also of what man thought of his situation, and something about how a knowledge of that situation may enable us to know him—for our own good. In the modern world man knows little about the cosmology and does not concern himself very much with it; it seems to let him alone, and he is disposed to let it alone. Con-

sequently he knows no way of saving himself, although it is generally admitted that he is still in need
of salvation. In other words, the philosophy of the
modern world lacks the unity, the integration, the intelligible practicality of the philosophy of the Renaissance. Man's equipment for gaining the power of
knowledge is greater than it was three hundred and
fifty years ago. He is certainly less bound down by
tradition and authority than he was then; he has more
intelligence about his surroundings; possibly he is
habitually more willing to suspend judgment until
decisive factors have appeared. In so far as he consciously follows—as he still does in large numbers—the
ancient theory of the nature and origin of man and
created things, with its various promises and threats,
duties and dangers, it will pay him to know better the
constitution and by-laws of the cosmogony of ancient
times, the Middle Ages, and the Renaissance. Even if
man does not consciously follow the ancient system, it
will be found to concern him, for it has never been
superseded and still governs a great part of his
life. Most of the older questions about the here and
the hereafter, often quite differently stated, persist and will probably continue to persist. May we
not therefore by knowing the past as it concerns us
today and by seeing 'the resemblance of things' within
it and to our new 'things,' and the subtler differences
as well, come to understand infinitely better the lives
and thoughts of modern men, of ourselves?

BIBLIOGRAPHICAL NOTES

CHAPTER I

[1] Philosophy of dualism. See E. Troeltsch, 'Idealism,' in Hastings, *Encyclopædia of Religion and Ethics*, with references; F. Ueberweg, *Die Philosophie der Neuzeit bis zum Ende des XVIII. Jahrhundert.* 12 Aufl., neubearbeitet v. Frischheisen-Köhler und Moog. Berlin, 1924, pp. 15-59, 88-112, 161-9, 182-93, 206-15; Sir Leslie Stephen, *History of English Thought in the Eighteenth Century*, 3rd ed. 2 vols. London, 1902, I, 34-90.

[2] Charron. *Of Wisedome Three Bookes*. Translated by Samson Lennard. Printed for Edward Blount and William Aspley, after November 6, 1612 (S.T.C.), pp. 24-5. (Bk. I, chap. vii).

[3] Cosmology. Contemporary works into which the theory of the cosmology enters: Sir Walter Ralegh, *The History of the World* (W. Burre, 1614 and later editions); Guillaume de Saluste du Bartas, *Bartas: his Devine Weekes and Workes*. Trans. J. Sylvester (H. Lownes, 1608, and later editions); Richard Hooker, *The Laws of Ecclesiastical Polity;* Sir John Davies, *Nosce Teipsum;* Louis Le Roy, *Of the Interchangeable Course of Things in the Whole World*. Trans. R. Ashley (C. Yetsweirt, 1594); Thomas Milles, *The Treasurie of Auncient and Moderne Times.* 2 vols. (W. Jaggard, 1613 and 1619); Robert Burton, *The Anatomy of Melancholy;* David Person, *Varieties: or, A Surveigh of Rare and Excellent Matters* (R. Badger for T. Alchorn, 1635); Thomas Heywood, *The Hierarchie of the Blessed Angels* (A. Islip, 1635). See Pierre Duhem, *Le système du monde, histoire des doctrines cosmologiques de Platon à Copernic.* 2 t. Paris, 1913-14, I, 28-101, 130-342; II, 267-390, 393-501; T. F. Troels-Lund, *Himmelsbild und Weltanschauung im Wandel der Zeiten*. Übersetzt v. L. Bloch. Leipzig, 1908, pp. 165-239, *et passim;* H. Nichols, *A Treatise on Cosmology*. Vol. I. Cambridge, Mass., 1904, pp. 33-133, *et passim;* H. Macpherson, *Modern Cosmologies*. London, 1929, pp. 1-18; Ernst Cassirer, *Individuum und Kosmos in der Philosophie der Renaissance*. Leipzig, 1927; A. N. Whitehead, *Process and Reality, an Essay on Cosmology*. New York, 1930, pp. 127-67, and *Adventures in Ideas*. New York, 1933, pp. 131-221.

[4] Perfect correspondences. See G. C. Joyce, 'Analogy,' in Hastings, *Encyclopædia of Religion and Ethics*, with references; George Berkeley, *Alciphron*, Dial. IV, chap. xxi. For typical

example of analogical reasoning see Edward Forset, *A Comparative Discourse of the Bodies Natural and Politique*. London. Printed for I. Bill. 1606.

5 Fideism. See Louis I. Bredvold, *The Intellectual Milieu of John Dryden*. Ann Arbor, Mich., 1934, pp. 73-85.

6 Montaigne. *Essays of Montaigne*. Translated by E. J. Trechmann. 2 vols. Oxford, 1927, I, 428, 480.

7 Prospero. See *The Tempest*, V, i, 54-7.

8 Raphael's advice. See *Paradise Lost*, VIII, 167-74.

9 Seventeenth century. See E. A. Burtt, *The Metaphysical Foundations of Modern Science*. London, 1925, pp. 1-44, *et passim*.

10 Before its ruin. See *Paradise Lost*, VII, 551-8.

11 Desdemona. See *Othello*, V, ii, 10-13.

12 John Jones. *The Arte and Science of Preseruing Bodie and Soule in al Health*. London. Printed by H. Bynneman. 1579, pp. 4-9, 12, 22-4.

13 Diagrams of macrocosm and microcosm. See reproductions in E. A. Grillot de Givray, *Witchcraft, Magic and Alchemy*. Translated by J. Courtenay Locke. London, 1932.

14 Fallacy of misplaced concreteness. See A. N. Whitehead, *Process and Reality*. New York, 1930, p. 6, *et passim*.

15 Henry Cornelius Agrippa. *De occulta philosophia libri tres*. Antwerp and Paris, 1531; *Three Books of Occult Philosophy*. Written by Henry Cornelius Agrippa. Translated out of Latin into the English Tongue by J. F. London, 1651. The quotations in the text are from the translation; see pp. 357, 341-2, also Bk. I, chap. xi.

16 Eve's question. See *Paradise Lost*, IV, 657-75.

17 Bacon. *The Advancement of Learning, Works*, ed. Spedding, Ellis, and Heath, 14 vols. London, 1857-74, III, 405, 408.

18 Seals or characters. See W. C. Curry, *Chaucer and the Mediæval Sciences*. New York, 1926, pp. 91-118, and notes; Agrippa, *Three Books of Occult Philosophy*, loc. cit., Bk. III, *passim*.

19 St. Augustine. *De civitate Dei*, lib. VIII, cap. viii, xvii, *et passim*.

20 Friar Laurence. See *Romeo and Juliet*, II, iii, 9-22.

21 The law of nature and the law of Scripture. *The Works of Mr. Richard Hooker*, ed. Keble. 7th ed. 3 vols. Oxford, 1888, I, 200 ff.: Jean Calvin, *The Institution of Christian Religion*. Trans. T. Norton. 3 pts. London. Printed by R. Wolfe and R. Harrison. 1561, many later editions, pt. II; Sir Walter Ralegh, *The History of the World, loc. cit.*, Bk. I; Henry Cornelius Agrippa, *Of the Vanitie and Vncertaintie of Artes and Sciences*. Trans. Ja. San[ford] Gent. London. Printed by Henry Wykes. 1569,

pp. 159ᵛ ff.; Milles, *op. cit.*, Vol. I, Bk. VIII, chaps. iii-v, *et passim;* Philippe de Mornay, *The True Knowledge of a Mans owne selfe.* Trans. A. Munday. London. Printed by I. Roberts for W. Leake. 1601, *passim.* See also R. Eucken, *Main Currents of Modern Thought.* London, 1912, pp. 195 ff.; É. Boutroux, *De l'idée de la loi naturelle dans la science et la philosophie.* Paris, 1895; J. B. Mullinger, *The University of Cambridge.* 3 vols. Cambridge, 1873, 1884, 1911, II, 125 ff., 423, *et passim* (on the study of law in the universities); J. W. Allen, *A History of Political Thought in the Sixteenth Century.* London, 1928, pp. xiv, 8-12, *et passim;* É. Doumergue, *Jean Calvin, les hommes et les choses de son temps.* 7 t. Lausanne, 1895-1927, V, 383-607; R. H. Murray, *The Political Consequences of the Reformation.* Boston, 1926, pp. 22, 35, 65-7, 84, 120-4, 155-6, 197-202, 228-36, 274-5.

²² Milton. See *Paradise Lost*, III, 129-30; V, 852-65; IX, 457-68.

²³ Iago. See *Othello*, I, iii, 322-30.

²⁴ Law as the outcome of the social contract. Hooker's *Ecclesiastical Polity*, Book VIII. With an introduction by R. A. Houk. New York, 1931, pp. 51-3, 67-8, *et passim;* Murray, *op. cit.*, 65-7, 75, 105-7, 119-23, 186-7, 203-9, with references.

²⁵ Brutus. See *Julius Caesar*, V, iii, 73-5.

CHAPTER II

¹ Astrology. E. B. Knobel, 'Astronomy and Astrology,' in *Shakespeare's England.* 2 vols. Oxford, 1917, I, 444-61, with bibliography; C. Camden, Jr., 'Astrology in Shakespeare's Day,' *Isis*, XIX, 26-73, and 'Elizabethan Astrological Medicine,' *Annals of Medical History*, N.S. II, 217-26; C. Clark, *Shakespeare and Science.* Birmingham, 1929, pp. 3-4, 38-59, *et passim;* H. Baron, 'Willensfreiheit und Astrologie bei Marsilio Ficino und Pico della Mirandola,' in *Goetz-Festschrift.* Leipzig, 1927, pp. 145-70. See three i.nportant early works: John Chamber, *A Treatise against ludicial Astrologie.* London. Printed by Iohn Harison. 1601; Sir Christopher Heydon, *A Defence of ludiciall Astrologie.* Cambridge. Printed by Iohn Legat. 1603; and George Carleton. ΑΣΤΡΟΛΟΓΟΜΑΝΙΑ: *The Madnesse of Astrologers.* London. Printed by W. Iaggard for W. Turner. 1624.

² Fulke Greville. *Life of the Renowned Sir Philip Sidney.* Oxford, 1907, p. 141.

³ Dr. John Dee. *The Private Diary of Dr. John Dee*, ed. J. O. Halliwell [-Phillipps]. London, 1842, pp. 2, 20.

⁴ M. W. Wallace. *The Life of Sir Philip Sidney.* Cambridge, 1915, p. 173. *Astrophel and Stella. The Complete Works of Sir Philip Sidney*, ed. A. Feuillerat. 4 vols. Cambridge, 1922, II, 253.

5 Gabriel Harvey. *Gabriel Harvey's Marginalia*, collected and ed. by G. C. Moore Smith. Stratford-upon-Avon, 1913, p. 163; see C. Camden, Jr., 'Elizabethan Almanacs and Prognostications,' *Library*, 4th S. XII, 83-108, 194-207; E. Bareste, *Nostradamus*. Paris, 1842; J. Ferguson, 'The Secrets of Alexis: a Sixteenth Century Collection of Medical and Technical Receipts,' *Proceedings*, Royal Society of Medicine, XXIV, 225-46.

6 Byron. See *Conspiracy of Charles Duke of Byron*, III, i, 106-10.

7 Helena. See *All's Well That Ends Well*, I, i, 232-3.

8 Cassius. See *Julius Cæsar*, I, ii, 140-1.

9 Hamlet. See *Hamlet*, I, iv, 23-38.

10 Prospero. See *The Tempest*, I, ii, 180-4.

11 Edmund. See *King Lear*, I, ii, 128-39.

12 Montaigne. *The Essays of Montaigne*. Translated by E. J. Trechmann. *Loc. cit.*, I, 442-3.

13 Occult aspects of psychology. Agrippa, *Three Books of Occult Philosophy*, *loc. cit.*, Bk. I, *passim;* Bacon, *The Advancement of Learning*, *loc. cit.*, p. 381; Robert Burton, *The Anatomy of Melancholy*, ed. A. R. Shilleto. 3 vols. London, 1896, I, 205-39, *et passim;* G. S. Brett, *A History of Psychology*. 3 vols. London, 1912-21, I, 72-9, 204-12, 272-90; II, 30-2, 90-113, 116-24, 143-53, *et passim;* L. Stein, *Die Psychologie der Stoa*. Berlin, 1886, 101-51.

14 Rosaline. See *Love's Labour's Lost*, IV, iii, 242-3.

15 Montaigne. *Essays, loc. cit.*, II, 222.

16 Induction or transfusion of soul. Cf. W. C. Curry, 'The Demonic Metaphysics of Macbeth,' *Studies in Philology*, XXX, 395-426.

17 Ghost of the murdered king. See *Hamlet*, III, iv, 112-15; cf. G. C. Taylor, *Shakespeare's Debt to Montaigne*. Cambridge, 1925, p. 13.

18 Gaunt. See *Richard II*, II, i, 31.

19 Lady Macbeth. See *Macbeth*, I, v, 27.

20 Agrippa's doctrine of the passions. See *Three Books of Occult Philosophy*, *loc. cit.*, Bk. I, chap. lxiv.

21 Evil magic—demonism. W. E. H. Lecky, *History of the Spirit of Rationalism in Europe*. 2nd ed. 2 vols. London, 1865, I, 1-154; G. L. Kittredge, *Witchcraft in Old and New England*. Cambridge, Mass., 1929, pp. 329-73; É. A. Grillot de Givry, *Witchcraft, Magic and Alchemy*. Trans. J. Courtenay Locke. London, 1931. See also many older works, particularly Maury, *Histoire de la Magie* (Paris, 1860), Thomas Wright, *Narratives of Sorcery and Magic* (London, 1851), Des Mousseaux, *Pratiques des Démons* (Paris, 1854), Madden, *Phantasmata* (London, 1857),

Le Comte de Gabalis (Paris, 1671), Glanvill, *Philosophical considerations touching Witches and Witchcraft* (London, 1666); and of course Jakob Sprenger, *Malleus Maleficarum;* Reginald Scot, *Discoverie of Witchcraft;* Jean Bodin, *Démonomanie des Sorciers;* Naudé, *Apologie pour les grands hommes soupçonnez de magie;* Hutchinson, *Essay on Witchcraft;* and Johann Wier, *De Præstigiis Dæmonum.*

22 Nor think...night. See *Paradise Lost,* IV, 675-80.

23 Religion. See articles in *Cambridge Modern History,* Vol. II, with bibliographies, particularly by A. F. Pollard (chaps. v-viii) and A. M. Fairbairn (chap. xi); Ronald Bayne, 'Religion,' in *Shakespeare's England,* I, 48-78, and article 'Disciplinarian Puritanism,' in edition of Hooker's *Laws of Ecclesiastical Polity,* Bk. V (1902); also Charles Beard, *The Reformation of the Sixteenth Century in Its Relation to Modern Thought and Knowledge.* New impression. London, 1927, pp. 112-46, *et passim;* R. W. Dixon, *History of the Church of England.* 6 vols. Oxford, 1895-1903, Vols. V and VI, *passim;* A. F. S. Pearson, *Thomas Cartwright and Elizabethan Puritanism, 1535-1603.* Cambridge, 1925, and *Political Aspects of Sixteenth Century Puritanism.* Cambridge, 1928; W. H. Frere, *The English Church in the Reigns of Elizabeth and James I (1558-1625).* London, 1904, chaps. vii, xii, xv, *et passim;* J. S. Flynn, *The Influence of Puritanism in the Political and Religious Thought of the English.* London, 1920; Mrs. E. Kirby, *William Prinne, a Study in Puritanism.* Cambridge, Mass., 1931; H. W. Schneider, *The Puritan Mind.* New York, [1930]; Walter F. Schirmer, *Antike, Renaissance und Puritanismus.* München, 1933; *Two Elizabethan Puritan Diaries by Richard Rogers and Samuel Ward,* edited by M. M. Knappen. Chicago, 1933; Doumergue, *op. cit.,* V, 3-380, *et passim.*

24 Robert Allott. *Wits Theater of the Little World.* London. Printed by I. R. for N. L. 1599, pp. 1r-4v.

25 Sir John Davies. *Works,* edited by A. B. Grosart, I, 45, 52-60; cf. Aquinas, *Sum. Theol.* p3, 92, Art. 1-2: man is compound 'ex anima et corpore, constituitur in unoquoque nostrum duplex unitas, naturæ et personæ.' For quotations, see *Nosce Teipsum. loc. cit.,* I, 101, 102.

26 Thomas Milles. *Op. cit.*

27 Religion in the education of the prince. Henry Peacham (the Younger), *The Valley of Varietie.* London. Printed by M. P. for Iames Becket. 1638, chap. xiii, pp. 107 ff. See Ruth Kelso, *The Doctrine of the English Gentleman in the Sixteenth Century.* Urbana, 1929, 111-64, with bibliography.

28 Bodin. *De la République.* Paris, 1576; Latin version, 1586; *The Six Bookes of a Commonweale.* By I. Bodin...Out of the

French and Latin Copies, done into English by Richard Knolles. London. Printed by G. Bishop. 1606. The references in the text are to Knolles' translation.

29 Regius. Louis Le Roy, *Of the Interchangeable Course, or Variety of Things in the Whole World*...Written in French by Loys Le Roy called Regius: and Translated into English by R. A[shley]. London. Printed by Charles Yetsweirt. 1594, pp. 1-17ᵛ.

30 Heathen philosophers (consonance between heathen philosophy and Christianity). Kurt Schroeder, *Platonismus in der englischen Renaissance vor und bei Thomas Eliot*. Berlin, 1920, pp. 16 ff., *et passim*; David Person, *op. cit.*; Le Roy, *op. cit.*, *passim*; St. Augustine, *De civitate Dei*, lib. VIII, cap. i-xvii; Sir J. E. Sandys, *A History of Classical Scholarship*. 3 vols. Cambridge, 1903-8, 1921, *passim*.

31 *The Feminine Monarchie*. Oxford. Printed by Ioseph Barnes. 1609. See chap. i, and Conclusion addressed to the Reader.

32 Person, *op. cit.*, pp. 80 ff.

33 Huarte. Juan de Dios Huarte Navarro, *Examen de Ingenios*. Baerça, 1575; *Examen de Jngenios. The Examination of Mens Wits*. Translated out of the Spanish tongue by Camillo Camilli. Englished out of his Italian, by R. C. Esquire. London. Printed by A. Islip for T. Man. 1594, p. 166.

34 Guilty conscience. See Lily B. Campbell, *Shakespeare's Tragic Heroes: Slaves of Passion*. Cambridge, 1930, pp. 10-24; and Thomas Beard, *The Theatre of Gods Judgements: or, a Collection of Histories*. Trans. Thomas Beard. London. Printed by A. Islip. 1597, and John Reynolds, *The Triumphs of Gods Revenege against the crying and execrable Sinne of Murther*. 3 vols. London. Printed by F. Kyngston for W. Lee. 1621, 1622, 1624, quoted and referred to by Miss Campbell.

35 Calvinism. A. M. Fairbairn, 'Calvin and the Reformed Church,' *loc. cit.*, with bibliography; R. H. Murray, *op. cit.*, pp. 80-128, 169-211, with bibliographical references; Doumergue, *op. cit.*, VII, 175-422; Q. Breen, *John Calvin: A Study of French Humanism*. Grand Rapids, Mich., 1931, pp. 146-64, with bibliography; P. Barth, 'Calvins Lehre vom Staat als providentieller Lebensordnung,' in *Wernle-Festschrift*. Basel, 1932, pp. 79-94; see also references under 'Religion' above.

36 Huguenots. See A. A. Tilly, 'The Reformation in France,' *Cambridge Modern History*, II, chap. ix, and 'French Humanism and Montaigne,' *ibid.*, III, chap. ii, with bibliographies; also Fairbairn and Murray as above; Doumergue, *op. cit.*, *passim*; Henry M. Baird, *History of the Rise of the Huguenots*. 2 vols. New York, 1889, *passim*, and *The Huguenots and Henry of Navarre*. 2 vols. New York, 1886, *passim*; E. Armstrong, *The*

French Wars of Religion. 2nd ed. Oxford, 1904, pp. 1-44; C. G. Kelly, *French Protestantism, 1559-1562.* Baltimore, 1918, with bibliographical references; Armand Garnier, *Agrippa d'Aubigné et le parti protestant.* 3 t. Paris, 1927, *passim; A. Huguenot Family of the XVI Century.* The Memoirs of Philippe de Mornay...written by his wife. Trans. Lucy Crump. (Broadway Translations.) London, n. d.; P. F. Willert, *Henry of Navarre and the Huguenots in France.* New York, 1904, pp. 1-148; Albert Guérard, *Literature and Society.* Boston, 1935, pp. 108, 109.

37 *Institutes.* John Calvin, *Institutes of the Christian Religion.* A new translation by Henry Beveridge. 2 vols. Edinburgh, 1863, I, 28 ff.; Doumergue, *op. cit.,* I, 500-16, 589-98; IV, 1-17, 21-416, *et passim.*

38 Aristotle's doctrine of form. J. L. Stocks, *Aristotelianism.* New York, 1925, pp. 30-62; H. H. Joachim, Introduction to *De Generatione et Corruptione* (Oxford, 1922); G. R. Mure, *Aristotle.* London, 1932, pp. 10-15, 107-16, 148-9, *et passim;* W. D. Ross, *Aristotle.* London, 1923, pp. 63-6, 70-5, 167-76; George Grote, *Aristotle,* edited by Alexander Bain and G. C. Robertson. 2nd ed. London, 1880, pp. 446 ff., *et passim.*

39 Philip Stubbes. *The Anatomie of Abuses.* London. Printed by Richard Johnes. 1595, pp. 19-20. See Furnivall's edition (N.S.S., 1877-9), p. 44.

40 *Areopagitica.* See *The Prose Works of John Milton.* London, 1888, II, 68.

CHAPTER III

1 Revolt against the Schoolmen. Bacon, *The Advancement of Learning, loc. cit.,* 285-7, 483.

2 Historical criticism. C. V. Langlois and Ch. Seignobos, *Introduction to the Study of History.* 3rd impression. London, 1925, pp. 63-70, 211-61, *et passim,* with references. The two main schools of historiographical methodology affecting the criticism of Renaissance literature are perhaps those of Dilthey and Croce. See 'Auffassung und Analyse des Menchen in 15. und 16. Jahrhundert,' *Wilhelm Diltheys Gesammelte Schriften.* Leipzig, 1914–, I, 1-89, 'Das natüraliche System der Geisteswissenschaften im 17. Jahrhundert,' *ibid.,* 90-245, 'Die Funktion der Anthropologie in der Kultur des 16. und 17. Jahrhunderts,' *ibid.,* 416-92, and *Der Aufbau der geschichtlichen Welt in den Geisteswissenschaften, ibid.,* VII, 1-291. A number of important articles elucidatory of Dilthey's methods are to be found in the files of *Die Deutsche Vierteljahrschrift für Literaturwissenschaft und Geistesgeschichte,* e. g., Kurt Riezler, *Über den Begriff der historischen Entwicklung,* IV, 193-225. Croce's works on the theory of historiography and literary criticism are numerous; see especially *Logica come scienza del concetto puro*

and *Teoria e storia della storiografica;* see H. Wildon Carr, *The Philosophy of Benedetto Croce.* London, 1917, 189-200, with bibliography.

[3] Validity of Renaissance science. See A. N. Whitehead, *Science and the Modern World.* New York, 1925, pp. 1-9, 270-92, *et passim;* Thorstein Veblen, *The Place of Science in Modern Civilization and other Essays.* New York, 1919, pp. 1-31, 55, *et passim.*

[4] Topsell ... Gesner. See Conradi Gesneri Medici Tigurini, *Historiæ Animalium.* Liber primus. Francofurti in Bibliopolio Camberiano. MDCIII, pp. 311-12; Edward Topsell, *The Historie of Foure-footed Beastes.* At London. Printed by William Iaggard. 1607, pp. 46-7.

[5] Sir Thomas Browne. See *The Works of Sir Thomas Browne.* 3 vols. Edited by Simon Wilkin. London, 1852, I, 273-6.

[6] Topsell's version. See Topsell, *op. cit.,* pp. 14-15; Gesner, *op. cit.,* pp. 864-5.

[7] Mind of the modern man. One notes in this connection the vast modern movement which is filling the world with popular handbooks, 'stories' of philosophy, of mankind, and of various arts and sciences. Popularization goes on in all ages, but possibly the twentieth century, like the sixteenth, displays a high degree of faith on the part of the common man in his ability to enter with some understanding into erudite fields and a corresponding willingness on the part of men of erudition to prepare primers for the unlearned.

[8] The literacy of the Elizabethan audience should not, however, be underestimated; see J. W. Adamson, 'The Extent of Literacy in England in the Fifteenth and Sixteenth Centuries: Notes and Conjectures,' *The Library,* 4th Ser. X, 163-93; Louis B. Wright, *Middle-Class Culture in Elizabethan England.* Chapel Hill, 1935, pp. 44, 103-4, *et passim.* See also Max J. Wolff, "Shakespeare und sein Publikum," *Shakespeare-Jahrbuch,* LXXI, 94-106.

[9] Elizabethan psychology. The word 'psychology' was not in use in English until long after the period of the Renaissance; see *N.E.D.* under *Psychology, b.* The subject of psychology was included in 'mental' or 'rational' philosophy and, since it was the study of the soul, was thought of as 'metaphysics.' As a matter of convenience the word 'psychology' is used in this book to denote the study of mental life in the Renaissance, both as science and as instrument.

[10] Applied sciences. See *Shakespeare's England.* 2 vols. Oxford, 1916, I, 112-27, 141-69, 346-80, 413-44; II, 334-83; *passim.*

[11] Science met with success. Cf. Burtt, *op. cit.,* 23-60.

[12] *Of the Laws of Ecclesiastical Polity.* See Bk. I, chap. lix-lxxxix;

also Bk. I, *passim*, and Bk. VIII, chap. i-iv. Cf. J. W. Allen, *op. cit.*; pp. 184-98; H. O. Taylor, *Thought and Expression in the Sixteenth Century*. 2 vols. New York, II, 135-58.

13 Ulysses. See *Troilus and Cressida*, I, iii, 75-136; for parallels in Montaigne see G. C. Taylor, *op. cit.*, pp. 17-18.

14 Telescope. See Marjorie Nicolson, 'The Telescope and Imagination,' *Modern Philology*, XXXII, 233-60, the first of a series of articles on the effects of the use of the telescope on imaginative literature.

15 Experimentation. L. Thorndike, *A History of Magic and Experimental Science during the first Thirteen Centuries of our Era*. 2 vols. New York, 1929, I, 11-13, 28-30, 55-7; II, chaps. lxiii-lxv, *et passim*.

16 Bacon. See Burtt, *loc. cit.*

17 Aristotle and the Aristotelians. J.-R. Charbonnel, *La pensée italienne au XVI* siècle et le courant libertin*. Paris, 1919, pp. 158-205, 220-388, 438-616, *et passim*, with bibliography and references; E. Renan, *Averroès et Averroïsme*. Paris, 1852; J. Owen, *Skeptics of the Italian Renaissance*. London, 1893; Ueberweg-Moog, *Grundriss*, III. *Die Philosophie der Neuzeit*. 12. Aufl. (1924), sects. 4-5, with bibliography.

18 Aristotle in the new *studium generale*. H. Rashdall, *The Universities of Europe in the Middle Ages*. 2 vols. Oxford, 1895, II, 254-6, *et passim*; Mullinger, *op. cit.*, I, 282-3, *et passim*.

19 The alchemist. Robert Steele, 'Alchemy,' in *Shakespeare's England*, II, 462-74, with bibliography; C. Clark, *op. cit.*, pp. 60-5. Special importance is to be attached to Elias Ashmole's *Theatrum Chemicum Britannicum* (1652).

20 The four elements. See *Paradise Lost*, I, 920-7; II, 890-1055; V, 180-4, 404-20; *Richard II*, III, iii, 54-60; *Julius Cæsar*, V, v, 73-5; *Twelfth Night*, II, iii, 10; *Antony and Cleopatra*, V, ii, 290-1; *Hamlet*, I, iv, 27; *Othello*, II, iii, 347-8. See also Lily B. Campbell, *op. cit.*, pp. 51-62, with citations of John Jones's translation (1574) of *Galens Bookes of Elementes*, his *Bathes of Bathes Ayde* (1572), and other works dealing with elemental aspects, such as humours and complexions.

21 Rule of Reason. Bacon, *De Aug. Sci.*, *loc. cit.*, I, 668; Abraham Fraunce, *The Lawiers Logike*. London. Printed by W. How for T. Grubbin and T. Newman. 1588, Bk. II, chap. xvii, *et passim*. See Charles Waddington, *Ramus (Pierre de la Ramée), sa vie, ses écrits, et ses opinions*. Paris, 1855, pp. 267-79, 341-7.

22 Medicine. Sir William Osler, *The Evolution of Modern Medicine*. New Haven, 1913, pp. 163-82; F. H. Garrison, *Introduction to the History of Medicine*. 4th ed. Philadelphia, 1929, pp. 271, 298-9, 379, 408-11; C. A. Mercier, *Astrology in Medicine*. Lon-

don, 1914; Camden, 'Elizabethan Astrological Medicine,' *loc. cit.*

23 Plague. F. P. Wilson, *The Plague in Shakespeare's London.* Oxford, 1927, pp. 1-3, *et passim; The Plague Pamphlets of Thomas Dekker,* edited by F. P. Wilson. Oxford, 1925.

24 Violence. Thomas Dekker, *The Seven Deadly Sins of London,* edited by Brett-Smith. Boston, 1922, pp. 50-9; G. W. Thornbury, *Shakespeare's England.* 2 vols. London, 1856, I, 180-372; E. P. Cheney, *History of England from the Defeat of the Armada to the Death of Elizabeth.* 2 vols. New York, 1914, 1926, I, 463-577; II, 24-36; G. B. Harrison, *An Elizabethan Journal.* London, 1928. *A Second Elizabethan Journal.* London, 1931, and *A Last Elizabethan Journal.* London, 1933, *passim;* Lilian Winstanley, *Hamlet and the Scottish Succession.* Cambridge, 1921, and *Macbeth, King Lear, and Contemporary History.* Cambridge, 1922, *passim.*

25 Jerome Cardan. Henry Morley, *Jerome Cardan. The Life of Girolamo Cardano, of Milan, Physician.* 2 vols. London, 1854, *passim.*

26 Shakespeare (and stoicism). See T. S. Eliot, 'Shakespeare and the Stoicism of Seneca,' in *Selected Essays.* London, [1932], pp. 126-44; Franck L. Schoell, *Études sur l'humanisme continental en Angleterre à la fin de la Renaissance.* Paris, 1926, pp. 99-131; R. M. Wenley, *Stoicism and its Influence.* Boston, 1924, pp. 139-59, with bibliography.

27 A recent writer. See W. P. Eaton. *The Drama in English.* New York, 1930, pp. 130-5.

CHAPTER IV

1 Ulysses. See *Troilus and Cressida,* I, iii, 197-210; III, iii, 153-60.

2 Early writers... Italy. See W. H. Woodward, *Education during the Renaissance.* Cambridge, 1924, pp. 1-78.

3 Melanchthon. K. Hartfelder, *Melanchthon als Præceptor Germaniæ.* Berlin, 1889, and *Melanchthoniana pædagogica.* Leipzig, 1892.

4 Practical subjects in Renaissance education. *Sir Thomas Elyot, The Boke named The Gouernour deuised by Sir Thomas Elyot, Knight,* ed. from the first edition of 1531 by H. H. S. Crofts. 2 vols. London, 1883, I, xxxix-xl, 72-86, *et passim;* Mullinger, *op. cit.,* II, 401-25, *et passim;* C. E. Mallet, *A History of the University of Oxford.* 3 vols. London, 1924-27, II, 85-6, 146-9, 321-3, *et passim;* R. T. Gunther, *Early Science at Oxford.* Oxford, 1923–, *passim; The Works of John Caius, M.D.* Cambridge, 1912, *Memoir,* pp. 1-54.

5 Sir Humphrey Gilbert. *Queene Elizabethes Achademy*, edited by F. J. Furnivall. E.E.T.S. London, 1869.

6 Vittorino da Feltre's program. W. H. Woodward, *Vittorino da Feltre*. Cambridge, 1897, pp. 7-8, 37-51, *et passim;* Elyot, *The Gouernour*, loc. cit., pp. 173-83, 203-69.

7 Glendower. See *1 Henry IV*, III, i, 121-6; *Hamlet*, III, i, 158-62; *Henry V*, I, i, 38-66.

8 Letters to Robert Sidney. M. W. Wallace, *op. cit.*, p. 208.

9 Foreign travel. *Complete Works of Sir Philip Sidney*, loc. cit., Vol. III, Letters X, XI, XXXVIII, XLII.

10 Wisdom of the ancients. Bacon, *The Advancement of Learning*, loc. cit.; *De Aug. Sci.*, II, xiii, loc. cit., II, 517-38; *De Sapientia Veterum*, loc. cit., VI, 605-764. See C. W. Lemmi, *The Classic Deities in Bacon: A Study in Mythological Symbolism*. Baltimore, 1933.

11 Erasmus. *The Apothegmes of Erasmus*. Trans. Nicholas Udall. Boston, Lincs., 1878, pp. xi, xix.

12 Primitive lives. See George Norlin, *Integrity in Education*. New York, 1926, pp. 49 ff.

13 Originators of scientific truth. Thorndike, *op. cit.*, I, 56-61.

14 Alchemy. Bacon, *The Advancement of Learning*, loc. cit., 289, 351.

15 Scepticism. George T. Buckley, *Atheism in the English Renaissance*. Chicago, 1932; F. von Bezold, 'Jean Bodins Colloquium Heptaplomeres und der Atheismus des 16. Jahrhunderts,' *Historische Zeitschrift*, CXIII, 260-315; F. Brie, 'Deismus und Atheismus in der englischen Renaissance,' *Anglia*, N. F. XXXVI, 54-98, 105-68; Charbonnel, *op. cit.*, *passim;* G. H. Sabine, 'The Colloquium Heptaplomeres of Jean Bodin,' in *Persecution and Liberty* (Essays in honor of G. L. Burr). New York, 1931, pp. 271-309.

16 Philostratus. *The First Books of Philostratus, concerning the Life of Apollonius Tyaneus*. Trans. Charles Blount. London, 1680, with notes; B. L. Gildersleeve, *Essays and Studies*. New York, 1890, pp. 251-96; F. W. G. Campbell, *Apollonius of Tyana*. London, 1908; Thorndike, *op. cit.*, I, 246 ff.

17 Sceptical rhetoricians. Thorndike, *op. cit.*, I, 268-86.

18 Rabelais, P. Stapfer, *Rabelais, sa personne, son génie, son œuvre*. Paris, 1896, *passim;* H. Hatzfeld, *François Rabelais*. Berlin, 1923, pp. 149 ff.; J. Boulanger, *Rabelais à travers les âges*. Paris, 1925, pp. 20-9; H. Bousson, *Les sources et le développment du rationalisme dans la littérature française de la Renaissance (1533-1601)*. Paris, 1922, pp. 179-91, 274-6; H. O. Taylor, *op. cit.*, I, 319-33.

19 Montaigne. P. Villey, *Les sources et l'évolution des Essais de*

Montaigne. 2. éd. 2 t. Paris, 1933, I, 5-52; II, 4-33, *et passim;* Bousson, *op. cit.,* pp. 434-57.

20 Man and the animals. Bacon, *The Advancement of Learning, loc. cit.,* 264-5, quoting *Gen.* i and ii; Thorndike, *op. cit.,* I, 236-7, 246 ff., 322-33, *et passim;* Camerarius, *The Walking Library.* Trans. Iohn Molle. London, 1621, Bk. II, chap. ii, *et passim;* Thomas Milles, *op. cit.,* I, 356, 658; II, 391-2, *et passim;* David Person, *op. cit.,* pp. 30-1; Charles Butler, *The Feminine Monarchie; or, a Treatise concerning Bees.* Oxford. Printed by Ioseph Barnes. 1609, chap. i; Pierre Boaistuau, *Theatrum Mundi, the Theatre or Rule of the World.* Trans. J. Alday. London. Printed by H. D. for T. Hacket. [1566?], Bk. I; G. B. Gelli, *Circes.* Trans. H. Iden. London. Printed by J. Cawoode. 1557, *passim;* Girolamo Cardano, *Cardanus Comforte.* Trans. T. Bedingfield. London. Printed by T. Marsh. 1573, 18ᵛ-20ᵛ; see also Du Bartas, *Divine Weekes and Workes, loc. cit.,* for many references to the lower animals.

21 Dr. John Caius. *The Works of John Caius, M.D., loc. cit.,* pp. 1-78; Mullinger, *op. cit.,* II, 245-6; W. L. Nathan, *Sir John Cheke und der englischen Humanismus.* Bonn, 1928, pp. 20, 68-77.

22 Sweating sickness. Caius, *Works, loc. cit.,* sigs. 13-3ʳ-15-4ᵛ.

23 *Englische Dogges. Social England Illustrated.* Arber's English Garner. Westminster, 1903, pp. 1-44.

24 Dr. Thomas Penney. On Penney, Moffett, and others mentioned see *D. N. B.;* also *Cambridge History of English Literature,* Vol. IV, chap. xvii. On Moffett see M. L. Farrand, 'An Additional source for *A Midsummer Night's Dream,'* *Studies in Philology,* XXVII, 233-43.

25 The Turners. See *D. N. B.; Turner on Birds,* ed. A. H. Evans, Cambridge, 1903, pp. vii-xiv.

26 Dr. Timothy Bright. W. J. Carlton, *Timothe Bright, Doctor of Physicke, a Memoir of 'the Father of Modern Shorthand.'* London, 1911, pp. 1-58, 180-9.

27 *Filum Labarynthi.* Bacon, *Works, loc cit.,* III, 621-40. Bacon prepared a number of schemes for the study of motion; see particularly *Novum Organum, loc. cit.,* I, 330-49 (IV, 214-32). The outline in the text is derived from an unpublished lecture by the author's colleague Professor W. D. Briggs.

28 Demonstration in circle. Bacon, *De Aug. Sci., Works, loc. cit.,* IV, 450-1.

29 Bacon's criticisms. *The Advancement of Learning, loc. cit.,* 358; see Virgil K. Whitaker, *Bacon and the Renaissance Encyclopedists.* Unpublished dissertation, Stanford University, sect. 4, 'Misuse of Logical Methods: the Final Cause.'

30 Agrippa. *Of the Vanitie and Vncertaintie of Artes and Sciences*, loc. cit., chap. xc, pp. 171ᵛ ff.

31 Bacon's interpretation of the Scriptures. *The Advancement of Learning*, loc. cit., pp. 483-90.

CHAPTER V

1 Ancient and mediæval psychology. G. S. Brett, *op. cit.*, Vol. I, and Vol. II, pts. i and ii; J. M. Baldwin, *History of Psychology*, 2 vols. London, 1913, I, 1-94; see article on the history of psychology by G. S. Brett in *Encyclopædia Britannica*, 14th ed., with references.

2 A *milieu* of expression. Hardin Craig, 'Shakespeare's Depiction of Passions,' *Philological Quarterly*, IV, 289-301.

3 Psychology in the *Faerie Queene*. Edward Dowden, 'Elizabethan Psychology,' in *Essays Modern and Elizabethan*. London, 1920, pp. 308 ff.; F. M. Padelford, 'The Virtue of Temperance in the "Faerie Queen,"' *Studies in Philology*, XVIII, 334 ff.; Edwin Greenlaw, 'The Castle of Alma (*F. Q.* Bk. II) and Alanus, *De Planctu Naturæ*,' *Studies in Philology*, XX, 216 ff.; M. Y. Hughes, 'Burton on Spenser,' *Publications of the Modern Language Association*, XLI, 545-67.

4 Milton. See *Paradise Lost*, XI, 526-37.

5 Man and man's life. L. Le Roy, *op. cit.*, pp. 16, 25ᵛ-32ᵛ, 113ʳ-26ʳ, et passim; Cardano, *Cardanus Comforte*, loc. cit., pp. 3 ff., et passim; Milles, op. cit., Bk. I, chap. vii; Bk. II, chap. xv; Bk. VII, chap. xxviii; Bk. VIII, chap. vi, et passim; Stephen Gosson, *The S[c]hoole of Abuse*. London. Printed by T. Woodcock. 1579, sig. Di ff.; Stubbes, op. cit., passim; Edward Reynolds, *A Treatise of the Faculties of the Soule of Man*. London, 1640, chap. i; et passim; Burton, *Anatomy of Melancholy*, loc. cit., I, 149-64, et passim.

6 Cardan. *De Rerum Varietate Libri XVII*, cap. lxv.

7 *The French Academie*. Edition of 1618. Bk. I, pp. 13-16, 28, 74-9; Bk. II, pp. 416-26, 437-76, 526-37, et passim.

8 Bright's Epistle Dedicatory. *Treatise of Melancholie*. London. Printed by T. Vautrollier. 1588.

9 Huarte. *Examen de Ingenios*. loc. cit., pp. 18, 69-90, 183-205, et passim; Anton Klein, *Huarte und die Psygnosis der Renaissance*. Bonn, 1913.

10 Vergerius. *De ingenuis et liberalibus studiis ad libertinum Carrariensis*. Basle, 1541, pp. 625 ff.

11 Vegius. *De educatione liberorum et eorum claris moribus libri VI*. Parrhisius. 1511.

12 Ford. See unpublished dissertation on Ford and Burton by Dr. G. F. Sensabaugh, University of North Carolina.

[13] Formal psychology in *Tamburlaine*. C. Camden, Jr., 'Tamburlaine, the Choleric Man,' *Modern Language Notes*, XLIV, 430-5.

[14] *Arden of Feversham*. Act III, sc. v, ll. 1 ff., *et passim*.

[15] *The Honest Whore*. *The Dramatic Works of Dekker*, Pearson reprint. London, 1873, II, 67-91, 86, 9, 12, 13, 16, 73, 30, 58, 35 (order of citations in the text).

[16] Claudius's repentance. *Hamlet*, III, i, 49-54

[17] Shakespeare. See *Macbeth*, I, vii, 59-61; III, ii, 27; 63-7; *Henry V*, III, i, 3-17; *Julius Cæsar*, III, i, 39-42; *Othello*, III, iii, 325-9.

[18] *A Woman Killed with Kindness*, ed. by Katherine Lee Bates. New York, 1917, as referred to in the text.

[19] Vives. *Vives and the Renaissance Education of Women*, edited by Foster Watson. London, 1912 (a translation of Vives' *De institutione feminæ Christianæ*, 1523), pp. 84-9, 94-102.

[20] Montaigne. See *Essays, loc. cit.*, II, 314.

[21] Favoured ideal of womanhood. H. S. V. Jones, *Spenser Handbook*. New York, 1930, pp. 223-30; A. S. Cook, 'The Amazonian Type in Poetry,' *Modern Language Notes*, V, 321-8; E. Koeppel, 'Florimel and Britomart's Saga,' *Archiv.*, CVII, 394 ff.; F. M. Padelford, 'The Women in Spenser's Allegory of Love,' *Journal of English and Germanic Philology*, XVI, 7 ff.; and 'The Allegory of Chastity in the "Faerie Queene,"' *Studies in Philology*, XXI, 367 ff.

[22] *Bussy D'Ambois*. *The Comedies and Tragedies of George Chapman*, Pearson reprint. Vol. II, pp. 1-96. See the author's 'Ethics in the Jacobean Drama: the Case of Chapman,' *Essays in Dramatic Literature: The Parrott Presentation Volume*. Princeton, 1935, pp. 25-46.

CHAPTER VI

[1] Harrison. *Harrison's Description of England*, edited by F. J. Furnivall. N.S.S. 4 vols. London, 1877, Vol. I, Bk. I, p. 78.

[2] Gabriel Harvey. *Marginalia, loc. cit.*, pp. 107-8, 156-7.

[3] Bacon. *The Advancement of Learning, loc. cit.*, 447-73; *De Aug. Sci.*, VIII, ii, *loc. cit.*, I, 749-91; quotation from *ibid.*, V, 70-1.

[4] History of logic. R. Adamson, *A Short History of Logic*. London, 1912; *The Organon of Aristotle*. Trans. Owen, London, 1853; M. Blundeville, *The Arte of Logike. Plainly taught in the English tongue, by M. Blundeuile of Newton Flotsam in Norfolke, as well according to the doctrine of Aristotle, as of all other moderne and best accounted Authors*. London. Printed by J. Windet. 1599; Thomas Wilson, *The Rule of Reason, conteining the Arte of Logique*. London. Printed by R. Grafton, 1552; M. De Wulf, *History of Medieval Philosophy*.

Trans. E. C. Messenger. 2 vols. London, 1926; G. Harms, *Geschichte der Logik.* Berlin, 1881; G. H. Lewes, *Aristotle: A Chapter from the History of Science.* London, 1864, and *The History of Logic from Thales to Comte.* 5th ed. 2 vols. London, 1880; C. von Prantl, *Geschichte der Logik im Abendlande.* 4 Bde. Leipzig, 1855-77; James Seth, *English Philosophers and Schools of Philosophy.* London, 1912; F. P. Graves, *Peter Ramus and the Educational Reformation of the Sixteenth Century.* New York, 1912; J. B. Mullinger, *The Schools of Charles the Great.* London, 1877; Friedrich Ueberwegs *Grundriss der Geschichte der Philosophie.* 12. Aufl. bearb. v. Frischhausen-Köhler und Moog. 3 T. Berlin, 1927.

5 Logic as an instrument. Grote, *op. cit.,* I, 298-377.

6 Ramus. Waddington, *op. cit., passim;* E. Bréhier, *Histoire de la philosophie.* 2 t. Paris, 1926, 1932, I, 771-5; J. Owen, *Sceptics of the French Renaissance.* London, 1893, pp. 493-558; A. Rickel, *Die Philosophie der Renaissance.* München, 1925, pp. 104-11, *et passim.*

7 Polonius. See *Hamlet,* II, ii, 97-104.

8 Wilson. *The Rule of Reason, loc. cit.,* fol. 111-23, *et passim.*

9 Ramus as an orator. Waddington, *op. cit.,* pp. 60-80, *et passim.*

10 Sidney a Ramist. Wallace, *op. cit.,* pp. 118-19; A. W. Osborn, *Sir Philip Sidney en France.* Paris, 1932, pp. 12, 16, 32-3.

11 Anthony Wotton. *Runne from Rome* (1624); quoted in *D.N.B.*

12 Logic in the Renaissance. P. S. Allen, *The Age of Erasmus.* Oxford, 1914, pp. 105-9; Friedrich Ueberwegs *Grundriss.* 3. T. *Loc. cit.,* pp. 22-35, 71-88, 161-9, 187-93; Stengel, 'Logik,' in Pauly-Wissowa, *Real Encyclopödie;* Riekel, *op. cit.,* pp. 83-90; M. Carriere, *Die philosophische Weltanschauung der Reformationszeit.* Leipzig, 1887, II, 11-75; Waddington, *op. cit.,* pp. 381-97.

13 Shakespeare and logic. See *Hamlet,* V, i, 9-22, 151-3; II, ii, 92-105; *1 Henry IV,* II, iv, 298-303, 535-45. See Hardin Craig, 'Shakespeare and Formal Logic,' *Studies in English Philology: A Miscellany in Honor of Frederick Klaeber.* Minneapolis, 1929, pp. 380-95.

14 Sir Henry Sidney. *An English Garner,* edited by E. Arber. 8 vols. Birmingham, 1877-97, I, 41-3.

15 Elyot. *The Gouernour, loc. cit.,* I, 1-4.

16 Bacon. *The Advancement of Learning, loc. cit.,* 295-7, 346-51.

17 Hooker. *The Laws of Ecclesiastical Polity, loc. cit.,* I, iv, 1, 2.

18 Arcadia. *The Complete Works of Sir Philip Sidney, loc. cit.,* I, xii, pp. 76-84.

19 Discovery of truth. For statement of the value of logic, see

preface to *Libellus Sophistarum ad usum Oxoniensem,* published by Pynson (1499-1500) and de Worde (1510, 1512, 1515?, 1524).

CHAPTER VII

[1] Chaucer and the rhetoricians. John M. Manly, 'Chaucer and the Rhetoricians,' British Academy, *Proceedings,* XXI, 95-113; Edmond Faral, *Les arts poétiques du XIIᵉ et du XIIIᵉ siècles.* Paris, 1924 (contains the Latin works referred to in the text).

[2] Colours of rhetoric. R. Volkmann, *Rhetorik der Griechen und Römer.* 3. Aufl., besorgt v. C. Hammer. München, 1901, pp. 639-76; J. M. Berdan, *Early Tudor Poetry,* 1485-1547. New York, 1920, pp. 60 ff., 124 ff., 442 ff.; H. W. Wells, *Poetic Imagery Illustrated from Elisabethan Literature.* New York, 1924; W. J. Courthope, *History of English Poetry.* 6 vols. London, 1895-1910, II, 178-200, 288-330; III, 103-9, *et passim;* F. Brie, 'Umfang und Ursprung der poetischen Beseelung in der englischen Renaissance bis zu Philip Sidney,' *Englische Studien,* L, 383-425; H. V. Canter, *Rhetorical Elements in the Tragedies of Seneca.* Urbana, Ills., 1925, pp. 99-125; C. S. Baldwin, *Medieval Rhetoric.* New York, 1928, *passim;* Walter F. Schirmer, "Shakespeare und die Rhetorik," *Shakespeare-Jahrbuch,* LXXI, 11-31. See *Wilson's Arte of Rhetorique,* ed. G. H. Mair. Oxford, 1909, pp. 169-209.

[3] Isocrates. La R. Van Hook, 'Alcidamas vs. Isocrates,' *Classical Weekly,* XII, 89-94; W. von Christs Geschichte der griechischen Literatur. 6. Aufl., bearb. v. Schid. München, 1924, I, 565-78, with bibliography. *Isocrates.* Translated by George Norlin. 3 vols. Loeb Classical Library. New York, 1928, I, ix-li, *et passim.*

[4] Rhetoric applied to theology. W. F. Mitchell, *English Pulpit Oratory from Andrewes to Tillotson.* London, 1932, pp. 41-4, *et passim.*

[5] Sidney's address to his troops. Wallace, *op. cit.,* p. 370.

[6] Sir Henry Wotton on Essex. *The Characters of Robert Devereux...and George Villiers...contrasted.* Lee Priory Press, 1824, p. 22.

[7] Ben Jonson on Bacon as an orator. *Timber or Discoveries,* edited by F. E. Schelling. Boston, 1892, p. 30.

[8] *A Discourse to the Queenes Majesty touching her Mariage with Monsieur. Complete Works, loc. cit.,* III, 51-60; quotation from p. 55. See *Wilson's Arte of Rhetorique, loc. cit.,* pp. 114-16, *et passim.*

[9] Polixenes. See *The Winter's Tale,* IV, iv, 97.

[10] Harvey's *Marginalia. Loc. cit.,* p. 122.

[11] Democritus to the Reader. *The Anatomy of Melancholy, loc. cit.,* I, 30-1; also I, 314, 304; II, 82.

12 *Timber. Loc. cit.*, pp. 54-5.

13 Aristotle, *Rhetoric*, I, i (6354a 1. 1).

14 John Hoskins. Brit. Mus. Harl. MS. 4604. See Wallace, *op. cit.*, p. 234; R. W. Zandvoort, *Sidney's Arcadia; a Comparison between the Two Versions*. Amsterdam, 1929, pp. 180-2, 189. See Hoskin's *Directions for Speech and Style*. Edited by Hoyt H. Hudson. Princeton, 1935, pp. 41, 93-4.

15 Aristotle, *Rhetoric*, III, xii-xiv (1414 a, b, 1415 b, 1418 b).

16 Plutarch. See *Lives*. Translated by North. Tudor Translations. London, 1895, II, 22.

17 Bacon on rhetoric. *The Advancement of Learning, loc. cit.*, 389-91, 409 ff.

18 Dekker. The references in the text are to the Pearson reprint. Vol. II. See II, 35-9, 150-5.

19 Wilson. *Op. cit.*, p. 113.

20 Language and thought. H. C. Warren, *Human Psychology*. Boston, 1919, pp. 314-29; William James, *The Principles of Psychology*. 2 vols. New York, 1904, II, 325-71; E. B. Titchener, *A Text-book of Psychology*. New York, 1924, pp. 521 ff.

21 Elizabethan expressiveness. H. O. Taylor, *op. cit.*, II, 238-387.

22 *Antonio and Mellida. The Works of John Marston*, ed. A. H. Bullen. 3 vols. London, 1887; *The First Part of Antonio and Mellida*, I, 1-93; *The Second Part of Antonio and Mellida [Antonio's Revenge]*, I, 95-191. The references in the text are to this edition.

23 Chapman. References to poems are from *The Works of George Chapman*. 3 vols. London, 1875; see Vol. II, pp. 8, 28-36, etc. References to plays are from *The Comedies and Tragedies of George Chapman, loc. cit.* See *Bussy D'Ambois*, Act I, sc. i, ll. 134-9, and Act III, sc. i, ll. 123-4 (Belles Lettres ed.); see (Pearson reprint) *The Conspiracy of Charles, Duke of Biron*, II, 187, 219, 220, 242; *The Tragedy of Charles, Duke of Biron*, II, 246, 254, 257, 258, 278, 306, 309; *The Gentleman Usher*, I, 258, 278; *Monsieur D'Olive*, I, 246; *Ovid's Banquet of Sense*, ll. 263, 266-7, 269, 270; see also *Hymnus in Noctem*, ll. 235 ff., 247 ff.

CHAPTER VIII

1 Renaissance attitudes of mind. Anticipations and suggestions of the ideas advanced in the text will be found in Whitehead and Veblen as cited, in Bury (see below), and in various brief passages scattered throughout many works of a historical and critical character.

2 Pastoralism. W. W. Greg, *Pastoral Poetry and Pastoral Drama*. London, 1906, with bibliography; H. Genouy, *L'élément pastoral dans la poésie narrative et dramatique en Angleterre*. Paris,

1929; Violet M. Jeffrey, 'Italian and English Pastoral Drama of the Renaissance,' *Modern Language Review*, XIX, 56-62, 175-87, 435-44; R. Bayne, 'Masque and Pastoral,' *Cambridge History of English Literature*, Vol. VI, chap. xiii, with bibliography.

³ Appreciation of nature. E. Blunden, *Nature in English Literature*. London, 1929, pp. 89-105; Elsa Berndt, *Dame Nature in der englischen Literatur bis herab zu Shakespeare*. Leipzig, 1923, pp. 55-100; F. W. Moorman, *The Interpretation of Nature in English Poetry from Beowulf to Shakespeare*. Strassburg, 1905, pp. 158-239; E. Voigt, *Shakespeares Naturschilderungen*. Heidelberg, 1909.

⁴ Montaigne. See Jonson's *Volpone*, III, iv, 87-90.

⁵ Romantic ideal. Jones, *Spenser Handbook, loc. cit.,* pp. 134-42, and 'The "Faerie Queene" and the Mediæval Aristotelian Tradition,' *Journal of English and Germanic Philology*, XXV, 283 ff.; W. P. Ker, *Epic and Romance*. London, 1897; J. W. Mackail, *The Springs of Helicon*. London, 1909, pp. 85 ff.; J. E. Spingarn, *Literary Criticism in the Renaissance*. New York, 1912, chap. iv; H. Maynardier, *The Arthur of the English Poets*. Boston, 1907, chap. xv; R. S. Crane, 'The Vogue of Guy of Warwick from the Close of the Middle Ages to the Romantic Revival,' *Publications of the Modern Language Association*, XXX, 125 ff.; J. B. Fletcher, 'Huon of Burdeux and the "Faerie Queene,"' *Journal of English and Germanic Philology*, II, 203 ff.; R. E. N. Dodge, 'Spenser's Imitations from Ariosto,' *Publications of the Modern Language Association*, XII, 151-204, and XXXV, 91-2; A. H. Gilbert, 'Spenser's Imitations from Ariosto: Supplementary,' *ibid.,* XXXIV, 225-32; C. B. Millican, 'Spenser and the Arthurian Legend,' *Review of English Studies*, VI, 167 ff.

⁶ Literature and life. See Elmer E. Stoll, *Shakespeare Studies*. New York, 1927, pp. 39-89; 'Literature and Life Again,' *Publications of the Modern Language Association*, XLVII, 283-302; 'Literature no "Document,"' *Modern Language Review*, XIX, 141-57.

⁷ Devices of thought. See Denis Saurat, *Literature and the Occult Tradition*. Trans. Dorothy Bolton. London, 1930, pp. 57 ff.

⁸ Roger Williams. *The Bloody Tenent of Persecution*, chaps. xviii-xxvi; *The Bloody Tenent yet more bloody*, chaps. xviii-xxvi.

⁹ Democratic thinking in the sixteenth century. J. W. Allen, *op. cit.,* 247-70, *et passim*, with bibliography; R. H. Murray, *op. cit.,* pp. 169-211; G. P. Gooch, *English Democratic Ideas in the Seventeenth Century*. Cambridge, 1927, *passim*; W. D. Briggs, 'Political Ideas in Sidney's *Arcadia*,' *Studies in Philology*,

XXVIII, 137-61, and 'Sidney's Political Ideas,' *ibid.*, XXIX, 534-42.

10 Idea of progress. J. B. Bury, *The Idea of Progress*, pp. 12 ff., 335-6, *et passim*, and 'The Perspective of Knowedge,' in *Selected Essays*, edited by H. Temperley. Cambridge, 1930, pp. 43-59; Sylvia Benians, *From Renaissance to Revolution, a Study of the Influence of the Renaissance upon the Political Development of Eurbpe*. London, 1923, *passim*; W. Lee Ustick, 'Changing Ideals of Aristocratic Character and Conduct in Seventeenth Century England,' *Modern Philology*, XXX, 147-66.

11 The nobility and the common people. Cheyney, *op. cit.*, II, 3-36, *et passim*.

12 Class and privilege. Muriel St. Clare Byrne, 'The Social Background,' in *A Companion to Shakespeare Studies*. Cambridge, 1934, pp. 187-318, and *Elizabethan Life in Town and Country*. London, 1925, *passim*; Kelso, *op. cit.*, pp. 31-41, with bibliography; Ustick, *op. cit.*; Sir E. K. Chambers, 'The Court,' in *Shakespeare's England*, I, 79-111. See Bodin, *The Six Bookes of a Commonweale*, *loc. cit.*, Bk. I, chaps. v-viii; Milles, *op. cit.*, Bk. I, chap. v; William Willymat, *A Loyal Subjects Looking-Glasse*. London. Printed by G. Elde. 1604, chaps. iii, vi; Jeronimo Osorio da Fonseca, *The Five Bookes of Civill and Christian Nobilitie*. Trans. W. Blandie. London. Printed by T. Marsh. 1576; Laurence Humphrey, *The Nobles, or Of Nobilitie*. London. Printed by T. Marsh. 1563.

13 Platonic academy. Martha Ornstein, *The Rôle of Scientific Societies in the Seventeenth Century*. Chicago, 1928, chaps. i-iii, *passim*.

14 Ethics of caste. Kelso, *op. cit.*, pp. 70-110. See Annibale Romei, *The Courtiers Academie*. Trans. I. K. London. Printed by V. Sims. 1598, pp. 78-128, *et passim*.

15 *Ars moriendi* literature. Lily B. Campbell, *op. cit.*, pp. 16-17, 113-14, 133-4, *et passim; The Axiochus of Plato translated by Edmund Spenser*, edited by F. M. Padelford. Baltimore, 1934, pp. 12-16; Hardin Craig, 'Hamlet's Book,' *Huntington Library Bulletin*, No. 6, November, 1934, pp. 17-37; J. Huitzinga, *Herfttij der Middeleeuwen*. Haarlem, 1921, pp. 231-54.

16 The Scriptures as interpreted. Charles Beard, *The Reformation of the Sixteenth Century in its relation to Modern Thought and Knowledge*. London, 1927, pp. 262-369; Wilhelm Dilthey, 'Die kirchliche Theologie, die historische Kritik und die Hermeneutik,' *loc. cit.*, II, 110-29; see notes on 'The law of nature and the law of Scripture' and 'Bacon's interpretation of the Scriptures' above.

17 Mythology in Renaissance thinking. Douglas Bush, *Mythology and the Renaissance Tradition in English Poetry*. Minneapolis,

1932, with bibliography; Schoell, *op. cit.*, pp. 21-42; Lemmi, *op. cit., passim;* H. G. Lotspeich, *Classical Mythology in the Poetry of Edmund Spenser.* Princeton, 1932, *passim.*

[18] Miranda. See *The Tempest*, I, ii, 457.

[19] Bacon on similarities and differences. *The Advancement of Learning, loc. cit.*, pp. 430 ff.; see also p. 418.

[20] Cruelty of punishments. *Hangmen's Diaries.* The Times, *Literary Supplement*, 24 June 1926, pp. 421-2, reviewing T. Hampe, *Crime and Punishment in Germany, as illustrated by the Nuremberg Malefactors' Books.* Trans. by M. Letts. London, 1929, with other works on crime and punishment.

[21] Sir John Davies. See *D. N. B.* under Davies, Sir John.

CHAPTER IX

[1] The advancement of Renaissance learning. Bacon, *The Advancement of Learning, loc. cit.*, pp. 306-8, *et passim; Novum Organum*, I, cxxviii-cxxix, *loc. cit.*, IV, 112-14; Le Roy, *op. cit.*, chaps. xii, xiii; Campanella, *The City of the Sun*, in Morley's *Ideal Commonwealths.* 10th ed., p. 263. See Whitaker, *op. cit., passim.*

[2] Shakespeare's meaning. Elmer E. Stoll, 'Anachronism in Shakespeare Criticism,' *Modern Philology*, VII, 557-75, 'Criminals in Shakespeare and Science,' *ibid.*, X, 55-80, "Falstaff," *ibid.*, XII, 197-240, and *Shakespeare Studies, loc. cit.*, pp. 90-146, 403-90; L. L. Schücking, *Die Charakterprobleme bei Shakespeare.* Leipzig, 1919 (3rd ed. 1932), who cites Rümelin and other continental critics. See review of Schücking's work by Karl Young, *Philological Quarterly*, I, 228-34. For the point of view of historical criticism, see Barrett Wendell, *William Shakespeare.* New York, 1901, introduction, *et passim;* John Corbin, *The Elizabethan 'Hamlet.'* London, 1895; C. M. Lewis, *The Genesis of 'Hamlet.'* New York, 1907; G. L. Kittredge, *Shakespeare.* Cambridge, Mass., 1916; J. M. Robertson, *The Problem of 'Hamlet.'* London, 1919, and other works by the same author; *The Works of William Shakespeare*, edited by R. Bridges. Stratford, 1907, Vol. X, pp. 321-4. See also Sir E. K. Chambers, 'The Disintegration of Shakespeare,' in *Aspects of Shakespeare*, edited by J. W. Mackail. Oxford, 1933, pp. 23-48; L. Abercrombie, 'A Plea for the Liberty of Interpreting,' *ibid.*, pp. 227-54; E. C. Knowlton, 'Falstaff Redux,' *Journal of English and Germanic Philology*, XXV, 193-215; Émile Legouis, 'La réaction contre la critique romantique de Shakespeare,' in *Essays and Studies by Members of the English Association*, XIII, 74-87.

[3] Changing conception of the Renaissance. R. H. Fife, 'The Renaissance in a Changing World,' *Germanic Review*, IX, 73-95, with references to the opinions of Taine, Burckhardt, K. Bur-

dach, W. Rehm (*Das Werden des Renaissancebildes in der dt. Dichtung vom Rationalismus bis zum Realismus*. München, 1924), E. Cassirer (*Individuum und Kosmos in der Philosophie der Renaissance*. Leipzig, 1927), E. Troeltsch ('Renaissance und Reformation,' *Historische Zeitschrift*, CX, 528 ff.), and others. See also H. W. Eppelsheimer, 'Das Renaissance-Problem,' *Dt. Viertel-jahrschrift für Literaturwissenschaft und Geistesge-schichte*, XI, 477-500; G. Weise, 'Der doppelte Begriff der Renaissance,' *ibid.*, XI, 501-29; F. Blaschke, 'Stendhals Begriff der Renaissance,' in *Goetz-Festschrift*. Leipzig, 1927, pp. 201-12; D. Frey, *Gotik und Renaissance als Grundlagen der modernen Weltanschauung*. Augsburg, 1929; Enrico Carrara, *Lineamenti dell' umanesimo*. Torino, 1930.

4 Commentaries and *spuria*. Material is widely scattered in such works as Sandys, *History of Classical Scholarship*, Manitius, *Geschichte der lateinischen Literatur des Mittelalters*, and Teuffel-Schwabe, *History of Roman Literature*, and in various studies of the influence of classical authors.

5 Elizabethan translators. See F. O. Matthiessen, *Translation, an Elizabethan Art*. Cambridge (Mass.), 1931, where there is made out a case for the superiority of certain Elizabethan transla-tions to their originals.

6 Scientific and moral subjects. *Gabriel Harvey's Marginalia*, loc. cit., pp. 160-3.

7 Jonson. *Timber*, loc cit., p. 49.

8 Poet and Painter. See *Timon of Athens*, I, i, 20-37.

9 Amatory conventions. Lu Emily Pearson, *Elizabethan Love Conventions*. Berkeley, Calif., 1933, pp. 30-102, *et passim*, with bibliography.

10 Conventionality of the sonnet. Sir Sidney Lee, 'The Vogue of the Elizabethan Sonnet,' in *A Life of William Shakespeare*. New and revised edition. New York, 1909, pp. 443-57, and *Eliza-bethan Sonnets*. 2 vols. Westminster, 1904, pp. ix-cx; Pearson, op. cit., passim, with bibliography.

11 Ethics for women. *Vives and the Renaissance Education of Women*, loc. cit., passim; Jones, *Spenser Handbook*, loc. cit., pp. 223-30, with references; P. S. Allen, op. cit., pp. 193-9; A. M. Clark, *Thomas Heywood: Playwright and Miscellanist*. Ox-ford, 1931, pp. 93-5; W. H. Woodward, *Studies in Education during the Age of the Renaissance*. Cambridge, 1906, pp. 21, 110, 205, 264-70. See also Miles Coverdale's translation of Hein-rich Bullinger, *The Christen State of Matrimonye*. 1541 and many editions; William Austin, *Hæc Homo, wherein the Ex-cellency of the Creation of Woman is described*. London. Printed by R. Olton for R. Mabb. 1637. See especially Louis B.

Wright, *op. cit.*, pp. 108-17, 201-27, 465-507, *et passim*, with many references.

[12] Passage from the Old Testament. Numbers xxx. 3-5; see Charles Gibbon, *A Work Worth the Reading* (1591), first dialogue.

[13] Courtly love and chivalry. See W. H. Schofield, *Chivalry in English Literature*. Cambridge, Mass., 1912, *passim*; E. B. Fowler, *Spenser and the Courts of Love*. Menasha, Wis., 1921, and *Spenser and the System of Courtly Love*. Louisville, 1934.

[14] Platonic love. C. R. Baskervill, 'Bassanio as an Ideal Lover,' in *Manly Anniversary Studies in Language and Literature*. Chicago, 1923, pp. 90-103; Pearson, *op. cit.*, pp. 30-57, 163 ff., *et passim*; with bibliography; J. S. Harrison, *Platonism in English Poetry of the Sixteenth and Seventeenth Centuries*. New York, 1903, *passim*; K. Schroeder, *op. cit., passim*.

[15] Polydore Vergil. See article in *D. N. B.*, with references; J. B. Mullinger, *Introduction to the Study of English History*. London, 1881, p. 302.

[16] Elizabethan criticism. J. E. Spingarn, *A History of Literary Criticism in the Renaissance*. 2nd ed. New York, 1908, pp. 253-81, with bibliography; G. Gregory Smith, *Elizabethan Critical Essays*. 2 vols. Oxford, 1904, I, lxvi-lxxxix, *et passim*; George Saintsbury, *A History of Literary Criticism*. 3 vols. London, 1928, II, 143-235; G. A. Thompson, *Elizabethan Criticism of Poetry*. Menasha, Wis., 1914, pp. 35-55, *et passim*.

[17] Exceptions. Jonson certainly shows in *Timber* and other writings an individual point of view in criticism; as also Shakespeare in some places, such as *Hamlet*, II, ii, 454-71.

[18] Michael Angelo. J. Huizinga, *The Waning of the Middle Ages*. London, 1924, p. 244.

[19] Invention of plots—imitation. W. L. Bullock, 'The Precept of Plagiarism in the Cinquecento,' *Modern Philology*, XXV, 293-312; W. G. Howard, 'Ut pictura poesis,' *Publications of the Modern Language Association*, XXIV, 44 ff.; M. W. Bundy, ' "Imagination" and "Invention" in the Renaissance,' *Journal of English and Germanic Philology*, XXIX, 535-45; Hermann Gmelin, 'Der Princip der Imitatio in der romanischen Literatur der Renaissance,' *Romanische Forschungen*, XLVI, 83-360; H. O. White, *Plagiarism and Imitation during the English Renaissance*. Cambridge, Mass., 1935, *passim*.

[20] History of Shakespearean appreciation. A. Ralli, *A History of Shakespearian Appreciation*. 2 vols. London, 1932, I, 9, 34, 80-1, 157-8, *et passim*; R. W. Babcock, *The Genesis of Shakespeare Idolatry*. Chapel Hill, 1931, pp. 45-126, *et passim*.

[21] J. M. Manly, 'Shakespeare Himself,' in *A Memorial Volume to Shakespeare and Harvey*. University of Texas Bulletin No. 1701.

Austin, Texas, 1917, p. 20; see *The Rape of Lucrece*, ll. 1361-1568.

22 Marlowe. C. Camden, Jr., 'Marlowe and Elizabethan Psychology,' *Modern Language Notes*, XLV, 298-9, and 'Tamburlaine, the Choleric Man,' *loc. cit.*

23 La Primaudaye. *Loc. cit.*, pp. 282-5.

24 Elizabethan psychology in the interpretation of character. A. C. Bradley, *Shakespearean Tragedy*. London, 1905, pp. 115-22, 171-4, 271-3, *et passim*; Lily B. Campbell, *op. cit.*, pp. 15, 22, 23, 110, 132, *et passim*; M. W. Bundy, 'Shakespeare and Elizabethan Psychology,' *Journal of English and Germanic Philology*, XXIII, 516-49; Ruth L. Anderson, *Elizabethan Psychology and Shakespeare's Plays*. Iowa City, 1927, pp. 154-76, *et passim*; E. E. Stoll, *Shakespeare Studies*, *loc. cit.*, pp. 90-146.

25 Mr. T. S. Eliot. See 'Hamlet' in *Elizabethan Essays*. London, 1934; for the general point of view see A. C. Bradley, 'Poetry for Poetry's Sake,' in *Oxford Lectures on Poetry*. London, 1909.

26 Jonson. See *Timber*, *loc. cit.*, pp. 24, 28.

CHAPTER X

1 Synthetic process. See A. N. Whitehead, *Adventures of Ideas*. New York, 1933, pp. 131 ff., and *Science and the Modern World*, *loc. cit.*, pp. 74-9, 219-51.

2 Recent writer. See P. J. Smith, *Bibliographia Burtoniana*. Stanford University, 1931, p. 6.

3 *The Anatomy of Melancholy*. *Loc. cit.*, I, 205-30.

4 Knowledge of Bacon's *Essays*. *Ibid.* II, 288.

5 Bacon. *Novum Organum*, I, lxxxii, lxxxv, cxxii, cxvii, lxii-lxv, cxvi; *Works*, *loc. cit.*, I, 80-1, 82-5, 108-9, 104-5, 63-6, 103-4; references given in the order of quotation in the text.

6 Humanism in England. *The English Works of Sir Thomas More*. Edited by A. W. Reed and others. Vol. I. London, 1931; J. A. Gee, *The Life and Works of Thomas Lupset*. New Haven, 1928; *The Poems of Sir Thomas Wiat*. Edited by A. K. Foxwell. 2 vols. London, 1913; *Supposes* and *Jocasta*, edited by J. W. Cunliffe. Boston, 1906; Anna B. Modersohn, 'Cicero im englischen Geistesleben des 16. Jahrhunderts,' *Archiv*, CXLIX, 33-51, 219-45; L. Rick, 'Shakespeare und Ovid,' *Shakespeare-Jahrbuch*, LV, 35-53, and *Ovids Metamorphosen in der englischen Renaissance*. Münster, 1915; A. E. A. K. Roeder, *Menechmi und Amphitruo im englischen Drama bis zur Restauration, 1661*. Leipzig, 1904; J. W. Cunliffe, *The Influence of Seneca on Elizabethan Tragedy*. London, 1893; Evelyn M. Spearing, *The Elizabethan Translations of Seneca's Tragedies*. Cambridge, 1912; *The Poetical Works of Sir William Alexander*. Edited by Kastner and Charlton. 2 vols. Manchester,

1921, 1929; F. L. Lucas, *Seneca and Elizabethan Tragedy*. London, 1927; J. S. Harrison, *op. cit.;* K. Schroeder, *op. cit.;* Martha H. Shackford, *Plutarch in Renaissance England*. Privately printed, 1929; *The Works of Thomas Kyd*. Edited by F. S. Boas. Oxford, 1901; F. L. Schoell, 'L'Helénisme française en Angleterre à la fin de la Renaissance,' *Revue de littérature comparée*, 1925, pp. 193-238, and *Études sur l'humanisme continental en Angleterre à la fin de la Renaissance*. Paris, 1926; H. M. Ayres, 'Shakespeare's *Julius Cæsar* in the light of some other Versions,' *Publications of the Modern Language Association of America*, XXV, 183-227, and 'Caesar's Revenge,' *ibid.*, XXX, 771-87; *Ciceronianism in English Literature*. Edited by G. Gordon. Oxford, 1912; Douglas Bush, *Mythology and the Renaissance Tradition in English Poetry*. Minneapolis, 1932. See also extended bibliographies in *Cambridge History of English Literature*, Vols. III and IV, and in *Shakespeare's England*.

7 Ascham. See *The Scholemaster*; passage modernized from *The English Works of Roger Ascham*. Cambridge, 1904.

8 Montaigne. See *Essays, loc. cit.*, I, 351-2.

9 Castelain. *Ben Jonson, Discoveries*. Thèse par Maurice Castelain. Paris, n.d. See Hoskins, *Directions for Speech and Style*, edited by Hoyt H. Hudson, *loc. cit.*, pp. xxvii-xxx.

10 Lyly's culture. See *The Complete Works of John Lyly*. Edited by R. W. Bond. 3 vols. Oxford, 1902; *Euphues*. Edited by Croll and Clemons. London, 1916; A. Feuillerat, John Lyly, *Contribution à l'histoire de la Renaissance en Angleterre*. Cambridge, 1910; V. M. Jeffrey. *John Lyly and the Italian Renaissance*. Paris, 1928.

11 Dekker. *Dramatic Works, loc. cit., Non-dramatic Works*. Edited by A. B. Grosart. 5 vols. Huth Library, 1888. See in the latter II, 240-1; III, 1-60; IV, 1-84; III, 88-90, 305-50; V, 54.

12 *The Whore of Babylon, loc. cit.*, II, 223-4.

13 Nashe's culture. *The Works of Thomas Nashe*. Edited by R. B. McKerrow. 5 vols. London, 1904-1908.

14 Shakespeare's scholarship. H. R. D. Anders, *Shakespeare's Books*. Berlin, 1904 (Review by E. Keoppel, 'Randglossen zu dem Anders'schen Werk über Shakespeares Belesenheit,' *Archiv*, CXIII, 49-55); Sir J. E. Sandys, 'Scholarship' in *Shakespeare's England*, I, 251-83, with bibliography.

15 Jonson. See *Ben Jonson*. Edited by C. H. Herford and Percy Simpson. Oxford, 1923—Vol. I, Appendix IV: Books in Jonson's Library, pp. 250-71.

INDEX

A

Actorides, 103
Agricola, Rodolphus, 90
Agrippa, Henry Cornelius, 16-21, 30, 43-8, 96, 98, 110, 111, 260
Alberti, Leo Battista, 90
Albertus Magnus, 17, 67
Alday, John, 119
Alexander the Great, 90
Alexis of Piedmont, 39
Allott, Robert, 50, 119
Ambrose, St., 57, 221
Anselm, St., 52
Anthony, St., 67
Antoniano, Silvio, 121
Apuleius, Lucius, 17
Aquinas, Thomas, St., 23, 248
Arcandam, 38-9
Arden of Feversham, 123, 124, 131, 229, 232
Ariosto, 186
Aristophanes, 258
Aristotle, 1, 7, 15, 17, 22, 23, 33, 39, 52, 57, 61, 71, 75, 76, 78, 82, 89, 104, 110, 113, 139, 140, 142-7, 157, 170-4, 185, 186, 199, 213, 214, 245, 248, 249, 253, 254
Ascham, Roger, 89, 100, 165, 166, 220, 251, 252
Augustine, St., 21, 22, 24, 52, 57, 221
Avicenna, 17

B

Bacon, Francis, 19, 26, 63, 75, 76, 78, 79, 95-7, 99, 100-2, 105-12, 114, 141, 142, 164, 167, 169, 174, 186, 190-2, 202, 203, 206-9, 237, 241, 243, 244, 249-51, 262-4; *The Advancement of Learning*, i, 1, 19, 32, 61, 87,

95, 99, 110, 113, 139, 141, 153, 159, 160, 174, 181, 202, 210, 238
Barckley, Sir Richard, 119
Bartholomew de Glanville (*De Proprietatibus Rerum*), 119
Beaumont, Francis, and John Fletcher, 123, 227
Berkeley, George, 1
Beza, Théodore, 190
Bible, 2, 52, 56, 99, 118, 145, 198, 199, 220
Boaistuau, Pierre, 119
Boccaccio, 161
Bodin, Jean, 53, 76, 246
Boethius, 142
Boethius, Hector, 102
Boiardo, 186
Borromeo, Charles, St., 189
Briggs, Henry, 100, 104
Bright, Timothy, 103, 104, 119, 120
Brinsley, John, 89
Browne, Sir Thomas, 67
Bruno, Giordano, 141
Buchanan, George, 190
Burton, Robert, 10, 116, 117, 119, 123, 159, 167-9, 243-51, 263
Butler, Charles, 54
Butler, Samuel, 41

C

Cæsar, Julius, 63, 90, 145
Caius, John, 100-3
Calvin, John, 52, 55-8, 143
Camden, William, 253
Camerarius, Joachim, 101, 109
Campanella, Tommaso, 210, 211
Cardan (Girolamo Cardano), 21, 77, 81, 98, 117, 197, 200, 245, 247

Carew, R., 119
Carleton, George, 41
Cartwright, Thomas, 189
Castelain, M., 255
Castiglione, 207
Caxton, William, 214
Cervantes, 208, 263
Chamber, John, 41
Chapman, George, 41, 68, 82, 122, 126, 136, 137, 179-81, 227, 236, 253, 261
Charron, Pierre, 1, 2, 79, 179
Chaucer, 115, 160, 161, 228
Cheke, Sir John, 100, 104
Chrysostom, John, St., 52
Cicero, 52, 98, 161, 165, 167, 171, 173, 195, 215, 253, 261
Clark, Cumberland, 238
Coeffeteau, Nicholas, 179
Copernicus, 71
Cornelius Africanus, 113
Cotton, John, 189
Crusius, David, 246
Cyprian, St., 57
Cyrus the Younger, 90

D

Damascene (Joannes Damascenus), 52
Dante, 63, 161
Davies, Sir John, 51, 52, 119, 205
Davies, John, of Hereford, 119
Dedekind, Friedrich, 255
Dee, John, 21, 34, 40
Dekker, Thomas, 123-5, 174-6, 195, 207, 221, 229, 255-8
Deloney, Thomas, 195
Denis, St., 50
Descartes, Réné, 1, 145
Dionysius Areopagitica, 52
Dionysius Pariegetes, 89
Donne, John, 136, 186, 236, 253, 263

E

Edwards, Richard (*Damon and Pithias*), 123, 231
Eliot, T. S., 234

Elizabeth, Queen of England, 193, 212
Elyot, Sir Thomas, 10, 89, 90, 119, 153
Epaminondas, 90
Epicurus, 199
Erasmus, 95, 100, 121
Erra Pater, 38
Euclid, 77, 89
Euripides, 115, 214, 258

F

Fairbairn, A. M., 56
Favorinus, 98
Ficino, Marsilio, 16, 95
Fleming, Abraham, 102
Fludd, Robert, 13, 40
Foquelin, Antoine, 150
Ford, John, 68, 123, 137
Fortescue, Thomas, 117
Foxe, John, 212
Fraunce, Abraham, 146, 149

G

Galen, 38, 101, 110, 113, 116, 118
Galileo, 74
Galsworthy, John, 194
Gassendi, Pierre, 245
Geffroi de Vinsauf, 161
Gesner, Conrad, 65-7, 101-4
Gilbert, Sir Humphrey, 90
Gonzaga, Aloysius, St., 189
Gosson, Stephen, 98, 229
Grafton, Richard, 39, 40
Greene, Robert, 6, 123, 149, 166, 185, 260
Gregory of Nyssa, St., 57
Greville, Sir Fulke, 33, 34
Grosart, A. B., 255, 256
Guarino da Verona, 90
Gunter, Edmund, 100

H

Harrison, William, 212
Harvey, Gabriel, 37-40, 140, 141, 149, 158, 167, 215, 216
Harvey, William, 79, 100
Hector, 99

Henri IV, King of France, 193
Heraclitus, 19
Herodotus, 214
Hesiod, 258
Heydon, Sir Christopher, 41
Heywood, Thomas, 125, 137, 195; *A Woman Killed with Kindness*, 128-36, 221
Hippocrates, 37, 101, 117
Holywood, John (Johannes de Sacro Bosco), 89
Homer, 258
Hooker, Richard, 14, 15, 23-30, 71-3, 151, 153, 159, 167, 169, 187, 190, 206, 263
Horace, 257
Horatius, 90
Hoskins, John, 171
Hotman, François, 190
Huarte Navarro, Juan de Dios, 55, 117, 119-21

I

Isocrates, 162, 167, 253

J

James VI, King of Scotland, 81
Jerome, St., 67, 221
John de Garlandia, 161
Johnson, Samuel, 236
Jones, John, 10, 11
Jonson, Ben, 41, 68, 83, 122, 136, 159, 164, 169, 170, 185, 207, 216, 217, 235-7, 253-5, 260-3
Justin Martyr, 52
Justinian, 117

K

Kepler, Johann, 71
Klein, A., 122

L

Languet, Hubert, 92, 93
La Primaudaye, Pierre de, 10, 119, 179, 232
Latimer, Hugh, 104
Lavater, Louis, 247

Leeuwenhoeck, Anthony van, 74
Lemnius, Levinus, 119
Lennard, Samson, 119
Livy, 214
Locke, John, 114
Lodge, Thomas, 229
Lorkin, Thomas, 103, 104
Loyola, Ignatius, St., 189
Lucian, 98
Lucretius, 30
Lully, Raymond, 21
Luther, Martin, 56
Lydgate, John, 214
Lyly, John, 207, 208, 213, 221, 253, 255

M

Machiavelli, 52, 141, 142, 194, 202
McKerrow, R. B., 259
Macrobius, 67
Manly, J. M., 160-3, 230
Marlowe, Christopher, 6, 41, 122, 123, 187, 224, 229, 230, 253, 258, 259
Marston, John, 82, 122, 126, 136, 177-9, 253, 261
Martial, 257
Martin, Richard, 205
Matthieu de Vendôme, 161
Maximus Tyrius, 246
Medici, Catherine de', 81
Medici, Cosimo de', 101
Mela, Pomponius, 50, 89
Melanchthon, Philipp, 89, 101, 119, 142
Melton, John, 41
Michelangelo, 223, 224
Middleton, Thomas, 83, 117, 123, 137, 194
Milles, Thomas, 52, 53
Milton, John, 90, 153, 158, 186, 187, 263; *Areopagitica*, 59, 60; *Paradise Lost*, 6, 7, 9, 19, 26, 49, 115, 116
Mirror for Magistrates, The, 231
Misfortunes of Arthur, The, 231

Moffett, Thomas, 103
Molle, John, 109
Montaigne, 4, 42-4, 98, 132, 185, 197, 244, 252, 253, 261, 263
Montanus, Johannes Baptista, 101
More, Sir Thomas, 195, 207, 225
Mornay, Philippe de, 190, 197
Munster, Sebastian, 101

N

Napier, Sir John, 100
Nashe, Thomas, 253, 255, 259, 260
Nemesius, 114
Newton, Sir Isaac, 8
Newton, Thomas, 119

O

Origen, 52
Ovid, 145, 215, 253, 257, 260

P

Painter, William, 226, 227
Paracelsus, 21, 247, 258
Pausanias, 67
Penney, Thomas, 103
Person, David, 54, 55
Petrarch, 161, 214
Petrus Hispanus, 142
Phidias, 239
Philemon, 52
Philostratus, 97
Pico della Mirandola, Giovanni, 16
Plato, 2, 3, 5, 15, 22, 23, 82, 110, 213, 221, 250
Plautus, 260
Pliny the Elder, 17, 50, 89, 96, 99, 257
Plotinus, 95, 246
Plutarch, 98, 173, 198, 212, 222, 257, 258
Pompey the Great, 90
Pomponatius (Pietro Pompon-azzi), 248
Pope, Alexander, 79
Porphyry, 142

Porretanus, Gilbertus, 142
Possevino, Antonio, 122
Proclus, 20, 246
Prynne, William, 229
Psellus, 246
Ptolemy, 33, 36, 38

Q

Quintilian, 162, 171, 173, 253, 261

R

Rabelais, 98, 263
Ralegh, Sir Walter, 97, 228
Ramus (Pierre de la Ramée), 78, 79, 100, 142-7, 240
Recorde, Robert, 35-7
Regius (Louis Le Roy), 54, 76
Reisch, Gregorius (Margarita Philosophica), 119
Reuchlin, Johann, 16
Ridley, Nicholas, 104
Romance of the Rose, The, 220
Rowland, William, 41

S

Sackville, Thomas, and Thomas Norton (Gorboduc), 123, 228, 231
Scaliger, Julius Caesar, 246
Seager, H. W., 238
Secreta Secretorum, 39
Securis, John, 39
Selimus, 123, 231
Seneca, 82, 98, 162, 195, 215, 257, 258, 260, 261
Shakespeare, William, 7, 63, 68, 82, 83, 115, 122, 126-8, 137, 157-9, 185, 187, 194, 195, 206-8, 211, 212, 215, 222-4, 228, 230, 233-5, 243, 253, 260, 261, 263; All's Well that Ends Well, 41; Antony and Cleopatra, 78, 233; Coriolanus, 233; Hamlet, 42, 45, 78, 80, 91, 124, 145, 151, 153, 197, 200, 234; Henry V, 91, 92, 127; 1 Henry IV, 91, 151, 152; 3 Henry VI, 124; Julius Caesar, 29, 41, 78, 127,

128, 163, 202; *King Lear*, 42, 80, 125, 233; *Love's Labour's Lost*, 44; *Macbeth*, 46, 80, 120, 127, 128, 232, 233; *Measure for Measure*, 221; *The Merchant of Venice*, 157, 200, 220, 221, 225; *Much Ado About Nothing*, 225; *Othello*, 9, 27, 78, 116, 128, 220, 225, 233, 256; *The Rape of Lucrece*, 230; *Richard II*, 45, 46, 157: *Richard III*, 225; *Romeo and Juliet*, 22, 41, 206, 220, 221, 224; Sonnets, 42; *The Tempest*, 6, 42, 101; *Timon of Athens*, 217; *Troilus and Cressida*, 72, 87, 88, 214; *Twelfth Night*, 78, 192, 221, 225; *The Winter's Tale*, 117, 166

Shepherds Kalendar, The, 38
Sidney, Sir Henry, 91, 153
Sidney, Sir Philip, 33-5, 56, 82, 88, 92-4, 100, 148, 149, 153-6, 158, 164-7, 185, 186, 190, 207, 208, 221, 223, 228, 231, 253, 261, 263
Sidney, Robert, 92-4
Smith, Sir Thomas, 100
Socrates, 199, 246
Solinus, 50, 89
Spenser, Edmund, 56, 82, 149, 186, 190, 207, 208, 215, 216, 221, 228, 230, 231, 253, 261; *The Faerie Queene*, 45, 59, 115, 200
Stow, John, 163, 212
Strabo, 50, 89
Stubbes, Philip, 58, 59, 158, 229
Sturmius (Johann Christoph Sturm), 89
Suetonius, 257

T

Tacitus, 257
Tasso, 186

Telesio, Bernadino, 248
Temple, Sir William, 149, 158
Terence, 167
Tertullian, 57
Theseus, 90
Topsell, Edward, 65, 67
Tourneur, Cyril, 117, 123, 206, 227
Turner, Peter, 103, 104
Turner, William, 104

V

Vegius, Mapheus, 121
Vergerius, Petrus Paulus, 121
Vergil, Polydore, 222, 223
Vesalius, Andreas, 101
Vicary, Thomas, 39
Virgil, 145, 215, 253, 260
Vittorino da Feltre, 90
Vives, Juan Luis, 89, 119-22, 131, 132

W

Wallace, M. W., 34
Warde, William, 38, 39
Webster, John, 68, 117, 123, 137; *The Duchess of Malfy*, 85, 226, 227
Wells, H. G., 63
Whitgift, John, 189
Wierus (Johann Weyer), 247
Williams, Roger, 189
Wilson, Thomas, 101, 146-8, 167, 176
Wotton, Anthony, 149
Wotton, Edward, 103
Wotton, Sir Henry, 163, 164, 171
Wright, Edward, 100
Wright, Thomas, 119, 179

X

Xavier, Francis, St., 189